The Last Four Weeks of the Civil War

Originally authored by

Edmund N. Hatcher
1848 -1917

And titled The Last Four Weeks of the War
Published 1891 in Columbus, Ohio

Re-Created, Edited, Illustrated and Re-published
With Addendum by

C. Stephen Badgley
Canal Winchester, Ohio
2012

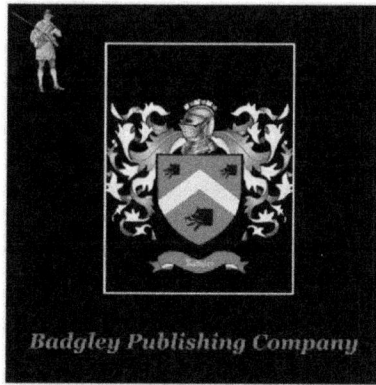

Badgley Publishing Company

This book is part of the Historical Collection of Badgley Publishing Company and has been re-created from the original. The original contents have been edited and corrections have been made to original printing, spelling and grammatical errors when not in conflict with the author's intent to portray a particular event or interaction. Annotations have been made and additional contents have been added by Badgley Publishing Company in order to clarify certain historical events or interactions and to enhance the author's content. Photos and illustrations from the original have been touched up, enhanced and sometimes enlarged for better viewing. Additional illustrations and photos have been added by Badgley Publishing Company.

ISBN 978-0985440381

THE LAST FOUR WEEKS OF THE CIVIL WAR

xi

INTRODUCTION

But for the cultivation of a fancy, this volume would not go to the public. The collection of material for this work began shortly after the close of the War, by seeking from both North and South, files of daily and weekly papers published during the activity of the two great armies of the Union and Confederate forces. Many difficulties were encountered in collecting files now in my possession, yet, after the lapse of more than a quarter of a century, the result of my collection is invaluable and cannot be duplicated. Having a desire, after having served in the field at a youthful age, to know more than I chanced to have seen, caused me to seek this channel for that I deemed more accurate and interesting than could come from the pen of a historian and to you is given the situation and expression on both Union and Confederate sides, to study over as I have done with great pleasure. I do not offer an apology for any article within this cover. I have given each as it came directly from the press sentiment on those dates. It has been found necessary at times to have concentrated letters and editorials, but the gist of each is retained and here given.

The contents are from the War Correspondents and editorials of the following papers: "The Tribune", "Herald" and "Times", of New York; "The Daily Rebel", "Confederate Union" and "Mobile Register", of Alabama; "The Raleigh Progress", and "Confederate", of North Carolina; "The Richmond Dispatch", "Sentinel", "Whig", and "Enquirer", of Richmond, Virginia; "The Daily Constitutionalist", of Augusta, Georgia;" The New Orleans Picayune", "Philadelphia Inquirer", "Washington Chronicle", "Baltimore American", and "The Cincinnati Commercial", "Gazette" and "Enquirer", as well as from files of many papers of less prominence, that were issued during the War, many of which have been for years extinct.

I trust, after the reader has carefully read,—and possibly wondered as to the accuracy of the contents,—that it will have been found interesting. Those who were witnesses and participants in the great struggle can vouch for the correctness of this compilation, while those who have since appeared on the stage may find herein food for the production of an imaginary picture of the closing days of the war that they will never be able to properly paint.

I launch this work with the belief that it will bring to many recollections that time has blurred, and recall the part you played in the great drama. With this accomplished, I have finished.

E. N. H.
Columbus, Ohio,
Sept. 30, 1891.

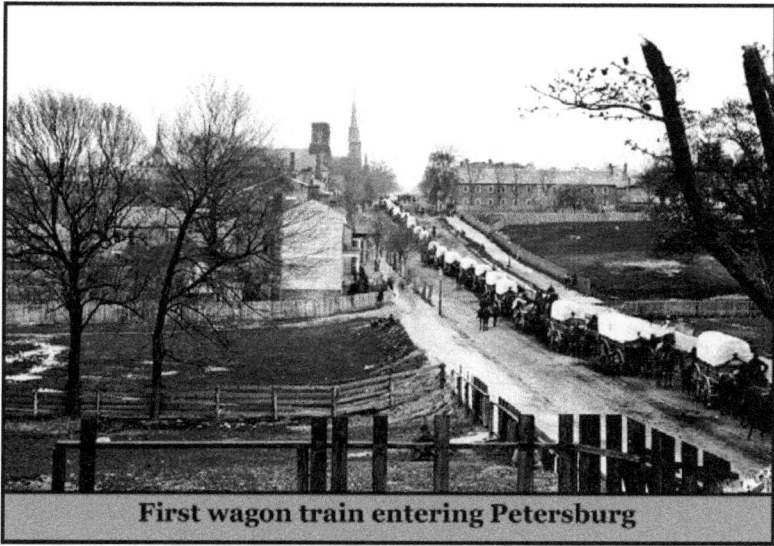

First wagon train entering Petersburg

As soon as the Rebels were forced to evacuate Petersburg, April 2, 1865, our troops took possession; the inhabitants of the city were in a very destitute condition, almost starving in fact. The U.S. Government at once began issuing rations to these starving people, and great trains loaded with provisions soon rolled into the city. The hated Yankees came to them with barrels of flour, pork, coffee, sugar, and other necessaries to relieve their suffering brought upon them by their friends (?) the Rebels.

Saturday, March 25, 1865

Army of the James, Bermuda Hundred, Virginia, Union Account

Turner's Division of Gibbon's, Army of the James, was dispatched to the Chickahominy for the purpose of supporting Sheridan in his crossing, in case of an attack by the enemy.

Ninth Army Corps in front of Petersburg, Va. Union Account

At 5 o'clock this morning the Rebels came in great force to capture Fort Steadman. The time occupied in crossing the ground between the lines was but a moment, when they were in the rear of the fort. Here they formed in line of battle, and while one portion advanced on the fort, the other swept the right, in toward the Appomattox River, expecting to flank and capture the whole line to that point. They were met by the Seventeenth Michigan and driven back, after a severe fight. The Rebels who attacked the fort were several times repulsed by the garrison, but their numbers being so superior to ours, they finally overpowered and took prisoners all who were in it. General Wilcox's command now came from the right, and drove the enemy from the line on the right of the fort. Gen. Hartranft's Division, on the left, was quick on the ground with reinforcements', and assaulted the fort from the rear, which the Rebels seemed determined to hold at all hazards. Three repeated charges were made, and then the fight was over. The Rebels surrendered.

Battery 11, to the left of Fort Steadman, was also in the enemy's possession, but they could not hold it but for a few moments.

Our loss in killed and wounded and prisoners, is believed to be about 500, one-third of whom are probably prisoners.

It was reported that the Rebels carried off three mortars, but this has proven a mistake. They took one over the side of the fort, but in their hasty retreat left it just outside our breast-works. It will be brought in tonight.

We have taken from the Rebels 1,800 prisoners, among whom are about forty officers. The Rebel General Terry, who had charge of the assault, is reported killed.

At one o'clock a flag of truce was arranged, between General Hartranft and the Rebel General Gordon, to bury the dead and care for the wounded, from two until four o'clock p. m. While doing so, the works on both sides were lined with soldiers, watching the proceedings.

The Third Maryland and the One Hundredth Pennsylvania exhibited great bravery today.

Five stands of colors were taken by General Wilcox's Division.

The Ninth Corps has, today, paid the Rebels back for their defeat at the Petersburg mine explosion, and in the future the Rebels will esteem them.

Inside Fort Steadman

Army of the Potomac in front of Petersburg, Va.
Union Account

At six o'clock this morning the enemy massed four divisions of General Gordon's Corps, consisting of Bushrod Johnson's, Evans' and Grier's commands, in front of the point of our line held by the First Division of the Ninth Army Corps. By a bold dash one of the enemy's divisions made a rush at Fort Steadman, capturing it with four guns, also our Batteries 9 and 10. Into the fort and Battery 10 they swarmed, shot down our gunners, and for a time held possession. They quickly turned the guns on our men as they fell back, firing canister into our ranks with fearful effect. This state of affairs, however, was brief. The Third Division of the Ninth Corps charged upon the rear of the captured works and quickly had possession of our complete works again, taking all the Rebels that were there. This discouraged the enemy, when he fell back to his line.

As soon as his attack was disposed of, a counter attack was made by the left of our line. The Second Corps advanced the left of its line, formed up the First and Third Divisions, with the Second Division in reserve. After very hard fighting, the left of the line gained about three miles of ground, the enemy falling back to his rear line of breast-works. The Second Corps is now near the Boydtown Plank Road, which is held by the Rebels.

President Lincoln, with Generals Grant and Ingalls, came up from City Point on special train. They went into the field and witnessed the attack made by the Second and Sixth Corps. This is President Lincoln's first appearance on a battlefield. The position he occupied was in range of the enemy's bomb-shells, several of which exploded near him.

The result of today's battle demonstrates the fact that the Rebels have lost heart in their cause. Large numbers are ready and willing to lay down their arms and give up the struggle. After they had gained possession of Fort Steadman, they began at once to plunder the baggage in the tents, in spite of their officers' protests. Those who remained in line fought with nothing like the enthusiasm exhibited last summer. When the Rebels determined to return to their line, hundreds of their men ran and hid in our bomb-proofs, waiting for our boys to take them prisoners.

Lee's Army, Petersburg, Virginia,
Confederate Account

At 11 o'clock this morning, General Lee attacked the Yankee Fort, Battery No. 5, near this city — the one that has been pouring its shells through this city for a long time, — and captured it with 700 prisoners and several guns. This will interfere with Grant's left wing, which is operating against the railroad.

It is reported that Grant is moving heavy bodies of troops toward Weldon, to reinforce Sherman.

It is very cold tonight. The wind is piercing to our brave Southerners on the picket lines in front of this city.

Augusta, Georgia,
Confederate Account

Our government has determined to avenge the recent official murder of Captain Beall, of Virginia, who was hung recently near New York City. It is said that the lot has fallen to Maj. Gen. Crook, of the Yankee army, who will certainly be made "pull hemp" as an atonement for the wicked murder of Captain Beall.

John Yates Beall
Executed as a spy

Cairo, Illinois,
Union Account

A desperate fight occurred between twenty of our troops and seventy guerillas, thirty miles from Paducah, Kentucky, on Wednesday night. Twenty guerillas were killed including McDougall, their chief. We lost Captain McGregor, who was killed. General Meredith has detachments out scouring the country with the expectation of cleaning the guerillas from the Kentucky shore.

Augusta, Georgia,
Confederate Account

The Yankees burned, destroyed and evacuated Dalton several days ago. About 1,000 of Woodford's cavalry command moved to a point about eighteen miles north of Dalton, on a tour of observation.

Louisville, Kentucky,
Union Account

Yesterday 118 prisoners of war, embracing several officers, 102 privates and two citizens, left the Military Prison here for Camp Chase in Ohio. Among the lot were four seamen, of the defunct

"Confederate States Navy," captured near Kingston, East Tennessee, while trying to burn the United States boats on that stream.

Goldsboro, North Carolina, Union Account

This is now a very important point. General Sherman entered the town, in person, while the bands played, the cannon boomed and the town generally was brim full of joy. On Thursday he reviewed the Army of the Ohio. Their appearance, he was frank to say, was not as gaudy as he had seen them, but, considering what they had done, and the time in which they had done what they did, he did not think they were an army to be ashamed of. He knew what they were worth and what they could do under such as General Schofield, and was proud of them.

Yesterday—Friday—that part of Sherman's Army in this city was also reviewed. Many would have failed to "pass muster" had it been any other place and any other time than this. Many were but half clad; some without hats; some barefooted; and others minus a coat, &c. They certainly looked like the tried and true of many battles.

General Sherman, in his speech today, said, *"We've whipped Johnston and can do it again."*

The entrance of Sherman's army into this place was a very comical affair. Carts with a half dozen mules hitched tandem, loaded with geese, turkeys, and chickens, all of which were adding their say in the movement, came in with the head, center and tail of the army.

~ 5 ~

Soldiers mounted on mules, some leading sheep, others with hogs before and behind them, and the general army carrying living supplies with them, was an amusing sight.

Army of the Potomac in Front of Petersburg, Va.
Union Account

At half past four o'clock this Army of the Potomac morning, the enemy, by a strong and sudden assault, captured Fort Steadman, but after a vigorous contest the fort was retaken by our troops, with 1,600 prisoners, two battle flags, and all the guns uninjured. Gen. McLaughlin was captured by the Rebels. The enemy afterwards assaulted Fort Haskell but was repulsed with severe loss. The Rebel prisoners we here captured number 2,700. The Rebels lost in killed and wounded, probably not less than 3,000. Our loss is estimated at 800. During the Rebel assault on Fort Haskell, General Humphrey's command opened up on the left with great promptness, capturing 100 Rebels, and causing the enemy to return the re-enforcements sent against Forts Steadman and Haskell.

At the point where the enemy charged, the main lines are only 150 yards apart. The ground between the lines is level and free from obstructions, except the usual rows of wire fastened near the ground to trip the ambitious Confederate or Yankee, in his effort to move forward with speed.

Montgomery, Alabama,
Confederate Account

A Federal column of from 1,500 to 1,800 strong, struck the Alabama and Florida Railroad seventy miles below here—in the neighborhood of Garland station—yesterday morning. The passenger train which left here Thursday afternoon was captured by the enemy. The passengers were robbed and the cars destroyed. They stated that they were on their way to Greenville, forty-three miles below here.

Mobile, Alabama,
Confederate Account

Our preparations for the protection of this city is complete. We are now able to meet any force Canby can get together to besiege the city. We have provisions for at least six months, and now the ship is ready—let the foe come on. He should, however, be met and whipped before he reaches our defenses. Once there, he will commence digging, and in a short time will have works as strong as those thrown up at Vicksburg. Let Canby be met, if possible, before he has an opportunity to accomplish much. If he be allowed to sit down, where he chooses, and there fortify himself, we will have a great deal of trouble, when the time comes, to move him. Shall we protect Mobile or not? This is in your hands and should be answered at once.

New York

Robert Cobb Kennedy, convicted of being a Rebel spy, was today executed at Fort Lafayette. He was shockingly profane, and sang a song while the executioner was adjusting the rope around his neck as follows:

"Trust to luck, trust to luck.
Stare fate in the face,
For your heart will be airy
If it's in the right place."

Robert Cobb Kennedy
Executed as a Spy

Gold is quiet. Prices opened at 157 1/2, but was found too high, and fell back to 153 1/2.

Newbern, North Carolina, Union Account

This place has become one of interest since Sherman's army is at Morehead City. Everything in the way of supplies is shipped here, and the town is fast assuming importance as a point of business. All supplies for Sherman, Schofield and Terry's armies must pass through here and be reshipped.

The special agent of the Post Office Department has just fitted up large rooms, as a distributing office for Sherman's army.

Petersburg, Virginia, General Lee's Letter, Confederate Account

"At daylight this morning Gen. Gordon assaulted and carried the enemy's works at Hare's Hill, capturing nine pieces of artillery, eight mortars, and between 500 and 600 prisoners, among them one Brigadier General and a number of officers of lower grades. The lines were swept for a distance of 400 or 500 yards to the right and left, and two efforts were made to recover the works which were handsomely repulsed, but it was found that the enclosed works in the rear could only be taken at a terrible sacrifice of life, and the troops were withdrawn to their original position. It being impossible to move the guns captured owing to the ground, they were dismantled and left."

Petersburg, Virginia, Confederate Account

Generals Bushrod Johnson and Gordon stormed the enemy's breast-works on our left this morning, and drove the enemy one mile, capturing his works and 500 prisoners. We captured the Yankee General McLaughlin and many other officers. The enemy massed his artillery heavily in the neighborhood of the captured fort, and was thus enabled to pour such a terrible fire upon our ranks as to cause our troops to fall back to their original position.

General Bushrod Johnson

Raleigh, North Carolina,
Confederate Account

Much unjust abuse has been heaped upon the cavalry under Gen. Wheeler. The marauding and plundering charged to them has been done by others. A more orderly or well-behaved set of men than Gen. Wheeler's cannot be found anywhere. We are of opinion that the Yankee sympathizers know more than Wheeler's men as to where, when, and how the plundering is done, as the woods here are full of them.

There are no less than from 300 to 600 deserters in the lower end of Pitt County, N.C., committing all sorts of depredations on citizens by stealing their horses, Negroes and provisions. It is reported they get $200 for every fine horse they carry to the Yankees; and $400 for every able-bodied Negro fit for service. They are stealing Negroes and horses every night in some portion of the country. They also take all provisions, such as bacon and pork, and leave families perfectly destitute.

General Joseph Wheeler
"Fightin' Joe"

Petersburg, Virginia,
Confederate Account

General Lee has broken through Grant's lines, carrying them by assault, capturing a large number of prisoners, thus opening the campaign in a different way from that Grant was looking for. General Lee's army is the same today as it was in the Wilderness, at Spotsylvania Court House and Gaines' Farm. The battle today demonstrates this. The Yankee army is a body of new recruits, as the old veterans have become disgusted and gone home. Those who have stayed in our neighborhood, sleep beneath a light covering of dirt, from the Rapidan to Hatcher's Run. Lee's veterans still confront the enemy, and when they make up their mind to do a thing, they do it, and do it right. Today has proven this.

Raleigh, North Carolina,
Confederate Account

So far everything is encouraging. In the affair which occurred a few days since, between Hardee's and Sherman's forces, we repulsed successfully five assaults upon our lines, and held the position until our object was effected. In drawing off we lost two guns, because the horses had been killed. Our loss was about 400 killed and wounded; the enemy's about 3,000. On Sunday we gained a decided advantage, the enemy being driven several miles with heavy loss. We captured some artillery and all told, did well. We learn today that Goldsboro, N. C, has been evacuated, but it is not official.

We also hear that some of our deserters are plundering the homes of the residents of Darke County, this State.

Richmond, Virginia,
Confederate Account

The Whig of today has an account of a meeting held at Wytheville for the purpose of receiving contributions of food for Lee's army in Richmond. The donations amounted to about one day's short rations for the army now in this city.

The Whig also says: "The check administered by Johnston to Sherman, at Bentonville, interferes essentially with the campaign of that *"cocawhoop"* leader and the combinations of Grant. The importance of the late battle at Bentonville will be appreciated. The blow struck there was as much a blow for the safety of the city as that delivered at Cold Harbor last year. General Johnston, and General Lee, under whom he acts, can be in no uncertainty as to the vital necessity of continuing to oppose an unmovable front to Sherman's advance. If he cannot be destroyed, as we devoutly trust he may be, he must, at any cost, be kept from coming forward—not that Richmond, as Richmond, is of so much value, but that, for reasons which need not be explained, its surrender to the enemy is a thing not to be thought of while its defense is possible. In this view we cannot award too much credit, or render too much gratitude to the gallant leader and devoted men who have said to Sherman, 'Thus far and no farther.'"

It is the talk here that Grant is sending re-enforcements to Goldsboro, N. C. This is not official, however, nor do we believe it is true. A single mistake by Sherman at this time, would result differently from his calculations.

The Yankee papers chronicle the rise in the price of flour here to $1,500 per barrel, which occurred a few days ago. This is certainly proof of the fact that every occurrence in Richmond is immediately known in Washington. How can success be possible, with every movement we make being known by the enemy the very instant it occurs? This city is evidently alive with Unionists, who no doubt, are in some way connected with a secret-service which is hard at work against us.

Considerable interest is felt in the movements of Pickett's division, and as to what their programme is. They have been ordered to the Petersburg Depot and to proceed to Petersburg. Indications point to a decisive movement of some nature. The marching of so many of our troops, through the streets of this city today, has led us to believe that there is foundation for the rumor afloat, that Lee is about to evacuate.

Washington, D.C.
Union Account

North Carolina refugees, who have just reached this city, say that two-thirds of the people of the State, in and about Fayetteville, are Unionists. The re-appearance of the Stars and Stripes brought to many tears of joy. Provisions they report as being plenty, but money is very scarce. Flour is worth, in Confederate money, $750 per barrel; corn meal, $60 per bushel; brandy, per glass, $10; whisky, per glass, $5; men's shoes, $250 per pair; men's felt hats, $150 each; shoddy coats are sold at $500 and other things in proportion. One dollar in gold is worth $125 in Confederate money. Clothing has been sent to Beaufort, N. C, for Sherman's army.

A gentleman just arrived from Richmond, says that the Rebels admit that Sherman's army has damaged them to the amount of $50,000,000. He represents the strength of the Rebel army at Richmond as all of 60,000, excluding 10,000 home-guards and emergency men. He does not believe that Johnston has to exceed 45,000 men, though he has drawn several divisions from Richmond. Deep gloom prevails in Richmond as everybody seems to believe that the day of reckoning is not far off.

Five hundred Rebel deserters have been received here since one week ago, all of whom have taken the oath of allegiance, and many are here provided with funds, as the government pays them for their arms.

Wautanga Bridge, Tennessee,
Union Account

General Stoneman's command has, in their rapid advance, uncovered over a hundred miles of railroad formerly controlled by the Confederates. They move along at a speed that the Rebels cannot check, and it is hard to tell just where they will not yet turn up. It is not an easy matter to follow Stoneman's boys.

Second Army Corps, in front of Petersburg, Va.
Union Account

This Corps was engaged at about dark, today. Over 400 prisoners fell into our hands. We are stationed near Hatchers Run.

It is reported that the Rebel General Gordon was seen urging his men to fight, and swearing at them for their cowardice, ending with, *"By God, just as I thought,—the men won't fight,"* after which he left and was not afterward seen.

General John B.Gordon

Sixth Army Corps, in front of Petersburg, Va.
Union Account

This corps made an attack today on the front of Fort Fisher. The Third Division led the assault. Shortly after noon the line of battle was formed and the order to advance was given. In a short time we had possession of the enemy's entire line of rifle pits, and captured nearly all of the occupants. We brought in over 600 prisoners. Our loss is small.

Another Account

The Sixth Corps pushed forward today to test the strength of the enemy's line along the center and right. The Rebel skirmish line fell back as the Sixth went on under a fierce fire from their batteries, and drove them into their defenses. We came to a halt and took steps to hold the ground we had gained. By this advance we are now entrenched in the Rebel picket-line and will stay there. We lost today about 100 men.

Confederates inside Fort Fisher at an area called "The Pulpit"

Ninth Army Corps, in front of Petersburg Va.
Union Account

Our losses are much larger than supposed. The First Division have in hospital 160 wounded and thirty are known to have been killed. The Third Division hospital has 166 wounded and about thirty-two killed. The Second Division was not regularly engaged, yet they have in the hospital 130 wounded.

The killed on both sides were exchanged late this afternoon, the Confederates showing more courtesy than heretofore.

Goldsboro, North Carolina,
Union Account

Information from Weldon shows that the Rebels have removed most of their guns from their works and are sending them to Richmond. The enemy has some 12,000 cavalry in our front, under Wheeler and Hampton. Yesterday they captured and hanged three of our foragers, within two miles of our outposts.

Kilpatrick boys were engaged yesterday evening. The firing was very heavy for two hours. Reports of the fight have not yet come in.

Large Rebel mails, just captured, show the utmost despondency throughout the South.

The first train from Kinston arrived here this morning.

Our loss in the fighting of last week is estimated at 1,500.

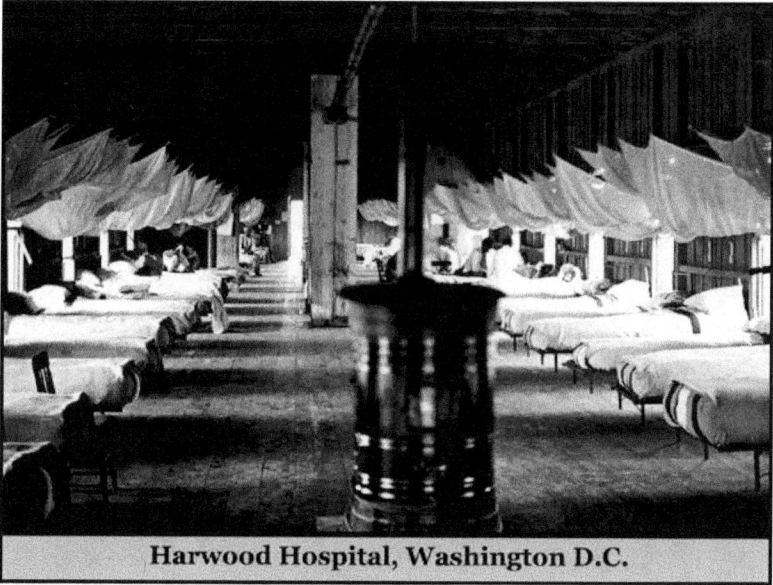

Harwood Hospital, Washington D.C.

Sunday, March 26, 1865

Bermuda Hundred, Virginia, Union Account

General Sheridan's whole cavalry force crossed the river at Deep Bottom today to join Grant. Everything goes to show that a decisive movement is near.

Major General Phil Sheridan

In front of Petersburg, Virginia, Union Account

Sheridan and his cavalry have just arrived and are moving to the left of the line of the Army of the Potomac.

Richmond, Virginia, Confederate Account

The weather this morning is very disagreeable. The night was very cold and this morning it is very windy, making one feel that summer is far away.

Five hundred Yankees, captured in front of Petersburg, were ushered into Libby Prison today.

Some say that Lee is a failure. That his position should not be one of defense and that he should pounce upon the Federals and drive them from our front. This comes from classes who have not Southern blood. They should be driven out of town.

General Breckenridge receives many dispatches from the front. He holds every message with a tight grasp, making us believe there is little encouragement in what he receives. Possibly we will, before night, get news from Lee that will please us. What a comfort it would be at this time.

News of importance from General Johnston is very scarce. Our whole interest is now in Lee and Johnston, who, we hope, will give us cheering news before the morrow.

Washington D. C.
Union Account

The forces in East Tennessee, under command of General Stoneman, have, in their rapid advance, recovered more than one hundred miles of railroad and are driving the enemy, which is in confusion, before them. General Stoneman is noted for putting in an appearance at a time when the enemy is not looking for him.

In front of Petersburg, Virginia,
Union Account

The Rebels are drawn up in double line of battle along their front from the Appomattox River to Hatcher's Run, in anticipation of an attack by our forces.

Considerable skirmishing, sometimes very heavy, has been the day's doings in front of the Second and Sixth Corps.

Our troops are massing on the left, preparatory to another movement on the South-side railroad. The Rebels are also massing on their right, to offset the movement we anticipate. Important movements are in progress that it would not be policy to state at this time.

Bermuda Hundred, Virginia,
Union Account

It is noticed that the enemy are weakening their force in our front. General Ord is wide awake and will possibly make an assault along this line from the James River to the Appomattox before the day is over. From the noise we hear on the Petersburg front our boys are still at it.

Appomattox River, Virginia,
Union Account

The march today of Sheridan's cavalry from Mrs. Wilcox's place, a mile and a half from James River, up along the Charles City Road, via General Ord's headquarters, and his pontoon bridge to this place, was not so pleasant as yesterday, the road not being so good, etc., but was not without interest.

A grand reception was given to General Sheridan's braves by the veteran Army of the James, on our entrance into General Ord's lines. The frowning, bristling battlements swarmed with his men, coming out to meet and welcome the recognized heroes of the Valley.

The bands of the forts struck up stirring martial airs, which were responded to by the bands of the cavalry host. Old comrades recognized each other after long separation, and fell upon each other's shoulders and wept of sheer joy at the grand reunion.

The pontoon bridge across the James, through which the River Queen, the Margaret Washington, and the George Steers had just passed, was soon swung into position, and the trampling host were seen winding down the hills on the north side, across the river, over the valley, and up the hills on the south side of the James, where, at this writing, they are going into camp, for probably a two days' stay, previous to further important operations.

Faysor Depot, North Carolina,
Union Account

General Sherman sent word to General Schofield that he would meet him at Faysor Depot on Sunday. He kept his word. We reached here last night.

We received this morning copies of the Richmond papers of Friday, filled with extracts from our Northern papers. They contain but little news from Mobile or Richmond.

Augusta, Georgia,
Confederate Account

"Broad Cloth. This article is now held at two thousand dollars per yard in this city. We have seen no one daring enough to indulge in the luxury of a new suit of broad cloth."

Gold, $60 stiff; silver buying at $55, selling at $60. Confederate securities dull. Cotton 99c per pound; very few sales. Flour $500 per barrel; coffee $60 per pound; sugar $20 per pound, crushed $25 per pound; rice $4.50 per pound; salt $4 to $5 per pound; iron $3 to $5 per pound; whisky $100 to $200 per gallon; calico $20 to $30 per yard; pepper $12 per pound; chickens $8 to $12 per pair; eggs $6 to $7 per dozen; butter $10 to $13 per pound; corn meal $40 per bushel, corn $35 per bushel. [From the market report of the Daily Constitutionalist, Augusta, Georgia.]

Mobile, Alabama,
Confederate Account

Preparations for defense are very complete, and provisions to last six months are in the city.

Montgomery, Alabama,
Confederate Account

A Yankee raiding party struck the Alabama and Florida Railroad, twenty miles below here, yesterday, and captured a train. The enemy then moved down the railroad. His force is said to be 2,500 strong.

Goldsboro, North Carolina,
Union Account

Everything is quiet. Kilpatrick's cavalry have been in a skirmish today with Hampton, above Cole's Bridge.

Sherman's bummers have foraged around this community so skillfully that the rooster fails to crow in the morning because he is not here, and if he was, the fence rail is not here upon which he can stand and flop his wings. The boys, however, claim that no roost has been tampered with, nor a fence been found.

Bermuda Hundred, Virginia,
Union Account

The Army of the James was honored by a visit today from the President, the Lieutenant- General, Admiral Porter, and several other civil and military officials of note. The coming of the President has always but briefly preceded activity in the army. He apparently desires to see the troops for himself, to examine into their discipline and general efficiency and to judge of their capabilities as soldiers for the performance of the work before them. At General Ord's headquarters everything was unusually active. The Howlett House Rebel battery keeps playing on Dutch Gap constantly. Very little damage is done by it, however.

Alexandria, Louisiana,
Union Account

The Rebels are reported in large numbers about here, and are strengthening Fort DeRussey. They have been seizing property of the citizens and have given the community, in general, dissatisfaction.

Canton, Mississippi,
Confederate Account

We are informed that the Legislature has decided that Georgia is going to operate against the government in arming Negroes. We guess the Negroes will go into the service regardless of the Legislature. This fight must be won, and the slaves must be used in it when necessary.

Lisbon, Portugal, March 26, 1865

The Confederate ram Stonewall has arrived here from Ferrol, where she left the Federal war steamers, Niagara and Sacramento, which are reputed to have shunned a conflict.

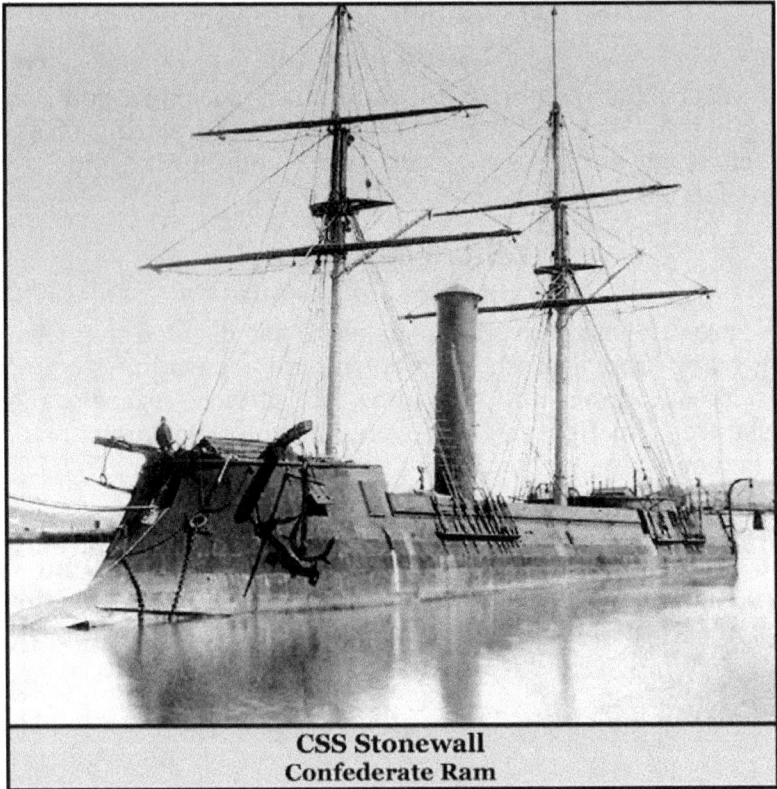
CSS Stonewall
Confederate Ram

Pensacola, Florida,
Union Account

General Steel's command, at Nutshell's Fork, today came in contact with about eight hundred Rebels. After a severe fight the enemy scattered in the woods, while many were captured.

Goldsboro, North Carolina,
Union Account

A detailed account of the battle fought by Sherman's army in their progress to a junction with Schofield and Terry:

The first fight is called the Battle at Moore's Cross Roads. General Sherman, after leaving Fayetteville, decided to form a junction near Goldsboro.

The enemy, General Hardee's forces, consisting of the Carolina and Georgia troops, released from Charleston and Savannah, had retired in the direction of Raleigh. It was necessary to deceive him as to the line of march, and make him believe Raleigh was the point proposed. Accordingly, the corps of General Slocum's command, the

Twentieth, moved up the road to a point twelve miles in advance, where it halted, and allowed Kilpatrick's cavalry to pass and take the front.

General William Hardee

As usual, he was in this case to cover the movement of the army in the direction of Goldsboro, by demonstrating and feigning well toward Raleigh. He had passed the Twentieth Corps, and reached a point four miles from Averysborough, when the foragers, mounted and dismounted, came dashing in from the front, reporting the enemy's infantry to be advancing in line of battle.

Kilpatrick deployed the Ninth Michigan Cavalry, and sent them rapidly forward to attack and hold the enemy in check until his troops could be brought forward and massed. Colonel Walker's Fifth Michigan Cavalry met and drove in the enemy's advance; he dismounted his entire regiment, and on foot forced the Rebel infantry back across a ravine which the following day became our line of battle.

Kilpatrick's cavalry had now been brought up and placed in position, dismounted, together with eight pieces of artillery. In the meantime word had been sent to General Williams, commanding the Twentieth Corps, for re-enforcements. Before these could reach our cavalry the enemy advanced in line of battle, with every intention of charging Kilpatrick's position.

Maj. Gen. Judson Kilpatrick

Colonel Walker fell back within the barricades when the line advanced, but received so heavy a fire from the artillery and carbines of the enemy that he fell back again to the ravine. A brigade of infantry now came up and was placed in position with the cavalry. Everything remained quiet during the night. In the morning Kilpatrick advanced with his whole force, the infantry under Holly having the center. The enemy was steadily forced back, and at last driven within his works near Moore's Cross Roads.

Casey's brigade of Ward's Division, Twentieth Corps, now came up and were shoved in upon the left and directed, together with Colonel Spencer's Cavalry Brigade, to assault the enemy's works upon the right. While these preparations were going on heavy masses of Rebel infantry moved upon Kilpatrick's right, and partly succeeded in turning his flank.

Colonel Jordan's Brigade of Cavalry, consisting of the Ninth Pennsylvania, Eighth Indiana, and Second and Third Kentucky, was pushed in on our right to prevent this movement.

The fighting at this point was very severe. The enemy's infantry charged our cavalry repeatedly, but the Eighth Indiana, Ninth Pennsylvania and Ninth Michigan dismounted, held the position, and resisted every attempt of the enemy to drive them from the trees and their heavily constructed barricade. In the meantime Major-General Williams came upon the field with a portion of the Twentieth Corps, and soon after Generals Sherman and Slocum arrived in person, and the infantry upon the left was ordered to advance. The enemy's works were carried, and he forced from his position with the loss of his guns and his caissons. One division after another of our infantry was now pushed in upon the right and left.

Kilpatrick's cavalry had gone to the right and had succeeded in reaching the Goldsboro road, which placed him directly in the rear of the enemy, when a heavy body of Rebel infantry, evidently re-enforcements, struck the Ninth Ohio Cavalry in front and flank, and notwithstanding the exertions of Colonel Hamilton and the bravery of his men, the regiment was thrown back upon the Ninth Pennsylvania Cavalry, which was also forced to retire, but so slowly as to give time for Colonel Selvidge, commanding the right of our infantry, to change front with his brigade.

The cavalry fell back on a line with our infantry, and the Rebel infantry in advancing received a cross fire from Colonel Selvidge's entire brigade, when Kilpatrick, with Colonel Jordan's cavalry brigade, charged straight upon the enemy, driving him in confusion down upon the Goldsboro road, and back to his original position.

This ended the fighting on the right and all further attempts of the enemy to turn our flank in that direction.

The enemy stubbornly fell back before each attack, and when night set in still held the cross-roads. During the night, however, he retired in the direction of Raleigh, leaving his killed and wounded on the field.

This was the first real hard fighting of the campaign. The troops did splendidly. The cavalry fought side by side with the infantry, mounted and dismounted, and were the admiration of the entire army.

The loss in the Twentieth Corps was quite severe, and in the cavalry particularly so, the Eighth Indiana, Colonel Jones, losing upwards of seventy killed and wounded.

General Atkins and Colonel Jordan, commanding the cavalry upon the right, deserve great credit for the skillful manner in which they fought their commands for the first time opposed to infantry.

The Rebel troops opposed in this fight were McLaw's division of cavalry and Folliver's and Rhett's artillery brigades. These are heavy artillery. They composed the Southern garrisons, and from Colonel Rhett, commandant at Fort Sumter, taken prisoner by Kilpatrick, it appears that these organizations were very full, his own regiment, for instance, at one time numbering not less than fifteen hundred men.

The road to Goldsboro being now apparently open, the left wing continued its march, without opposition, until the 19th.

Meanwhile, Johnston having become completely satisfied that Goldsboro was the real object, hastily called in Hardee and moved from Smithfield down the road to Bentonsville, where he entrenched himself, his line of works extending from Mills Creek on the upper side, and including the village, returned to the creek again.

This position the Fourteenth Corps in advance discovered. General Slocum immediately formed a well chosen line, flanked upon the left by a ravine, where he posted the artillery, and upon the right by a swamp and open field.

The third battle is called the battle at Morris's Farm. From this admirable line, Morgan's Division having moved forward with the intention of establishing another line a half-mile in advance, the enemy, who had been retiring toward their own line for several hours, here suddenly advanced with overwhelming numbers, and attacked the brigades of General Robinson and General Buell, comprising Morgan's Division, and drove them back in some confusion to the line of the railroad already marked by General Slocum's prompt and skillful eye as the proper rallying ground for the emergency.

Here, by the exertions of our officers and the great bravery of the men the enemy was checked. A hasty work of rails and dirt was thrown up, and the whole of the Fourteenth Corps and Colonel Selvidge's Brigade of the Twentieth Corps, and General Kilpatrick's cavalry arrived and took up a position, Colonel Selvidge upon the left, the cavalry in the rear. This was at four o'clock p. M., and now began a series of desperate charges by the enemy, only equaled by those at Franklin, and mainly directed against the right, by the diversion of the Georgians who had just before been flanked and doubled down to this line.

The enemy charged in three columns, one after another, each following up the other's repulse, making at one time three charges in thirty-five minutes, and with such desperation that when night closed in upon their defeat not only was the ground in our front strewn with their wounded, but their dead were packed up in numbers within our lines, even around the headquarters of the Generals.

On the other hand, our men fought as only this army can fight. Not a man left his post in line of battle, and each time the enemy was hurled back in confusion from in front of the very men whom overwhelming and outflanking numbers had only forced to retire in the morning.

The fighting in this engagement has been surpassed by no other during the war.

It was a grand spectacle as described by a general officer himself, from his position on the left, an eye witness of the whole; the battle-field was in full view, and notwithstanding the confusion of a sudden attack and the rapidity with which the position had been taken, a better could not have been found.

Considering these facts, and that General Johnston commanded in person with a force of 40,000 men, outnumbering our troops, Major-General Slocum, commanding, deserves great credit, and as he merits, will, doubtless, receive the thanks of the nation.

The next morning, with all dispatch, starting at three o'clock, the right was brought up from its camp, in the neighborhood of Falling Church, and by night a position had been taken, directed by General Sherman in person.

The Fifteenth and Seventeenth Corps and Kilpatrick's cavalry upon the extreme left, reached to Mill Creek, and were ready to take the offensive.

Tuesday was spent in entrenching, with the skirmishing attendant upon feeling the enemy in column, and when night came down, Howard's guns, far upon the extreme right, could still be heard long after dark. Late in the evening the programme for the following day reached the rear, which was for an advance, to be covered in the rear by the cavalry and a brigade of infantry.

This amounted to a flank movement, the virtue of which was apparent when in the morning the enemy was found to be retiring without a skirmish to Smithfield, leaving Sherman's progress to his base unopposed. The order of approach to Goldsboro was then, that the left wing, the Fourteenth Corps in advance, followed by the Twentieth, the troops that had borne the battle, should pass through the right wing, and cross the river first.

No land in the world is less favorable to a forced march than that which has been traversed by Sherman's noble army. The rains of winter and spring caught by the clay underlying the land, forms one vast and horrible quagmire, utterly impassable except in the way the marvel was accomplished, by almost one entire bridge from Savannah to the present base, over felled, trampled forests.

Union Soldiers in the Trenches
In Front of Petersburg, Virginia

Monday, March 27, 1865

Richmond, Virginia,
Confederate Account

The Enquirer of this morning says: The situation in North Carolina becomes more and more interesting. With his army scarcely half organized, General Johnston has been able to resist the advance of the enemy, from the time he left the Cape Fear. On three occasions he has given Sherman a severe lesson in the art of war, while at Kinston he was severely punished by General Bragg. The Battle of Bentonville, on Sunday the 19th, was a triumph to our arms. On the 20th the enemy was entrenched, and no fight occurred. On the 21st there was heavy skirmishing and some severe fighting, in which the enemy were badly handled. General Johnston maintains his position, and will be ready to meet the enemy at all points."

New York

"The World" of this morning, in its editorials, advises the Confederacy to lay down their arms at once and trust to chances.

Raleigh, North Carolina,
Confederate Account

"Judging from what we hear of the position in the eastern and middle part of North Carolina, we consider the signs more encouraging, if not decidedly cheering. Sherman will be prevented from crossing the North Carolina Railroad. Sherman and the Yankee nation will soon learn that marching through a country is not conquering it."

White Oak, North Carolina,
Union Account

Early this morning heavy firing began and continued throughout the day. Our advance scouts this evening report that citizens and scouts from Sherman's main army, say that Kilpatrick is fighting the Rebel General Hampton, between Goldsboro and Smithfield. Our cavalry are driving the enemy and at dark the firing grew more indistinct. We do not know as to the result. The sudden sweep of Kilpatrick's cavalry upon Hampton must be a surprise.

We are on the banks of the Neuse River, half-way between Goldsboro and Kinston. The country is well kept and supplies are abundant.

Baltimore, Maryland

The Flag of Truce boats, New York and Manhattan, arrived today with thirteen hundred and fifteen paroled prisoners and fifty officers from Varina Landing on the James River. The most of the men were captured in North Carolina.

Flag of Truce Boat New York

City Point, Virginia,
Union Account

President Lincoln is still here. Yesterday, in company with General Grant, he rode out to the front and witnessed the fighting on our left. It is said he will go to Washington tomorrow.

Over two thousand Rebel prisoners have been sent in from the front who witnessed the fighting at the left of our line. They will be shipped to the prisoners' camp at Point Lookout.

Last night thirty-nine Rebel deserters came into our lines on the Petersburg front and Army of the James, bringing their muskets with them.

In Front of Petersburg, Virginia,
Union Account

An engagement took place this morning which, though confined to a small portion of the line and of short duration, was of quite a severe character to the Rebels. A party of them, who pretended they wished to desert, was allowed to approach our lines, when they made a fierce attack on the front of the Sixth Corps, just before daybreak, for the purpose of recovering the advanced works from which they were driven on Saturday.

The assault was so sudden and furious that the Sixth Corps was for a moment forced back, but they instantly rallied, repulsed the enemy at all points, and recovered the ground lost. The Rebels lost heavily during the short fight, while our corps met with very light loss. The entire first line of Rebel works captured on Saturday by the Sixth and Second Corps we now hold and propose to hold, regardless of the Johnnies' desire to regain them.

Newbern, North Carolina,
Union Account

Five hundred and fourteen bags of mail arrived here yesterday and today for Sherman's army.

Army of the Potomac,
Union Account

Orders were today received at the various field hospitals to remove the sick and wounded to City Point and keep the hospitals in readiness for any emergency that may arise.

13th and 16th Corps,
Union Account

Our army began to-ay the bombardment of the Spanish Fort. This is the Rebels' strongest fortification at this point. It has sixteen heavy guns. The enemy has been expecting this movement no doubt.

The Rebel force in Mobile is reported at six thousand in the city, and the same number at Blakely, on this side of the bay of Mobile.

Daily skirmishing with a band of Guerillas has been the programme since the Thirteenth Corps left Fishing Creek on Saturday.

Generals Canby, Granger and Smith are at their posts and we hope soon to say that Mobile's lights are out.

Richmond, Virginia,
Confederate Account

The strength of Sherman's army was found in the headquarters of one of his Generals, after its owner had left. This represents its strength without Schofield's troops which have since joined it:

Ninety-six field pieces, none of which are more than twenty-two pounders.

Fourteenth Corps, Jeff. Davis in command, nine thousand strong; six four-gun batteries.

Fifteenth Corps, Logan in command, thirteen thousand strong; six four-gun batteries.

Seventeenth Corps, Blair in command, ten thousand strong; six four-gun batteries.

Twentieth Corps, Williams in command, ten thousand strong; six four-gun batteries, in small pieces. Right wing is under command of Howard; left wing is under Slocum.

Each regiment averages two hundred men; each brigade eight hundred men; each division three thousand men; each corps twelve thousand men, the whole army forty-two thousand men.

Davis

Logan

Williams

Blair

Schofield

Selma, Alabama,
Confederate Account

There is a report prevalent that a cavalry force, eight thousand strong, was coming from the north, by way of Tuscaloosa. Forrest no doubt will be able to take care of this party, should there be any truth in this report.

There seems to be three Federal columns—one from four thousand to six thousand last heard of at Pollard— another operating on Spanish Fort, probably ten thousand in number, and the North Alabama column, if there be one, of eight thousand. We do not believe the Federals could raise such a force.

Richmond, Virginia,
Confederate Account

There is but one regiment of Yankee infantry this side of Martinsburg, and that is about Kernstown and Winchester. Our scouts, who were in Winchester last week, report that this regiment had been ordered to another field, and that they were preparing to leave.

Thirteen hundred Yankee prisoners were sent off by flag of truce yesterday morning.

Five hundred prisoners, captured at Petersburg, were given accommodations in Libby prison last night.

City Point Virginia,
Union Account

General Grant's report of this morning says: On the 25th instant we met with the following losses: Second Corps, fifty-one killed, four hundred and sixty-two wounded, three hundred and two missing; Ninth Corps, sixty-eight killed, three hundred and thirty-eight wounded, five hundred and six missing. The Second Corps captured three hundred and sixty-one prisoners; the Sixth Corps four hundred and sixty-nine, and the Ninth Corps ten hundred and forty-nine.

The Second and Sixth Corps pushed forward, and captured the enemy's strong entrenchments, and turned its guns against him, and still hold it.

General Humphreys estimates the enemy's loss at three times greater than ours.

Richmond, Virginia,
Confederate Account

General Lee telegraphs that his attempt to break the Federal lines on Saturday was not successful. A full report of the result is not known here, but quite enough is current to convince us that the army of Northern Virginia has had a severe blow. From the report, which is from an official source, General Gordon assaulted the enemy's works at Hare's Hill, capturing several pieces of artillery and mortars, as well as many prisoners. The General's dash upon the enemy was a success. He swept a portion of their line, capturing several prominent and annoying forts and batteries, but was not able to hold them without being compelled to withstand heavy assaults, so it was deemed best to fall back upon our own works, which was done. Our troops behaved most handsomely. The sharp-shooters of General Gordon's corps, who led the assault, deserve the commendation of all loyal Southerners.

Even in face of this news, General Lee's dispatch is expressive of a nervous feeling on his part. We will pray for news not in keeping with that from General Lee, and hope tomorrow to state that General Lee's dispatch was but a rumor.

Washington, D.C.
Union Account

Recruiting is dull everywhere and drafting will be again resorted to, to obtain men. The draft began in Baltimore this morning.

Bermuda Hundred, Virginia,
Union Account

It is this morning known that Turner's and Foster's Divisions of the Twenty-fourth Corps and Birney's Division of the Twenty-fifth Corps, all under command of General Ord, will today join the Army of the Potomac, going by the pontoon bridge across the Appomattox at Point of Rocks. May God's blessing accompany them, and their next few weeks' efforts be crowned with glory.

City Point, Virginia,
Union Account

Sheridan's long column of troopers have this afternoon gone in the vicinity of Hancock Station, keeping well to the rear of our works, so that the enemy cannot see their movement. The air, tonight, is full of all kinds of reports. Some say that Goldsboro, North Carolina, will be Sheridan's aim; others that it is the

Southside Railroad, while others say that the Petersburg front will be entirely abandoned and that our army will swing in another direction. General Grant no doubt knows all about it and for us to state a thing properly it would be best to await his action. It is certain that a few days more will chronicle a change. We are inclined to think that it will be one pleasing to every loyal man.

Fayetteville, North Carolina,
Confederate Account

We are in great distress. Yankees have nearly destroyed both town and country. There will be left not more than fifty head of four-footed beasts in the country, and not enough provisions to last ten days. Many houses were burned and everything destroyed. Every store and house in town and country have been robbed.

Washington, D.C. March 27, 1865

"A special messenger who left Goldsboro, N. C., on the 22d arrived here today, and reports the occupation of that place by General Schofield's forces.

"He also brings the highly important information that General Sherman formed a junction with Schofield and Terry at Coxe's Bridge on the Neuse River, a few miles west of Goldsboro on the 21st.

"The Fourteenth Corps of Sherman's army had a fight with Hardee, at Averysborough, on the 16th inst., in which the latter was handsomely defeated, leaving all his dead in General Davis's hands, and retreating to Bentonville.

"At Bentonville on Sunday, the 12th inst, one division of the Fourteenth Corps was attacked by Johnston, and for a while turned back, but on being re-enforced by the rest of the divisions drove the enemy back, and during Sunday night he abandoned Bentonville and fell back across the Neuse River to Smithfield some ten miles west of Goldsboro.

"It is the merely temporary success in the first part of the fight which the Rebels are boasting over as a great victory. Sherman's loss will not exceed one thousand. The army is in excellent condition.

"Detailed accounts of the foregoing, dated Goldsboro March 21st, have also been received.

"On the 22d, Schofield moved out to Coxe's Bridge on the Neuse River, six miles beyond Goldsboro, where General Terry's forces were discovered laying pontoons to cross the river, having marched all the way from Wilmington. In a few moments some of Sherman's trains of the Twentieth Corps were discovered moving from

Bentonville to Coxe's Bridge, and the junction of the right wing of Sherman's army with Terry's and Schofield's forces was permanently made.

"General Sherman had notified Schofield that he would be at Goldsboro on the 22d of March, and he kept his word. Some of his staff were there during that day.

"After his repulse at Bentonville, Joe Johnston fell back to Smithfield, to cover Raleigh. Desertions of North Carolina troops from his army were numerous."

Petersburg, Virginia,
Confederate Account

"I expect this campaign will be the hottest fighting of the war. Ol' Abe will have to whip us this trip or close up his shop and quit. The exchange of prisoners was the clearest kind of an admission of weakness on his part, and it was the best thing in the world for us. Every Yankee prisoner we can produce now will bring us a good fighting man. Would it not have been a most excellent idea to have saved the clothes of the doodles we buried at Andersonville, and dressed up a little of the Georgia militia and traded them as Yankees for good fighting men. Many of the young men of Augusta, Georgia, who have disgraced themselves could be made useful to their country and the cause in the same way—for they are dead beats now."— [From a letter to the Daily Constitutionalist, of Augusta, Georgia.]

Baton Rouge, Louisiana, Union Account

General Bailey, with about one thousand cavalry, made an advance from Baton Rouge toward Clinton, a few days since. He had several fights and skirmishes with the Rebels thereabouts, and killed two and captured four. Our loss was thirteen wagons.

Tuesday, March 28, 1865

Washington D.C. March 28, 1865

The Fourth Army Corps, under General D. S. Stanley, is reported on its way to Knoxville to join in the West Virginia campaign, and its strength is estimated at from fifteen thousand to eighteen thousand men.

A cavalry force, estimated at six thousand, has left Knoxville under General Stoneman and is moving also toward West Virginia.

City Point, Virginia, Union Account

President Lincoln, Generals Grant, Sherman, Sheridan, Hancock, Meade, and all the leading Generals in the Army of the Potomac and the Army of the James, had a private consultation on board the President's boat, "The River Queen," this forenoon, which revives the story about Lee's desire to surrender.

White Oak, North Carolina, Union Account

We moved out from Kinston early this morning, General Cox accompanying us. Ruggles' First Division of the Twenty-third Corps with McQuiston's Brigade led the column. The Twelfth New York Cavalry headed the procession and are now forward looking for game.

Washington D.C. March 28, 1865

General Robert Anderson reached here today on his way to Fort Sumter to raise the same flag he was obliged to lower to the Rebels four years ago on the 14th of April.

New York, March 28, 1865

Gold opened at 154, went up $154^{5/8}$ and fell again to $154^{1/4}$. Brown sheetings are quoted at 30 cents per yard; bleached sheetings, New York mills, at 45 cents per yard. Calicoes are jobbing at 20 cents. Nails are $6.50 per keg.

Richmond, Virginia, Confederate Account

"This afternoon, four hundred and eighty-seven Yankees—part of the several thousand hived by General Johnston's army in the successive blows struck Sherman's horde in South Carolina by Hampton and Wheeler—were received from Fayetteville. The dirty blue line crawled its way down Main Street, coiling itself up in Libby Prison. No description could convey the utter horror and loathing with which their appearance was regarded by our citizens. Dirty, begrimmed, ragged, scores of them barefooted and bare-headed, with stolen toweling bandaged about their feet and heads, limping, hobbling and cursing, they appeared the scabs, scavengers and scum of all creation, not a face or feature on which was not written 'thief,' 'murderer,' 'house-burner' and 'woman ravisher.' Never since the war began has such a crew of hell-born men, accursed and God-forsaken wretches, polluted the air or defiled the highways of Richmond with the concentrated essence of all that is lecherous, hateful and despised. And these are a part and parcel of that human *fungi* Johnston's noble army are confronting. These are some of those who robbed, burned, plundered and murdered in the fair homes of Georgia and South Carolina. If we cannot successfully resist them, God help Richmond and her citizens. Devils from hell would show mercy when these would strike and rob, murder, pillage and destroy. The only way they can be permitted to come, must be on the terms that those come today—as prisoners of war. The majority of the horde that came in today were captured from Kilpatrick's thieves, and they may not inaptly be called Kil-devils."

Goldsboro, North Carolina,
Union Account

The grand combinations in the Carolinas are now reaching their final development. The roar of artillery from our three grand columns is reverberating this evening. This tells us that a fight is now on and that Johnston's army is resisting our further advance.

At 10 o'clock P. M., word comes to us from General Sherman saying the battle just fought was all right for us, and our loss light.

Trans-Mississippi Department,
Confederate Account

Military matters beyond the Mississippi are entirely at a standstill. Our forces hold the lower portion of Arkansas, along the Washita River, commanding the greater portion of the Red River.

Washington, D.C.
Union Account

A letter received today from one of Sherman's men says: Our men are beginning to grow feathers on the calves of their legs, having feasted so long on chickens, turkeys, geese and ducks,"

Newbern, North Carolina,
Union Account

Supplies are rapidly going forward from this place to General Sherman's army. Quartermaster-General Meigs is personally superintending the transportation.

A general payment of all the troops in this department has been ordered to be made up to December 31.

All is quiet at the front. The enemy show no signs of life. Where they are and what they are doing is a matter of indifference to us just now.

Goldsboro, North Carolina,
Union Account

Bodies of Rebel cavalry are prowling about our lines, picking up foragers and unprotected squads that venture out beyond our lines.

Mobile, Alabama,
Confederate Account

General Murray, in command here, has issued an order to the people to send away all non-combatants, and prepare for a vigorous defense against the Federal troops.

Bermuda Hundred, Virginia,
Union Account

A selection of tried veteran regiments was today made from the Army of the James, or rather from the Twenty-fourth Corps, and under command of General Ord they crossed the pontoon at Point of Rocks at dark, bound for the Petersburg front.

Our line from Dutch Gap to the Appomattox is quiet. Rain is coming down in torrents.

Army of the Potomac,
Union Account

Everything has been quiet along this entire front, except the usual picket firing at night. As General Sheridan's cavalry were passing an exposed point yesterday, the Rebels opened upon them with shell, but, with a single exception, their shot fell short and did no damage.

Sheridan's men and horses look remarkably well considering their service, and the men are ready and anxious to show us how they do things. They will have an opportunity to do this very soon if there is anything in appearances, as they are, at this time, on the black-board for an advance.

City Point, Virginia,
Union Account

At twelve o'clock last night, the whole Army of the Potomac was placed under arms and held in readiness for movement at a moment's notice. It is not known as to General Grant's plans, but it is settled to a certainty that the campaign now on, he intends making the final one of the war. Keep your eyes open.

Between Selma and Montgomery, Alabama,
Union Account

General Wilson's command met Forrest and Taylor's Rebel forces today between Selma and Montgomery, where a display of the skill of both sides was shown in the fierce engagement. The Rebels were totally defeated, and a large number of prisoners were captured by General Wilson's cavalry.

Army of the Potomac,
Union Account

General Ord, with the tried portion of the Army of the James has taken a position on our left and is temporarily encamped behind the line of the Second Corps on Hatcher's Run. They reach us to participate in what we hope will be the closing campaign of the war. Everything is activity. No telling what a day will bring forth. The Army of the Potomac is ready for the issue and hope to change position in spite of Lee's protests. Every indication points to an advance on our part. Where will we be in a week from now?

In Front of Spanish Fort,
Union Account

We have been peppering away at Spanish Fort since yesterday morning. Our skirmish line is within two hundred yards of it, and our artillery within three hundred. We have it encompassed on the three land sides. Bartman's Brigade of the Thirteenth Corps is holding the extreme left near the bay; Veach's division next and Benton's next, all of the Thirteenth Corps. General A. J. Smith's Sixteenth Corps is holding the right, so the only chance the Rebels have to escape is by water. If our gunboats can get up the torpedoes and get within range, we have them on the hip.

General Steele's forces have captured two trains loaded with supplies, at Pollards, taking in also the whole of the Sixth Alabama (Rebel) Cavalry.

Richmond, Virginia,
Confederate Account

President Davis, this afternoon, paid the veterans at Camp Lee a visit. The President carries an expression of anxiety upon his face, so different from that generally found there. It is no doubt his opinion that Lee and Johnston are in a very uncertain position and that with the Yankee armies re-enforced, we are likely to be overpowered and forced to yield. He says but little to others than those of his immediate official circle, but the news we daily receive, lead us to imagine that he is more concerned about the Confederacy than his expression shows.

The day is one of clouds and sunshine. The weather is fairly pleasant, yet cold enough to make it uncomfortable for our veterans now in the trenches fighting for the Confederacy.

Jefferson Davis
President, CSA

Wednesday, March 29, 1865

In front of Petersburg, Virginia,
Union Account

At four o'clock this morning the Fifth and Second Corps were put in march upon the right of the enemy's line, the Fifth moving by the Quaker road. On coming to a point called Skunk's Hollow, and mounting the brow of the opposite slope, a breastwork was found abandoned by the enemy. Passing about three-fourths of a mile beyond this, the head of the column, at half-past five o'clock, met a line of the enemy posted on the edge of a thick pine-wood belting or clearing. Here a sudden and heavy fire was opened upon our skirmish line, and it was driven back upon a line formed of the First Brigade, First Division, which at first fell back, but, on being supported by the Second Brigade, rallied, and drove back the enemy, with some loss in prisoners. In the meantime, General Warren drew up the rest of the First and the Third Divisions of the Fifth Corps in line, in order to support the attack. After an action of about three-quarters of an hour, the enemy retreated in haste, leaving his dead and most of his wounded on the field. The force of the enemy engaged was one division of their Fourth Corps, under General B. Johnson, its strength being about six thousand men. Our loss was three to four hundred men killed and wounded. That of the enemy, in killed and wounded, appeared to be about the same, but the number of prisoners—some one hundred and fifty to two hundred—renders their total loss greater than ours. Lieutenant Patterson, of the Seventh Michigan, was killed in the engagement.

Major McCuen, of the One hundred and ninety-eighth Pennsylvania Regiment was also killed. At the close of the day our original line, which extended on the left to Hatcher's run, had been prolonged beyond the Run, westward across the Vaughn and Quaker roads, facing northward to within about two and a half miles of Dinwiddie Court House. In the meantime, our cavalry corps under General Sheridan, made a detour east of the Vaughn road, sweeping around the left of our infantry at four o'clock p.m., toward Dinwiddie Court House.

The route taken is the same over which a portion of the army has traveled several times heretofore, namely: The Vaughn and Halifax roads, running southwest across Hatcher's Run. Rebel prisoners said that the move had been a complete surprise to them as they had expected an attack in the vicinity of Fort Steadman, and that their troops had been massed there to meet it.

General Grant's headquarters were this evening established on the Vaughn road, near Gravelly Run, General Meade being in the same vicinity.

A large portion of the Army of the James, under General Ord, was withdrawn from the north side of the Appomattox River, which, with the Sixth and Ninth Corps, was left in charge of the works before Petersburg.

Army of the Potomac,
Union Account

The route taken by a portion of this army is the same over which it has several times traveled, by way of the Vaughn and Halifax roads, running southwest across Hatcher's Run.

The column started at three o'clock this morning. Sheridan's cavalry took the Halifax road toward Dinwiddie Court House. The infantry crossed Hatcher's Run on the Vaughn road, but met with no opposition until they reached within a short distance of the Boydtown Plank Road, when the enemy's pickets were found and driven back. Griffin's Division went up the Quaker road and about three o'clock this afternoon a division of the enemy were encountered. They did not know as to the strength of our force when they formed in line and charged. They were repulsed with heavy loss.

A number of prisoners brought in say that they were taken by surprise, as they expected an attack in the vicinity of Fort Steadman and their troops were there massed to meet it.

It is believed the Rebels were hurrying their troops toward the South-side Railroad all this afternoon, in hopes of being able to prevent Sheridan taking possession of it. Sheridan is breaking for that point and we hope will succeed in cutting off the supplies from Lee's army.

Petersburg Front,
Union Account

The Fifth Corps had a sharp encounter with the enemy on the Quaker road today. We lost less than three hundred men and drove the Rebels nearly a mile, with serious loss to them and a number of prisoners.

Washington, D. C.
Union Account
General Thomas is moving upon Richmond from the southwest with a heavy force. The enemy will be pressed so as to compel him to give instead of receive a battle.

Hatcher's Run,
Union Account
Turner's Division of the Twenty-fourth Corps made a junction with the right of the Second Corps just as the sun peeped out this morning. This connection was made without fighting. It was not expected, however, that we should long exist in a quiet state. Hardly had we become in position when our services were needed. The gallant commands of both Foster and Turner made an assault on the enemy's line and captured their rifle pits with all that was in them. This advance was made within six hundred yards of the enemy's main works. Birney's Division held the right of Foster, and the assault was simultaneous. Cheer after cheer went up all along the line over the work of the gallant Twenty-fourth Corps. Our loss cannot tonight be given accurately, but is heavy.

Covington, Kentucky,
Union Account
A large number of Rebel soldiers belonging to Kentucky regiments, who have been confined in prison, have recently taken the oath, and pass through here daily, bound for their homes.

Augusta, Georgia,
Confederate Account
Messrs. W. A. Ramsey & Co., at their auction sale on Friday last, obtained the following prices: Harness, $3,000 to $3,500 per set; carriages, $4,000 to $6,000 each; Negro boys, $3,000 to $3,500; Negro women, $3,700 to $4,100; woman and two children, $4,500; silver spoons, $1,200 to $1,300 per dozen ; sewing machines, $500 to $1,500.

Mobile, Alabama,
Confederate Account
Scouts report a force landed at Cedar Point today. The Yankee fleet fired a number of guns, occupying all day. Cause not reported.

Newport, Kentucky,
Union Account

Rebel Guerillas have again made their appearance in the upper end of this county and are committing many depredations. They are reported at Twelve Mile Creek, where they are ransacking stores, burning property and doing about as they choose.

City Point, Virginia,
Union Account

The downfall of the Confederacy is near at hand. Recent advices give assurance that neither Lee nor Johnston can either retreat or offer battle without great destruction to their armies. It is understood that steps will be taken at Richmond at once, to convince General Lee that to longer attempt holding the Confederacy together means the loss of thousands of lives. We will likely know the result of both Grant and Lee's intentions in a very few days.

Collecting Remains of the Dead

This is a ghastly view showing the process of collecting the remains of Union soldiers who were hastily buried at the time of the battle. This is a scene on the battlefield months after the battle, when the Government ordered the remains gathered for permanent burial. The grinning skulls, the boot still hanging on the fleshless bones, the old canteen on the skeleton all testify to the hasty burial after the battle.

Looking on this scene you can easily understand why, in all National Cemeteries, there are so great a number of graves marked "Unknown". These are the "unknown heroes of the war, who "died that our Nation might live."

Near the Boydtown Plank Road,
Union Account

We are now here, but we do not promise to stay here very long. General Meade's headquarters, near the Aiken House at Park Station, were broken up at six o'clock and at eleven General Grant, accompanied by Generals Williams and Ingalls, a number of his staff and several civilians, arrived on a special train at Humphrey Station, the terminus of the railroad, within a mile of Hatcher's Run on the Vaughn road. Here Grant and his modest cortege mounted their horses, and after visiting the headquarters of General Ord, nearby, moved down to the new line which had been formed, in compliance with orders, south of Hatcher's Run. General Meade and staff had already preceded him by several hours, and were superintending the formation of the Second Corps line, which in the afternoon was advanced over a mile northward.

The Rebel pickets across the run fell back before the advance of the Second Corps, and. the new line was assumed without any opposition. Entrenching tools were brought into requisition, and in a short time the position was rendered secure against any attack. During this time the Fifth Corps was moving down the Goshen road, a little west of south and several miles east of the Vaughn. Five miles from the point of starting, the corps struck another road, known as the Old Stage road, leading west to the Vaughn, which it crossed on a by-road to the Quaker or Military road, leading north to the Boydtown Plank Road. Meanwhile, Sheridan was moving still farther to the left, in the direction of Dinwiddie Court House.

Moving up the Quaker road, through a wooded country, with occasional clearings and small streams, the Fifth crossed Gravelly Run at 2:30 P. M. and on arriving at May's farm, a short distance beyond, found a line of Rebel earthworks and a number of huts deserted by the enemy's pickets. A few hundred yards beyond this point the Rebel skirmishers were encountered by our flankers, who gradually advanced, followed by the column, pushing the enemy before them, until they reached another clearing. Here the brigade of General Chamberlain, which had led the column, was disposed in line of battle and advanced across the clearing. When well in the clearing the enemy opened from the woods beyond, driving back our skirmishers upon the line of battle, which now became hotly engaged. A sharp engagement lasted for fifteen minutes, when the enemy, who had used no artillery, showing no disposition to retire, Battery B of the Fourth United States Artillery, was brought up and posted on the right of the road, to compel a retrograde movement on their part. A few rounds, well directed, and the fire of the enemy slackened. Chamberlain's brigade was then directed to charge, which it gallantly did, the enemy falling back hastily up the Quaker toward the Boydtown Plank Road. General Warren then formed his corps in line of battle, placing the left in reserve, and moved up to the Rainie House at the junction of the Quaker and Boydtown roads. Our loss in the engagement was from three to four hundred in killed and wounded, while the casualties of the enemy might have been fewer, owing to his sheltered position. The capture of one hundred and forty prisoners, however, probably made his loss greater than our own. And thus ends the history of today. Sheridan is near Dinwiddie, Warren at the junction of the Quaker and Boydtown roads, in connection with the Second, whose line extended from his right nearly eastward past Dabney's Mills to the vicinity of Hatcher's Run. The new line had been formed, and with the exception of a little skirmishing along portions of the front, and the fight of the Fifth Corps, all has been quiet during the day. Tonight the headquarters of Generals Grant and Meade are near Gravelly Run, on the Vaughn road.

Petersburg, Virginia,
Confederate Account

At nine minutes past ten o'clock tonight the Federals opened on our extreme left, near the Appomattox River, with a fearful artillery fire, while a simultaneous movement was made on the part of their infantry, the men charging upon our breastworks in great masses. Our men, under the gallant Gordon, were wide awake and received the charge with a coolness and precision which caused the assailants to recoil with evident dismay and consternation. The enemy made five assaults between that time and midnight, the time I write this. In each assault the "blue-bellies" were sent reeling back. We know that the enemy has expended his greatest effort and we are satisfied with the result. They came in swarms, supposed to be several lines of battle deep, and in no instance did they even get through our obstructions. The slaughter was fearful. Our loss is light. It is very dark at this time, being impossible to see farther ahead than twenty paces.

Lisbon, Portugal, March 29, 1865

The Confederate ram Stonewall has sailed from this port. The Federal war steamers, Niagara and Sacramento, have arrived here. The Portuguese authorities prohibit their sailing for twenty-four hours.

At 10: 25 A. M., the Federal frigates, Niagara and Sacramento attempted to sail before the expiration of the time fixed by the Portuguese authorities, and were fired upon by the Beleu Fort.

The Niagara was struck on the poop, and a seaman was killed. The vessels thereupon anchored.

Richmond, Virginia,
Confederate Account

Mosby has six hundred men doing good work in the northern part of this State. Three hundred are in Louden County, and the same number in Prince William, or all near Washington City. The daring deeds of Mosby and his braves will never be forgotten by the true Southerner. His work of destruction of Yankee property goes right on.

Colonel John S. Mosby
"The Gray Ghost"
43rd Battalion, Virginia Cavalry

Mosby's Rangers
43rd Battalion, Virginia Cavalry

Goldsboro, North Carolina, Union Account

The Armies of the Tennessee and Cumberland have not been supplied with clothing and shoes since they left Atlanta. Through the stupidity and bad management of someone, supplies for the army did not reach Savannah until the armies had moved out. The men are in great need of everything.

About half of this army are mounted; it rather don't care to do much more walking. Nearly everyone has his own coach, cab, buggy, cart or wagon, drawn by horses or mules—blind or lame—colts or old worn-out horses or mules, anything that can draw something after it, was "pressed in" and the result is, General Sherman could now advertise a livery stable extensive enough to supply the whole country, provided they were not choice as to "rigs." A few soldiers turned out this morning in a fine-looking coach, behind four fat, sleek mules decked with silver-plated harness, with the following card on the door:

"All aboard for Richmond via Camp Fifteenth Army Corps. Fare (hard-tack and sow-belly) free." It is now foregone that a soldier is not worthy of respect unless he has his own coach and a span of trotters—jackasses preferred.

The rear of the Seventeenth Corps presents a very novel appearance. A number of vehicles were seen there this morning, leading one to believe that there was a funeral on hand, but the character of the occupants soon convinced us of our mistake. One of the boys said "it was the funeral of the Confederacy." The owners of the trotting stock fed by this army have not yet come after them, so we just try to enjoy them a little for a change. Our feet are sore and we can't walk quite so well as we could before we struck so many things on wheels.

Mobile, Alabama, Union Report

The Spanish Fort opened early this morning, and the guns on the south side were silenced by our sharpshooters. As soon as a Rebel made his appearance at a gun, he was picked off. At about half past ten o'clock all was quiet. Our boys, getting tired of doing nothing, gave a yell, as if about to charge, which proved a successful ruse, for immediately the Rebel heads made their appearance above the works, to look for the last time.

Several siege-guns and mortars have arrived from Fort Morgan.

Our loss, up to tonight, numbers fifty killed and two hundred wounded. The Rebel loss is not known.

The Rebel battery near Dog River, opened fire on the gunboat Scotia, early this morning. The Scotia was not hit. The iron-clad Milwaukee put in an appearance and drove the Rebel battery back.

Thursday, March 30, 1865

Richmond, Virginia,
Confederate Account

A sudden change of the weather has brought rain upon us in torrents. It is very warm. Possibly the Almighty has seen fit to give us this change of weather, to defeat Grant in his efforts to destroy General Lee's communications and source of supplies. It is our prayer that such is the case, as we surely need help from above at this time.

Reliable news reaches here this morning that General Thomas's Army is rapidly advancing from East Tennessee into Virginia. Where next will the Yankees strike? With Grant in front of us, Sherman in our rear and Thomas coming in on the southwest, how can we long expect to get supplies? Their armies are tenfold greater than ours. Appearances go to show that we are short lived as a Confederacy, but we will yet show them that we are able to hold Richmond in spite of their immense force, for a long time to come.

Washington, D.C.

Deserters arrived today from Lee's Army and report that Negroes are being placed in the fortifications in and about Richmond, and that the Richmond citizens do not like it, while the Confederate troops laugh at them. The Negroes improve every opportunity to desert, while many have succeeded in making their escape. At Belle Isle several thousand Negroes are being drilled with sticks in lieu of muskets.

The transport Connecticut brought about four hundred wounded here today, including fifty-eight Confederates, which were sent to the different hospitals. The Confederates report their loss at Fort Steadman will amount to nearly four thousand.

An Alabama planter who arrived here today, states that the Rebel authorities have placed Negroes in the trenches around Richmond, but they are afraid to trust them in large bodies.

The telegraph between here and City Point has not been working for five or six hours and if there is any fighting it is unknown here. It is believed, however, that a heavy battle took place today.

In Front of Petersburg, Virginia,
Union Account

At four P. M. yesterday the enemy was seen to be massing in front of that part of our line held by the First Division, Ninth Corps. This led General Wilcox to strengthen that point, and to put his pickets on the alert. At 10:15 a rocket shot up from the Rebel lines, and at once a heavy fire was opened from their batteries on the right and left of the point menaced. A little later this was followed by a heavy musketry fire from the nearest line of their defenses, distant about one hundred and seventy-five yards from our line. For some time this fire was kept up with vigor, and our batteries replied to it as vigorously, while the Second and Third Brigades of the division lay quietly ready to meet any attack. Then the enemy showed outside of their defenses the head of a strong column, as if to make an attack upon Battery n and the line about it, but the fire of our artillery forced the column to get hastily under cover again. The firing was kept up some time longer upon our defenses between Battery 11 and Fort Steadman, and finally ceased at 1:10 A. M.

This section of our line is that which was carried by the enemy on the 25th instant, and which they were forced to relinquish after a short struggle.

The object of the enemy in this attack appears to have been to feel the strength of our line at the point mentioned, and to draw off troops from our left, by an attack, if the point was found to be weak, or by a show of attack in case the line was found strong. The latter seems to be the most likely, for they made a show of the attack which they would not have done if any real effort was meant, as on the 25th instant, when their attack was quiet and sudden.

All the firing being done in the dark, the loss was small on our side and could not have been great on that of the Rebels. Only fifty-one men were hit on our side, the only officer of rank killed being Major Brown, Eighteenth New Hampshire Volunteers.

On the side of the Rebels the loss may. not have exceeded two hundred men, their force having been only at one time from under cover.

Army of Northern Virginia, Confederate Report

Headquarters, March. 30, 1865 *General J. C. Breckinridge, Secretary of War:* General Gordon reports that the enemy, at eleven P. M. yesterday, advanced against a portion of his line, defended by Brigadier-General Lewis, but was repulsed. The fire of artillery and mortars continued several hours with considerable activity. No damage on our lines reported. *R. E. Lee.*

Petersburg, Virginia, Confederate Account

At an early hour this morning a heavy force of the enemy, consisting of cavalry, infantry and artillery, supposed to be headed by "Cavalry Sheridan," made a detour around our lines and advanced toward the Boydtown Plank Road, and, between seven and eight o'clock, struck this thoroughfare some six miles beyond Dinwiddie Court House. Toward eleven o'clock we understand this force was in the vicinity of the Court House, our forces skirmishing heavily with their advance.

Richmond, Virginia, Confederate Account

General Anderson, commanding our extreme right, demonstrated against the enemy's works in his front for the purpose of ascertaining his strength at that point, and, if possible, their intentions. In pending operations our forces met with a vigorous resistance. The object of the demonstration gained, they fell back, the Yankees not pursuing. Late in the afternoon, however, the enemy commenced advancing and skirmishing with our forces. Some severe fighting may have occurred. Meantime let us all keep cool, wait results, and trust in God, General Lee and the gallantry of our brave troops for success.

Gravelly Run, Virginia,
Union Account

An advance was made this morning along our whole left or operating wing, the enemy giving way after indulging in some spiteful sharpshooting, to his main works across the Boydtown Plank Road. Our movement has developed portions of his line, and discovered the fact that he still maintains, with a bold front, his old earthworks covering the Southside Railroad. Our advance was perhaps most hotly contested opposite General Birney's division and north of the intersection of the Vaughn road with Hatcher's Run, where the enemy used considerable artillery, doing us but little damage, however. A battery was likewise unmasked beyond Dabney's Mill, in front of Smyth's brigade of the Second Corps, and several shots thrown at our advance.

A reconnaissance was made to White Oak Grove this morning by Merritt's Division of Cavalry, and the enemy found to be guarding the different avenues approaching the Southside Railroad.

Our casualties in the skirmish today have been few, and will not probably foot up to more than forty or fifty at the highest estimate.

Our present line in general direction is the same as yesterday. The whole movement thus far cannot, perhaps, be more comprehensively explained than by saying that our left or movable wing has executed what is known in military evolutions as *a right wheel* with the pivot of the wheeling line resting near the Vaughn road at the point where it crosses Hatcher's Run. We now have possession of the Boydtown Plank Road several miles north of Dinwiddie Court House, and five and a half or six miles from the Southside Railroad. From the point where our left cuts the Boydtown plank our line extends nearly eastward, almost the entire distance through thick forests of pine saplings, across Hatcher's Run to our original line and with it forming an obtuse angle. South of and cutting the Boydtown Plank Road a quarter of a mile above the junction, the left of our line rests.

Richmond, Virginia,
Confederate Account

Reliable intelligence from City Point represents the presence of fifteen monitors and forty ironclad vessels in the James River below Dutch Gap. Since our attempt to pass the Yankee obstructions, the enemy has doubled his vigilance and increased his force.

Sheridan and his cavalry have passed around Lee's right.

It is evident that April will witness a decisive turn, one way or the other, to Grant's campaign. All we need is to sustain our army and keep the Stars and Bars flying for one month, when the mighty effort of the Federal power will have been made and will have failed, as usual.

Hatcher's Run, Virginia,
Union Account

There is no room on this line for else than men of snap. The Twenty-fourth Corps has been under fire all day long and it has been rattlety-bang from morning until night. Birney's Division has been in battle most of the day. Their losses are heavier than the balance of the Corps. It is acknowledged on all sides that the Twenty-fourth Corps contains pluck and that their coming here at this time means that they will make use of it.

Tonight our boys are busy strengthening their works, and before morning will have a line that the Johnnies will find "a hard road to travel."

City Point, Virginia,
Union Account

Last night a heavy rain storm set in making the treacherous soil one vast slough all along and in the rear of our works. Through the woods leading to the front, caissons, guns, wagons and ambulances might be seen at short intervals mired in mud, and it at once became evident that no advance would be made, from the fact that no artillery could be thrown forward through the woods until the roads were corduroyed.

Newbern, North Carolina,
Union Account

General Sherman issued the following this morning: "All mail for officers and soldiers in the army now with Major General Sherman, will, after this date, be sent to Fortress Monroe for distribution. No mail for civilians will be delivered unless addressed to the care of some officer to whom they are personally known."

Goldsboro, North Carolina,
Union Account

The first serious attempt at raiding or scouting around our lines since our occupation was made today by Hampton's cavalry, upon the right and center of our lines, northwest of Mosely Hall, eight miles from here.

A party of Kilpatrick's cavalry had been sent out on a scouting expedition, when they fell in with a force of Hampton's cavalry who attacked them. A sharp skirmish followed, our men fighting and falling back. A squad of the Twenty-third Michigan arrived just in time to save our men, who were outnumbered three to one. We captured two prisoners. A detail went out from the Second Brigade to bring in the wounded and bury the dead.

Richmond, Virginia,
Confederate Account

This morning's Sentinel says: "Obviously there is extreme need for every exertion which we can possibly put forth. General Lee needs men and needs provisions. He needs every man and every ration we can give him. We must now give him the militia, the reserve and the local troops to the last man. We must all lend our efforts also, to the encouragement of the enlistment of colored troops. We must yield our slaves and encourage them to volunteer, and do so speedily. We must, at whatever sacrifice, supply Lee's army with provisions. It is superfluous to say that this is absolutely necessary. There is no time to dole or to measure out our contributions. Lee's army must be fed, or we shall be overtaken with speedy disaster and inevitable ruin."

Mobile, Alabama near Spanish Fort,
Union Account

Admiral Thatcher's fleet, in conjunction with General Canby's forces, moved up the bay above Howard's Landing and opened a heavy fire at once, upon the Rebel gunboats and transports, compelling them to retire to a safer position.

The Thirteenth Corps under General Gordon Granger drove the enemy back and secured a strong position upon the left center and left, in this way opening communication with the bay, and completely flanking the Rebel right center, and right. The Sixteenth Corps under General Smith also succeeded in flanking the enemy's left center and left. Thus about four thousand Rebels were hermetically sealed in Spanish Fort. We are now within thirty yards of Spanish Fort, behind strong breastworks, dealing death to every Rebel who has the temerity to raise his head above their works.

Montgomery, Alabama,
Confederate Account

There is no doubt that the enemy in heavy force are moving down into the interior of the state from points on the Tennessee River. From department officers just arrived from Selma, we learn that a Federal force of six thousand has started from Tuscumbia. They divided at Jasper, one column moving in the direction of Tuscaloosa, and the other toward Montevallo. The troops, under the Yankee General McCook, had with them a wagon train and artillery. They came through Elyton and burned everything there. They also burned the Red Mountain Iron Works.

We have information that the wires are being tampered with by McCook's operators. The following message came in today: "How are you? Will call on you in Montgomery soon."

Savannah, Georgia,
Union Account

Since Sherman's capture of Savannah, two hundred and sixty brigs and sixty-six schooners have entered the port. Quite a number of adopted citizens were forced into the Rebel ranks by one reason or another during the progress of the war, and since Sherman's march through Georgia, large numbers of them have found their way back and are now peaceable citizens, apparently glad that Savannah is again beneath the good old flag.

Petersburg, Virginia,
Confederate Account

"A heavy fight has been progressing all day at Dinwiddie, near Hatcher's Run, eight miles from the city. Nothing official, but reports up to five o'clock, deemed reliable, state that three furious assaults were repulsed.

At half past two o'clock the Yankees came up in overwhelming numbers and drove Bushrod Johnson's Division one mile and a half.

We were then re-enforced, which turned the tide of the battle, and we drove the enemy with great slaughter to and beyond their original position in the morning. The ground was strewed with dead and dying, and seven hundred prisoners were sent to the rear.

The affair last night for roar of cannon and musketry, which lasted two hours, exceeded anything ever heard in this vicinity. It turned out today that both belligerents conceived the idea that they were being charged behind their works, when in fact, neither had left their entrenchments. Hence the lavish expenditure of ammunition. It was one of the most novel events of this remarkable war.

The loss was small on our side, and not supposed to be large with the enemy. All quiet in front today.

Lynchburg, Virginia,
Confederate Account

The advance of Thomas's Army is said to have been at Carter's, within twenty miles of Bristol, on Sunday evening last. Telegraphic communication is open to Bristol.

Thomas no doubt is preparing to invade Southwestern Virginia with a large force. There are large quantities of provisions in that section that should be promptly removed, or they will certainly be appropriated by Thomas if he succeeds in his expedition.

First Army Corps near Charleston, Virginia,
Union Account

Mosby still hovers around, occasionally dropping upon our pickets and outposts. We hope to gobble up this band of Guerillas and their man Mosby very soon, and give them a severe thrashing before doing so.

Friday, March 31, 1865

Washington, D. C. March 31, 1865

Substitutes are today receiving eight hundred dollars a head, and there is a good demand.

Goldsboro, North Carolina,
Union Account

"The Rebels have completed all preparations to evacuate Raleigh. All depots of the State Government have been removed to Gronsborough, as well as all surplus military stores. General Schofield has levied a contribution of one hundred thousand rations of meat and flour upon the citizens. A Newbern dispatch of the 28th says that the armies in North Carolina are taking a brief repose. Sherman's forces were much in need of shoes, clothing and other necessaries prior to striking the finishing blow to the Rebel Confederacy. All is quiet at the front. The enemy shows no signs of life. Where they are or what they are about, appears to be a matter of indifference just now. General Sherman's headquarters are to be removed from Savannah to Newbern. General Howard's headquarters, from Beaufort, S. C, are also to be removed to this point. Another batch of five hundred Rebel prisoners arrived in Newbern from Goldsboro on the 26th ultimo. They left on the 27th for the North. More than half of them desire to take the oath of allegiance."

Goldsboro, North Carolina,
Union Account

A most imposing military execution has just taken place about half a mile in front of the field works, fronting the Provisional Division, and running almost parallel with Little River' stream.

The condemned, James Preble, of the Twelfth New York Cavalry, was executed for a rape committed on an aged woman on the 16th inst., in the vicinity of Kinston.

The whole of the Provisional Division of Schofield's command was paraded on the occasion, and was, together with the arrangements for the execution, under the command of Colonel Classon, of the One Hundred and Thirty-second New York Volunteers.

The division arrived on the ground at precisely one o'clock, and was formed in two ranks in three sides of a square, the rear rank ten paces in rear of the front rank, which came to an about face when the unfortunate condemned one was paraded through the ranks.

At about twenty minutes to three o'clock, the procession which attended the unfortunate man who was soon to be summarily summoned into the presence of his Maker, made its appearance in the following order: A detachment of the One Hundred and Thirty-second New York and Seventeenth Massachusetts Volunteers, under command of Captain Keenan, Acting Provost Marshal, four men carrying a coffin, an ambulance containing the condemned man and his two spiritual advisers, the Reverend H. M. Bacon, Chaplain of the Sixty-third Indiana, and the Reverend Mr. Dodd, Chaplain of the Twenty-fifth Massachusetts. Upon arriving on the ground the unfortunate man was taken from the ambulance and escorted in mournful procession with Drum Corps playing the dead march through the ranks forming the three sides of the square.

James Preble did not appear to be more than twenty years of age, and about six feet in height; his appearance in no way gave indication of the brutality which would be naturally supposed to characterize the appearance of one proved to have been guilty of so heinous an offense. He marched with a remarkably steady step all the way round the square, and but seldom raised his eyes from the ground.

In the center of the space in the open side of the square, Preble's grave was dug, and on arriving at it, after marching around the square, the procession halted, and the proceedings and sentence of his court-martial, together with the order for his execution, was read by the Provost-Marshal, after which he knelt down by his coffin, with the Chaplain in attendance, and prayed for about five minutes, when his eyes were bandaged with a white handkerchief, and the firing party, consisting of twelve men from the One Hundred and Thirty-second New York and Seventeenth Pennsylvania, were formed in line about twelve paces in front of him. At precisely five minutes past three the order to "make ready, aim and fire," was delivered in a clear, audible tone by the Acting Provost-Marshal, and the unfortunate man fell down dead, pierced with four balls, one through the neck and three through the breast. He was immediately examined by the Provost Marshal and the surgeon in attendance and pronounced dead. The whole division then marched past the corpse, which was placed on top of the coffin, by columns of companies, and filed back to their quarters. This will doubtless prove, as it is intended it should, a warning to evil disposed and reckless men, and they well know that acts of barbarity will not be tolerated in an army whose purpose is to restore law and order.

City Point, Virginia, Union Account

Along General Ord's front, withstanding the disadvantage of the mud, an advance of several hundred yards was made by Turner's West Virginians and Foster's Division, supported by Birney's colored command of the Twenty-fifth Corps. Sheridan also pushed forward on Tuesday, and night found him in the vicinity of Sutherland's Station, on the Southside Railroad.

Not relishing Sheridan's alarming proximity to the Southside Railroad, the enemy, having been re-enforced by Pickett's Division, made an impetuous attack upon him in front and on the flank, and at night had pushed, back our troops after heavy fighting, compelling us to leave behind in the enemy's hands many of our dead and wounded. As the Fifth Corps had, on the night previous, assumed a line stretching nearly westward from the Boydtown plank, where its right connected with the left of the Second, by the repulse of Sheridan, and his retirement through Dinwiddie Court House on Friday afternoon, it was at once seen that a change of front of at least the Fifth Corps would be necessary, in order to meet any attack by a large force of the enemy on its left and rear. Accordingly, at midnight the Fifth, leaving an interval to be supplied by Miles's Division of the Second, left its position, and, moving down the Boydtown plank toward Dinwiddie, massed at the Butler House for the purpose of seizing the White Oak road, which, several miles above the junction of the Quaker and Boydtown, runs west from the latter until it strikes the Claiborne road leading to Sutherland Station.

Early in the morning the Fifth moved forward, while the Second commenced demonstrating its front for the purpose of masking our real intention, viz., the possession of the White Oak road. The charge of the Fifth was temporarily successful, the enemy being pushed back to a point near the coveted road, when he rallied, and in turn assaulted the Fifth, which retired somewhat hastily to the vicinity of the Boydtown road, where it took shelter behind a line of temporary works. At this junction the division of Miles was directed to strike the victorious enemy on the flank, and massing his brigades in echelon, he began moving to the left and west from his position on the Boydtown Plank. The remainder of the Second was meanwhile engaged in heavy skirmishing across the Boydtown Plank. General Humphreys moved his headquarters to the Rainie House, at the junction of the Boydtown and Quaker Roads, and it was near this point that his A. A. G., Major Miles, was killed by a round shot from one of the enemy's batteries.

At about half past ten o'clock in the forenoon, the column of Miles struck the Rebel left in front of Warren, surprised it, and moving rapidly forward, drove the enemy like frightened sheep down Warren's front, capturing prisoners, guns, and colors, and then wheeling to the right, still pursuing the flying enemy, established himself on the White Oak Road, across which Warren afterward formed his command, facing northeast, and connecting with Miles's Division of the Second. Thus, after a severe engagement of several hours, we had, at the cost of several hundred lives, compassed our original intention.

In Front of Petersburg, Virginia, Union Account

Army of the Potomac
Friday Night
March 31, 1865

There was severe fighting today. Notwithstanding the disadvantageous circumstance of mud, the left of our line was pushed forward at daybreak this morning, bringing on a heavy engagement in front of the Fifth Corps and General Miles's Division of the Second, the final result of which was the pushing back of the enemy across the White Oak Road and its occupation by our troops.

At daybreak this morning Griffin's Division of the Fifth Corps, the left of which rested on the Boydtown Road, a short distance above the Quaker Road, moved by the left flank down the Boydtown Road to the Butler House, where it was massed behind the commands of Generals Crawford and Ayres, for an advance upon the enemy, covering the White Oak Road.

The object of the advance was the possession of this road, which, diverging from the Boydtown Road, several miles north of its junction with the Quaker Road, runs westward to the Claiborne Road, leading northwest to the Southside Railroad.

At about eight o'clock this morning, the Division of General Ayres, supported by those of Crawford and Griffin, began their advance upon the enemy, which was immediately resisted by the Rebel skirmishers, who were slowly pushed back, however, to within a mile of the White Oak Road.

At this juncture the enemy, gathering all his available force, and with his usual yell, charged our advancing columns, which, wavering for a time, finally gave way to the impetuous assault, retiring slowly toward the Boydtown Plank Road, and halting only when they arrived at the brow of a hill, where supported by Griffin's Division, which had just reached that point, they took shelter in the temporary breastworks constructed by them last night. Several ineffectual attempts were then made by the enemy to dislodge them, our fierce musketry fire, aided by Batteries D and H of the First New York Artillery, meanwhile pouring death and destruction into their ranks.

The firing on either side soon subsided into heavy skirmishing and the rapid interchange of solid shot and shell, lasted until one o'clock this afternoon, our troops in the mean time retaining possession of their original line.

At this hour the Division of General Miles, which had been thrown to the left of Boydtown Plank Road to close the interval made by the withdrawal of Griffin in the morning, was ordered to strike the enemy in front of Warren on his left flank, while the Fifth Corps again essayed to obtain possession of the White Oak Road by advancing simultaneously. The second advance of Warren was led by General Chamberlain's Brigade of Griffin's Division, and that of Miles on the right moved in echelon in the following order from right to left:

General Nelson A. Miles

First Brigade, Colonel Scott, of the Sixty-first New York commanding; Irish Brigade, Colonel Nugent, Sixty-ninth New York; Third Brigade, General Medill; Fourth Brigade, General Ramsey. At one o'clock, as before mentioned, Warren's Corps again moved forward upon the enemy, who stubbornly held his ground for some time, when the rapid volleys from the right, and the loud cheer that followed, told of the successful issue of Miles's attack on the Rebel flank as he rolled up the enemy's line now broken, routed and falling back incontinently, followed by Warren, who was soon in possession of the coveted White Oak Road, which we now retain.

While all this was going on, heavy skirmishing was taking place on our line as far as Hatcher's Run. Under cover of a strong skirmish line, Turner's Division during the afternoon advanced several hundred yards, strongly entrenching, and with its Sharpshooters silenced the guns of several batteries in its front. The brigades of General DeTrobriand and McAllister, of the Third Division of the Second Corps, were likewise heavily engaged in skirmishing during the day, and succeeded in assuming an advanced line.

Our casualties will probably reach eighteen hundred or two thousand, of which the Fifth Corps is believed to have sustained the loss of nearly one-half.

Major Glenn, of the One Hundred and Ninety-eighth Pennsylvania, has the honor of capturing with his own hands, during the engagement of the Fifth Corps today, one stand of Rebel colors, belonging to Horral's brigade of Pickett's Division. General Miles also displayed at his headquarters, this afternoon, a Rebel color taken by his division.

Near Hatcher's Run, Virginia,
Union Account

From nine o'clock this morning until dark the Second Division of the Twenty-fourth Corps were engaged with the enemy in front of that part of our lines lately held by the Second Corps. The enemy in our front was found to be their Third Corps under Hill, and the division engaged that of Heth.

The ground held up to last evening by the pickets of this force was won by the Second Division, Twenty-fourth Corps, which at once threw up a strong line of log breastworks.

At an early hour today a strong skirmish line was sent out, which pushed up to within a few hundred yards of the Rebel batteries and kept up such a deadly fire that the gunners were unable to work their guns for a time. They tried to fire, but the men were shot off as fast as they showed the least part of their bodies. Finding our fire to be so deadly the enemy quickly lay under cover of their defenses, only returning a sharp fire of musketry.

At eleven o'clock this morning the fighting along our line from the center of the left was sharp. The left of the Twenty-fourth Corps connected with the Second Corps, which had the Fifth on its left, and along the front of those three bodies there was for some time an incessant fire, the artillery on the left being loud, but in front of our center, where the Twenty-fourth Corps fought, it was nearly silent. By this incessant and deadly fire the First and Second Divisions of the Twenty-fourth Corps gained some ground, and steps were taken to hold it. The line of Sharpshooters kept the Rebel guns silent, while a strong line was pushed forward, and, under cover of this fire, threw up a new line of breastworks. Behind this our line lay while the skirmish line gained, step by step, but very slowly, more ground.

The Second Division of the Twenty-fifth Corps, under General Birney, was held in reserve to the line of the Twenty-fourth all day, and was not called upon to fire a shot, but the colored troops were steadily engaged and showed no lack of spirit. Two brigades of the division were held in line behind the rear breastwork, while the other two—there being four in the division—stood further to the rear in reserve.

The ground was a mixture of pine and clearings, like most of the scenes of action in Virginia. A long line of woods hid the Rebel batteries from view, and in those woods was drawn up one line under cover of its log breastworks, with the skirmish line thrown out in front close to the Rebel works. In the rear of the woods the ground was open and along it, about three-quarters of a mile from the woods, ran the old line of defenses lately held by the Second Corps.

At six o'clock in the afternoon it was thought by General Gibbons, of the Twenty-fourth Corps, that by a sudden charge the First Division might be able to carry the batteries in its front, as the skirmish line had pushed up so near to them that the line would have only a few hundred yards to cross to reach the works, and the loss would be small. Dusk was thought a good time to make this attempt. After some consideration it was decided to defer this attack until a more proper moment. It may be that the possibility of there being some rear defenses which would command those in front, if taken, General Gibbons, who is a careful man, concluded to wait until he could better see what defenses were to be met. At daybreak tomorrow the attack may be made, and if the enemy have weakened their line to send troops to their right, the attack will, it is likely, succeed.

The loss of the Twenty-fourth Corps in this day's fight will not exceed two hundred men, and the only officer of any rank in the list of casualties was Captain G. H. Brown, of the Sharpshooters, who was wounded fatally and died ten minutes after he was struck. The loss of the enemy it is not easy to guess, as their artillery must have lost a good number of men; but their line was kept well under cover of their defenses, so that their total loss could not have been great.

About two hundred men came in from the Rebel line during the day, and there was an evident wish on the part of their men to desert when a chance offered.

Goldsboro, North Carolina,
Union Account

A detachment from General Lilly's command was sent out on a reconnaissance today beyond Little River. They found the enemy's cavalry in considerable force, but drove them back some three miles, returning without any loss whatever. The Rebel forces are north of Tar River.

Newbern, North Carolina,
Union Account

While Generals Sherman and Palmer were out riding today in a carriage, the horses took fright and ran away. Fortunately they escaped without injury.

The Rebels we locate today, for the time being, between Smithfield and Raleigh.

When General Sherman returned to Newbern, be said, *"There is no such thing as peace with the Rebels by negotiation. The issue must be fought out. Even this in face of the fact that it will be but few days until I lose a portion of our troops and muster out of the service, at the expiration of four months, one of the bravest and best armies that ever trod the earth."*

Raleigh and Weldon are being strongly fortified by the Rebels. They cannot imagine when and where Sherman will turn up.

City Point, Virginia,
Union Account

At half-past twelve o'clock today General Grant telegraphed President Lincoln as follows:

"There has been much hard fighting this morning. The enemy drove our left from near Dabney's House, back well toward the Boydstown Plank Road. We are now about to take the offensive at that point, and I hope will more than recover the lost ground."

Later he telegraphed again, as follows:

"Our troops, after being driven back to the Boydstown Plank Road, turned and drove the enemy in turn and took the White Oak Road, which we now have. This gives us the ground occupied by the enemy this morning. I will send you a Rebel flag captured by our troops in driving the enemy back. There have been four flags captured today."

Goldsboro, North Carolina,
Union Account

General Sherman returned last night after an absence at City Point of nearly five days. He has had a consultation with General Grant and the President, and doubtless ere long the points of that consultation will be made manifest to the world.

General Meigs arrived here in a special train with General Easton, the Chief Quartermaster of the military division of the Mississippi, on Wednesday afternoon. They are using every exertion and straining every nerve to expedite the forwarding of supplies to this army.

When General Sherman held his review of the troops composing his army, on the occasion of their marching into and occupying this town, a large portion of the men were barefooted, coatless, and some few actually pantless. By the almost superhuman exertions of the various Quartermasters having this important matter in charge the army is now nearly entirely clothed and shod, and it will not be many days before they will be fully prepared to take the field.

The railroad to Wilmington has been thoroughly repaired and is now in working order. We captured eight engines and forty-five freight cars on the occupation of Wilmington, which have been turned to good account in assisting in bringing up the needful supplies to this army.

There has been some considerable excitement in camp over the rumor that General Grant has had a severe fight with Lee at Richmond, defeating him with a loss of some twenty thousand killed and wounded and fifteen thousand prisoners. It is impossible to trace the origin of this story, which is doubtless, like many other camp stories, the work of some imaginative wag.

The men composing this army are confident that the war will be over in sixty days, and are already calculating on the probabilities of their being mustered out of service by the Government, in consequence of a lack of occupation for them.

Extensive fortifications and field-works have been erected all around Goldsboro, and are of the most formidable dimensions of any your correspondent has ever seen. If Lee and Johnston should both unite their forces with all the others in Rebeldom they could be easily kept at bay by the impregnable works which have been erected by Sherman's army since its arrival at this place.

Refugees continue to go north in great numbers; not a train leaves here but is loaded down with them. They are principally destitute white people and contrabands going to the plantations at Beaufort, S. C., and other places set apart by General Sherman for their benefit, and where white people are prohibited from settling.

Baltimore, Maryland, Union Account

The western mail train from here for Wheeling, yesterday, was captured by Mosby's Guerillas, and all the cars except five were burned. The passengers were all robbed.

Cairo, Illinois, Union Account

Rebel deserters in the vicinity of Meridian, Mississippi, defy the authorities and threaten to annihilate the militia, and to burn their houses if they attempt to oppose them. On the other hand, Forrest declares if the militia fails to arrest deserters, he will go there in force and hang every organized deserter that is around.

New Orleans, Louisiana, Union Account

It is certainly believed here that we shall soon have news from Texas that will startle and gratify the whole country. It is known that a message has been received at Washington from the Trans-Mississippi Department, proposing that enough cotton should be shipped down the river to pay off the Rebel troops in greenbacks, and that they should then be disbanded and allowed to take the oath of amnesty. A new Legislature is then to assemble, fresh from the people, to decide the question of independence or of return to the Union. The Rebel chiefs are, in consideration of a special amnesty for themselves, to exercise their influence in electing a Legislature favorable to reconstruction.

Great anxiety is felt to learn the result of General Lew Wallace's mission to Brownsville, and as to the purport of the late communications with Galveston.

Prominent refugees from that State who are in this city, who profess to have information from officers, are highly excited, and anxiously awaiting news from the pending negotiations at Galveston.

Saturday, April 1, 1865

City Point, Virginia,
Union Account

The establishment of General city Grant's headquarters today, on the Vaughn road, about half a mile west of Hatcher's Run, certainly means that more than usual is calculated on for today or possibly tonight.

Richmond, Virginia,
Confederate Account

The weather is cool and pleasant. Excited couriers have arrived from off the line of the Southside Railroad and report the Yankees as fighting their way through our lines, and their numbers as so great that we cannot much longer hold Petersburg.

The number of Virginians reported absent from their regiments without leave, will, this morning, exceed fifty thousand. What can this mean? A few more days will certainly decide as to whether we will succeed in longer holding together the Confederacy. With Sherman's army seemingly driving northward, and now reported at Goldsboro, N. C, it will be but a short time, in case Johnston does not crush him, until Lee will be completely pocketed.

News reaches us tonight that General Pickett has lost control of his troops at Five Forks, and that the Yankees are gradually moving toward Richmond. It seems that our troops have become discouraged and are easily confused. The Yankee assault on Pickett's Division has completely demoralized it, if reports are true.

Goldsboro, North Carolina,
Union Account

General Sherman returned this morning from his consultation with General Grant at City Point, Va., accompanied by his brother, John Sherman, and Edwin Stanton, son of Secretary Stanton.

Major General Cox assumes command of the Twenty-third Corps today. This Corps has won for itself an enviable reputation, and certainly is one of the finest bodies in the war. General Cox's appointment is pleasing to all of our boys.

Troops sent down from Grant's army, to capture the Rebel Fort Fisher, have arrived.

Our reorganization is about perfect and we are ready to begin movements toward a final campaign.

~ 71 ~

A reconnaissance was made yesterday by Anderson's Third Brigade, and Reilly's Third Division of the Twenty-third Corps. They crossed Little River, drove back Wheeler's Rebel Cavalry pickets and a Rebel forage train. They secured an abundance of corn and came back grinning from ear to ear.

Deserters from Johnston's army say that he has concentrated a force at Two Rivers, where, with a heavy detail of Negroes, he is fortifying his army and felling trees across the roads to impede our northward march. This is in anticipation of our movement to connect with Grant, at or near Petersburg, Va. Johnston's army is still in the direction of Smithfield. His supplies, we understand, have been moved to Raleigh.

A deserter from Johnston's army, who arrived here today, reports Johnston to have said that he lost five thousand men in the battle at Bentonville.

The weather is pleasant and the roads are in excellent condition. We are in splendid spirits and ready for the command, Forward!

Knoxville, Tennessee,
Union Account

The advance of General Stoneman's force entered and captured the town of Boone, N. C, at twelve o'clock today. The Rebels lost ten killed and sixty-five wounded and taken prisoners.

The Twelfth Kentucky Cavalry lost a few men. Stoneman's command is going straight into the northern portion of North Carolina, and if not checked will soon strike the very heart of the Rebellion.

Sheridan's Army in front of Petersburg, Va.
Union Account

Sheridan has changed his position of yesterday and has gone east of Dinwiddie Court House, rendering a change of front on the part of the Fifth Corps imperative. The troops under Warren's command were, in consequence of Sheridan's change moved across the White Oak road at midnight, and down the Boydtown Plank Road to the Butler House, where they took a road leading west toward the Southside Railroad.

Fifth Army Corps in front of Petersburg, Va.
Union Account

We are waiting the development department of Sheridan's attack upon Pickett's Rebel troops, which will decide our movement. The constant and fierce rattle of musketry and artillery is gradually coming near us, which means that Sheridan is driving the enemy towards us. The signal department keeps Warren informed and we are waiting orders to move toward the enemy.

3:30 O'clock p.m. We are advancing northwestward and are but a few hours from an engagement as the Rebel troops are in front of us in large numbers.

5 O'clock p.m. The enemy has taken a determined stand to check Warren from further advancing.

5:30 O'clock p.m. A desperate battle is now raging, with our forces advancing steadily. The enemy is fighting bravely, but is yielding slowly while our troops are taking every advantage possible.

9 O'clock p.m. The fight of this afternoon has been one of the most furious of the war and continued until dark. The cannonading has ceased and we are considerably nearer the Southside Railroad than we were at five o'clock. The loss of both sides is very heavy.

As nearly as can be understood, the left of our line has changed from its former position. Miles is reported to have retired from the left of the Second Corps and is now on Warren's right, holding his line along the Boydstown Plank Road.

General George Pickett

Twenty-fourth Army Corps, Petersburg, Va.
Union Account

With the exception of an assault of Foster's Division of the Twenty-fourth Corps supported by two of Ord's Brigades, on Ft. Gregg at one o'clock this afternoon, the rest of our line has remained undisturbed during the day.

The enemy first attacked Foster upon his advanced position gained yesterday, about an hour before daybreak, and succeeded in capturing thirty of our men and a portion of the works held by the One Hundredth New York. This lasted but a moment, when the gallant Eleventh Maine and Tenth Connecticut immediately charged, retaking our former position, driving the Rebels back and capturing one hundred prisoners. The battle was desperate and of great interest to our army.

Robert S. Foster

Goldsboro, North Carolina,
Union Account

The Rebels have completed their arrangements to evacuate Raleigh. All the departments of the State government have been removed to Greensboro.

Richmond, Virginia,
Confederate Account

It is evidently the intention of President Davis and the Confederate Government officers to move from this city. An evacuation and surrender of the capital is not far off. The assets of the banks have been sent off by the Danville Road; the machinery of the percussion cap factories have gone, and much of the Tredegar Iron Works machinery is being placed on the cars ready to leave.

Our army is reported not to have to exceed ten days' supplies in this city.

Nothing has been heard from Alexander H. Stephens, who seems to have deserted President Davis.

Flour is fifteen hundred dollars per barrel; tea, one hundred dollars per pound; coffee, fifty dollars; bacon, eighteen dollars; beef, fifteen dollars; and eggs are this morning quoted at thirty-five dollars per dozen.

Army of the Potomac in front of Petersburg, Va.
Union Account

The effort of the enemy today to carry our line in front of the Twenty-fourth Corps, having been unsuccessful, it is noticed that there is unusual activity on their side at this hour, nine o'clock in the evening. The rays of light from their camp fires show that a movement of some sort is anticipated.

Our left is quiet. Our right on the line directly in front of Petersburg is in action at this time. The constant roar of cannon tells of an unusually fierce artillery duel. Considerable musketry is also heard and it is not improbable that a charge is being made near the Appomattox River.

The general impression current here this evening is that an assault will be made on the entire Rebel line before daybreak. Our boys are in excellent spirits and are anxious to enter into what they hope may be the closing conflict of the war.

New York

Gold is one dollar and fifty-one cents today. Sales have been made at one dollar and fifty-two and one-half cents and one dollar and fifty-three cents, but the demand was not large. Flour, eight dollars and twenty-five cents for family; wheat, one dollar and fifty to one dollar and sixty cents; oats, sixty cents; rye, one dollar; barley, one dollar and twenty-five cents; clover seed, twelve dollars and seventy-five cents; lard, seventeen and one-half cents; coffee, thirty-one cents; sugar, thirteen cents; butter, thirty cents; eggs, eighteen cents; hay, twenty-seven dollars.

Goldsboro, North Carolina,
Union Account

Clothing has been issued and our boys in new uniforms present a more cheerful appearance. To see Sherman's army in its dress of today is a striking contrast from that of its entrance into Goldsboro.

The health of the army is all that could be desired. Few are sick and our hospital accommodations are ample.

Petersburg, Virginia,
Confederate Account

The enemy, we understand, has thrown up entrenchments on the line of his recent extension, and still occupies the position on the Boydtown Plank Road. It is believed that the enemy is still at Dinwiddie Court House. Thursday afternoon General Fitz Lee attacked and dislodged a division of Sheridan's cavalry from a position it had taken between the plank road and Southside Railroad, and drove the Yankees some distance.

A few prisoners were captured who reported themselves as belonging to Merritt's Division. On Friday forenoon the enemy then attacked the position on White Oak road, to the right of Burgess's Mills, and were met by a charge of our troops and handsomely driven back. They were pursued some distance south of the plank road, where they took refuge behind the main line of their works. It was deemed impracticable to attack them there, and our troops retired. The charge of our men is said to have been one of the most beautiful of the war. They advanced in perfect order and swept the opposing ranks before them like chaff. We sustained some loss, but not heavy. We captured upward of three hundred prisoners yesterday morning, who will probably reach this city today.

The enemy keeps his flank well guarded.

Our lines are secure against all attacks of the enemy. On the whole, all goes well with us, and ere long we hope to be able to chronicle a glorious victory for our arms and a crushing defeat to the enemy.

Army of the Potomac in front of Petersburg, Va.
Union Account

A courier just arrived from Sheridan's front with glorious Sheridan's cavalry and Warrens infantry advanced against the enemy this afternoon, driving them several miles and capturing about five thousand prisoners and several pieces of artillery. The Rebels fell back to Two Forks, where they were flanked by a part of the Fifth Corps, which had gone down the White Oak road. It was here that a desperate fight was held and the captures made. The Johnnies then retreated south along the White Oak road, and were hotly pursued by Sheridan, while McKenzie's cavalry, from the Army of the James, advanced west on the Ford road toward the Southside Railroad, which they expect to strike before morning. Should the Rebels lose this railroad tonight, what will become of them? This is their only line of supply and with its capture they will be compelled to abandon both Petersburg and Richmond.

Heavy cannonading is now—midnight—heard in the neighborhood of the Sixth Corps. An engagement on that part of the line is generally desperate and the result is anxiously awaited.

General Meade has decided to give the enemy no time to send re-enforcements against Sheridan. At nine o'clock tonight Meade orders the Second, Twenty-fourth, Sixth and Ninth Corps to make a simultaneous attack on the enemy. Only Meade and the Corps Commanders are aware of the movement at this hour, half past nine. Messengers are in front of Meade's headquarters with their horses ready to carry dispatches to each command, and before morning a great conflict can be expected.

Fourth Army Corps, Shields Mills, Tennessee, Union Account

General Thomas has ordered a lot of half broken-down horses to be sold to the people for farming purposes.

Our First Division made a march here from Strawberry Plains without burning a rail or stealing a chicken. For the first time in the history of this Division has any kind of poultry had the cheek to cross our path without paying the penalty of death.

A large squad of our men, who have escaped from Salisbury and Columbia Rebel prisons, passed through here today.

The condition of our troops is the best. Although we are not as actively engaged as are some of our brothers, yet we look upon the strife with approving satisfaction, and that what glory has been achieved in the Carolinas and Virginia, we helped bring about in the masterly destruction of Hood's army.

Second Army Corps in front of Petersburg, Va.
Union Account

All day long this corps has fought the enemy with vigor, and gradually fixed its line firmly in spite of their sharp firing. The left of our corps extends beyond the Boydtown road and rests on the White Oak road, where we connect with the Fifth Corps. In our front is a part of Hill's (Rebel) Third Corps; the other part of that corps lies in front of the Twenty-fourth Corps, which is on our right.

The ground on which our corps has fought all day is mostly thick with woods. While it affords what might be called good cover they were unfavorable for the action of our line in close order, and the ground was, in fact, more favorable to the enemy than to us.

Twenty-fourth Army Corps, Hatcher's Run, Va.
Union Account

At four o'clock this morning the Rebels made a fierce attack on our corps, with their usual yell, in the hope of taking us by surprise. At one point they were successful, driving the One Hundredth New York picket line back from our line, but they could not hold it long. The Eleventh Maine and the Tenth Connecticut came down upon the enemy and quickly forced them out of the point gained and back to their own line. Another attempt was not made by the enemy today.

A sharp firing has been constant along our front all day. Our Sharpshooters are picking off the Rebel gunners nearly as fast as they dare approach their batteries, making it hard work for them to keep their heavy guns in action.

Sixth Army Corps in front of Petersburg, Va.
Union Account

The day has been what might be termed a quiet one on this front, the Rebels seemingly being content with the idea of being allowed to hold their line at this point. Our corps has laid all day in readiness for activity if deemed advisable, while it is noticed that the enemy was weakening their line, which we deem prudent to observe closely.

Ninth Army Corps in front of Petersburg, Va.
Union Account

Quietness has reigned along the front of this corps for the greater part of the day. Only a few shots have been fired on the picket line as compared with former days. We are ready for an attack and expect orders for a move forward every moment. Our line, on both sides, has been in action today, and, from what can be learned, has been successful.

10 O'clock p.m. Firing is now heard in front of the Second Corps, which is rapidly coming this way.

10:30 O'clock p.m.   The Rebel batteries have opened in front of the Second Corps and the pine woods resound with the din of a heavy fight on their front.

11 O'clock p.m. The firing has reached us and cannonading and musketry are heard in every direction. A great battle is now raging and many dead and wounded are being carried to the rear.

Second Army Corps in front of Petersburg, Va.
Union Account

10:15 O'clock p.m.   The few shots of fifteen minutes ago on the picket line on our front have now grown into a desperate rattle. All of the Union and Rebel batteries are active and a fierce battle is now on.

11 O'clock p.m.   The fight still continues and the heavens glitter from the explosion of mortar shells in the air and the flash of powder from along our line.

12 O'clock Midnight. Firing on our front has nearly ceased. Our boys are cheering. The Johnnies received the worst of it.

Twenty-fourth Army Corps, Petersburg, Va.
Union Account

At ten o'clock tonight we are again engaged in battle. The guns on both sides are as active as it is possible to find them The bomb proofs are vacant and the rear of every sand bag on this front is hugged by our infantry men with their rifles working.

11 O'clock p.m. Cheers are heard from the position of the Second Corps, which means that we have again repulsed the enemy.

11:45 O' clock p.m. Firing has died down.

Sixth Army Corps in front of Petersburg, Va.
Union Account

10 O'clock p.m. The quietness of today has now changed. Every gunner on both sides is now hard at work and a terrible battle is now being fought. The air is a stream of fire from the explosion of mortar shells.

11:50 O'clock p.m. The line on our front has quieted down and firing nearly ceased.

Petersburg, Virginia, Confederate Account

Flour sold today at the moderate price of $1,100 per barrel. Sugar and bacon are equally reasonable in price.

Pensacola, Florida, Union Account

General Steele's command has met with much opposition, but no regular battle was fought until it reached Mitchell's Fork on Tuesday morning, March 28, when the enemy, numbering about eight hundred, made a stand, and after a severe fight were repulsed and scattered in the woods, many being captured.

New Orleans, Louisiana, Union Account

Rebel steamers ply regularly between Mobile and the Spanish Fort, conveying re-enforcements and guns. Two of our men have been injured by torpedoes near Mobile.

Washington D.C. Union Account

General Grant telegraphs at half past four this afternoon that he had a continuous line of troops and in a few hours would be entrenched from the Appomattox below Petersburg to the river above. The whole captures since the army started out would not amount to less than twelve thousand men and probably fifty pieces of artillery.

It is stated here that Grant promised the entry of President Lincoln into Richmond within the next twenty-four hours.

New Orleans, Louisiana, Union Account

Information received today states that a portion of Canby's army was within five miles of Mobile and siege guns were in position from which shells could be thrown into the suburbs of the city. The attack on Fort Blakely, the main defense of Mobile, had already commenced.

Maury is in command at Mobile, and Gen. Dick Taylor commands the Spanish Fort. Generals Canby and Granger were up Fishing Creek on the twenty-fourth. Our gunboats were shelling the woods at the mouth of Fishing Creek.

Knoxville, Tennessee,
Union Account

The East Tennessee and Virginia Railed has been completed to Bull's Gap, fifty-five miles east of here. Trains are now making regular trips.

Baltimore, Maryland,
Union Account

The schooner St. Mary was today boarded by a gang of pirates in Pawtuxet River, who said they had captured eight schooners that were lying at anchor in various rivers between here and Point Lookout. The crews were paroled and released.

In Front of Mobile, Alabama,
Union Account

We have advices that the Rebel loss inside Spanish Fort is five hundred killed and wounded, out of four thousand. Our total loss, based on the estimates of two corps, is probably the same. The proportion of killed is small.

The Seventh Corps is investing Fort Blakely, six miles above Spanish Fort.

General Thomas, with the Fourth Corps and a corps of cavalry, are expected in the rear of Mobile.

The Sixteenth Corps is laying a pontoon bridge over the river near Fort Blakely. We think it is the Tombigbee River.

Selma, Alabama,
Confederate Account

The Yankees, yesterday, were at Randolph, on the Blue Mountain Railroad, coming toward Selma.

Look for a fight near Selma today or tomorrow. We feel sanguine. Trains are running through to Pollard.

Forrest is in front of the enemy with considerable force. The big fight will probably be at Plantersville.

Mobile, Alabama,
Confederate Account

The enemy invested Spanish Fort on the east and have erected a heavy battery south of the fort, from which he keeps up a steady fire.

The enemy, today, moved up toward Blakely, and it is expected that he will attack the place tomorrow.

Firing has been heavy all week, but the Yankees made no impression on our works. Our loss is light, while that of the enemy is heavy.

All things go well.

Sunday, April 2, 1865

In Front of Petersburg, Virginia,
Union Account

At one o'clock this morning, General Wilcox had orders demonstrate on the right of the line so as to draw the Rebels from the left, preparatory to operations in that quarter. Shortly after this Admiral Porter and all the artillery in the works on the right, were also set to work. Wilcox's skirmish line was advanced, the Rebels were aroused, and soon sharp volleys of musketry were heard, indicating that they were also at work. Amid the noise and smoke the skirmishers pushed on until reaching the outskirts of Petersburg, where they met a heavy body of Rebels advancing upon them.

A brisk fight followed, but we were overpowered and compelled to fall back. General Wilcox then massed for an attack on the Rebel Fort Mahone. While this was being done, similar dispositions were making for the line to the left of Fort Mahone. A system of signals had been agreed upon by cannonading, fixing a time of starting, that all might assault simultaneously. Owing to a heavy fog on the field, the enemy failed to observe our movement closely. At four o'clock the signal was given. The men, with fixed bayonets, advanced steadily and in perfect order. That it was a calculation to advance and hold any position was proven by seeing a detachment of heavy artillery accompany the infantry that they might be prepared to turn and work the enemy's guns.

Presently musketry was heard, and the Rebel picket line was reached; now a hearty cheer, followed by the roar of musketry. Soon the whole line was in action. Now came the report of the artillery on both sides, where two hundred big guns belched forth their thunder and missiles of death. Brigadier General Harriman, of the Thirty-seventh Wisconsin, gave the order to charge; up and away our noble boys went, over breastworks, rifle-pits, abatis, chevaux-de-frise—the parapet of the first, into the main works, and the deed was accomplished. The thunderstruck Rebels looked but an instant and then took to their heels, but our boys were too fleet for them and captured two hundred and fifty. Nine guns were found in this fort, and, quickly turned, were set at work on the Rebel batteries. This, with the simultaneous action further left, cut the Rebel line in two, took from them their commanding position and many of their heavy guns. Scarcely did we recognize our position, when the Rebels reorganized their forces and came upon the fort determined to regain it. The assault they made was desperate, and in the face of terrific discharges of grape and canister and withering volleys of musketry. It was no use; they were sent back in disorder and suffered very heavily. The Rebel General Hill is reported as having been killed in this assault while leading his men up to retake their lost ground. Meantime the Sixth and Twenty-fourth Corps, having broken through the Rebel lines in their front, were swung around to their rear, and, coming down both upon their rear and flank, it was evident that Petersburg was lost to the Rebellion. The movements of the Sixth Corps were so rapid that General Lee himself narrowly escaped capture. As it was his headquarters fell into our hands.

Cheval-de-Frise
Anti-Cavalry Placements

Sixth Army Corps,
Union Account

At half past four o'clock this morning we left our lines to attack the Rebel left center. We moved in echelon, so as to enable us to throw forward our left and flank the works of the enemy one after another. In a moment a battery of four guns opened upon our First Division, but by a rapid change of the First Brigade it was immediately captured. The enemy's batteries now opened from every point, but on, on went our gallant braves. The left soon reached the enemy's works in their front, and one by one they fell into our hands. At half past ten o'clock a grand picture of war presented itself. The line of our corps with its left in advance was sweeping on toward two heavy Rebel forts. The Rebels plied their guns vigorously, and shells were bursting everywhere on our line. On pushed the left division until it struck the Southside Railroad. Against the two Rebel forts went the Second Division, our artillery playing its part well on the Rebel forts, from a commanding position, until we were close up to them. Then came a dash of our line which was met by a terrible storm of canister, compelling us for a moment to realize where we were. Again we pounced upon the Rebel line and met with success; but so resolute were the Rebels that some of them used the bayonet for a short time. When we had possession, such a cheer as went up from our line cannot be pictured; the enemy meanwhile flying to their inner lines, there to stay a further advance from us. Just here General Sheridan appeared on the field amid the cheers of the Sixth Corps. Our entire line was changing its long front to the right, and slowly before it the enemy gave way and fell back upon their inner defenses.

Against the line to which they fell back a heavy force was now pitted, composed of portions of the Twenty-fourth, Sixth and Twenty-fifth Corps. A lull took place and when the force was ready to move it was plain that a distinct action was to be fought. Dusk is now upon us and to reasonably predict the action of this army before the morning's rays of light appear would be impossible.

The Second Corps, connecting with the right of the Fifth Corps, was also victorious, notwithstanding they had, perhaps, the roughest ground to fight over, and a brave and desperate foe in tha Rebel Third Corps on their front.

The line of the Ninth Corps was stronger than at any other point. It delivered many assaults during the day and met with severe loss. Tonight it is close up to the main line of defenses, but unable to go further. The First Division of the Tenth Corps aided the Ninth Corps greatly.

In Front of Petersburg, Virginia, Union Account

Today came bringing with it a sun dimmed only by the battle smoke of the four days preceding and the Indian-summery haze which for a week had hung over the two armies. Sheridan's legion of prisoners began to arrive at Humphrey Station on their way to City Point, seemingly well pleased with the change in their condition. A grand right wheel of the whole line south of the Appomattox had been decided upon by General Grant. The Sixth and Ninth Corps, the latter east and the former southeast and south of Petersburg, had been ordered to make a grand and combined assault upon the enemy's works in their front, while the command of General Ord on both sides of Hatcher's Run moved to their support, followed by the Second, which was to connect on the left of the Sixth, southwest of the town.

Early in the morning Turner's and Foster's Divisions of Ord's command, moved to the support of the Sixth Corps, leaving Birney, of the Colored Division, to charge the enemy simultaneously with the Second on its left. The charge of the Second Corps and of Birney's Division of the Twenty-fourth was almost a bloodless one; no enemy but a few pickets were found in their front, and Birney's and the Second and Third Divisions of Humphrey's Corps continued their grand right wheel, and at or about eleven o'clock in the morning were on the line of the Sixth, southwest of Petersburg. But the gallant old Sixth and Ninth had already accomplished the work assigned them. The Sixth, supported by Ord, had advanced two miles, carried a complete line of formidable works, including a number of forts, and had seized the Southside Railroad, while the Ninth, almost as successful, had, by a series of assaults, forcibly possessed three almost impregnable salients, and occupied Fort Mahone in front of Fort Hell, the three Corps alone capturing thirty-two guns, nearly three thousand prisoners, and an indefinite number of colors. And thus it was accomplished.

Dead Confederate Artilleryman at Petersburg

Glorious news has just arrived from Sheridan. He has struck the Southside Railroad, which he now holds. In the engagement yesterday afternoon he captured four thousand prisoners and several batteries of artillery.

The Fifth Corps, which was supporting the cavalry, have also taken fifteen guns and about two thousand prisoners, enabling Sheridan to drive back the force which in the latter part of yesterday checked his advance in the vicinity of Dinwiddie Court House.

On receiving the news it was determined to give the enemy no time to send troops to their right, and at once a simultaneous attack was ordered all along the lines by the Ninth, Sixth, Twenty-fourth and Second Corps.

The order was given about nine o'clock at night, and in less than an hour a furious assault began on the Rebel entrenchments in the fronts of their several commands, resulting in the enemy being driven in confusion from their first into their second line of works, with a loss of over five thousand prisoners, several forts and about twenty pieces of artillery.

The Second Corps was engaged all day with the enemy in their front, and in spite of the terrible fire of musketry poured into their ranks by the Rebels behind their works succeeded in maintaining their new line several hundred yards in advance of the line they occupied in the morning. Two divisions of Hill's Corps held the Rebel line in front of the Second Corps, the other division being opposed to the Twenty-fourth Corps, which joins the Second on the right; the ground over which the Second Corps fought was for the most part covered with pine forests, which, while affording good shelter to our men, were unfavorable for flank movements and the maintenance of our lines in close order.

The Twenty-fourth Corps occupies the center of our line, holding the position previously occupied by the Second, its left connecting with the Second at Hatcher's Run, and its right joining the left of the Sixth Corps.

Before daylight this morning the Rebels made a furious, assault on this position of our line, driving a portion of the Third Brigade from their breastworks, and capturing about eighty or a hundred prisoners. Their success, however, did not last long, the Two Hundred and Sixth Pennsylvania, by a gallant charge, compelling them to abandon their position and driving them back beyond their first battle line. A sharp fire was kept up all day by both sides. Owing to the hot fire by our Sharpshooters, the enemy was unable to work his guns, and consequently very few casualties occurred on our side from shells. Our batteries, however, rained an incessant fire into their entrenchments, which must have caused them some loss.

There was little fighting in front of the Sixth Corps until night, when considerable shelling occurred.

Quiet also reigned along the Ninth Corps front.

So matters stood until ten o'clock, when the Second Corps were started into sharper attention by a few shots on their front, soon swelling into battling volleys. The batteries joined their deep bass to the martial music and the pine woods rang with the clamor, and were fitfully illuminated by the glare. The firing spread rapidly to the front of the Twenty-fourth Corps, and on to the Sixth, then away to the right till it reached the Ninth Corps, about eleven o'clock, by which time the fighting was at its height. Presently cheers broke out on the front of the Second, as the fire slackened. By half past two the fire had nearly ceased along the whole line, but at four o'clock in the morning it suddenly broke out again, nearer than ever to the Second Corps, while sharp artillery practice was heard far to the right, and again the crash of battle sped from end to end of the line.

The battle is raging fiercely, and thank God the colors are advancing all along the line.

Richmond, Virginia,
Confederate Account

The tocsin this morning early was heard and the militia ordered into the fortifications to relieve some regiments belonging to Longstreet's Corps that were posted on this side of the James River. They were hurried to Petersburg, where no doubt they will be engaged today.

Rumors afloat are to the effect that our loss near the Southside Railroad yesterday was fearful, and that our troops were overpowered by the Federals. There is evidence of truth in this report, as unusual activity all through the city in military and Government circles proves it.

At one o'clock intense excitement is found in every section of the city. Reliable information is in circulation that President Davis received a message from General Lee, while listening to the Rev. Dr. Hoge, at St. Paul's Church, stating that it was impossible to longer hold out against Grant, and that the surrender of Petersburg was imperative. This news spread so quickly that the congregations in all of our churches were dismissed before the completion of religious service. A notice was given from the pulpit by Dr. Minnegerodo that General Ewell desired all local forces in this city to assemble at three o'clock in the afternoon. This will result in no further service in the churches today.

Excited women are moving about with fear, in anticipation of what the next twenty-four hours may bring forth.

It is reported that Mrs. Davis has sold all her furniture. This is not true. Not a single piece has been taken away, nor will it be. Some pieces, rather dilapidated, were sent to the different stores some time ago for disposal, but none that were of modern construction or of particular value.

Shields Mills, Tennessee, Union Account

Last night a squad of twenty-five hearty, able-bodied Negroes came in, fleeing from Rebel conscription.

We pride ourselves on being in the best condition of any corps in the army, both as to numbers and efficiency. The First Division under General Kimball try to claim that they are the most perfect in the corps but they must admit it as a whole and not in pieces.

We are about seventy miles from Knoxville. Lee will possibly not come down this way. Should he try it, he will find the Fourth Corps ready for action on a moment's notice.

Augusta, Georgia,
Confederate Account

Nine thousand Federal troops attacked Selma this evening. They drove our forces from the entrenchments, and turned our left flank. Our loss in prisoners is very large. The Yankees have possession of Selma.

Gen. Nathan Kimball

Monday, April 3, 1865

Petersburg, Virginia,
Union Account

The first number of a newspaper, twelve by twenty inches, printed on one side only, has been started here and called "Grant's Petersburg Progress." Its motto is, "Eternal vigilance is the price of liberty."

The leading editorial has the appropriate heading, "We are here," and under the firm of "We, Us & Co." they say: "Our intentions are strictly honorable. We intend to publish a live paper as long as circumstances will permit; that is, as long as we can steal the paper and get men detailed to set the type. Our terms will be ten cents a paper and invariably in advance, except to Lieutenant, Major and Brigadier Generals; no credit given to others on any consideration, except immediately before the advent of the Paymaster.

"We are not particular as to the medium of exchange, and will take hard-tack, greenbacks, cigars, postage stamps, and in fact most any available currency, Confederate bonds and contrabands always excepted.

"For politics, the color of our cloth will be a sufficient guarantee that we are not very deeply imbued with a sense of the beauties of the secession firm in the village north of us. We believe in the United States, one and indivisible; in Abraham Lincoln, our adopted , father, in U. S. Grant, Captain of the Hosts, and ourselves as the principal sojourners in the Army of the Potomac; and the Freedom of the Contraband, the speedy extinction of the Rebellion and the perdition of Jefferson Davis here and hereafter."

Richmond, Virginia,
Union Account

Richmond has fallen. It was surrendered to our troops by the mayor of the city at eight o'clock this morning. The Second Brigade of the Third Division of the Twenty-fourth Corps, commanded by General Ripley, led the advance upon the town, Major General Weitzel and his staff heading the column.

Upon entering the suburbs of the city, General Weitzel sent a small detachment of the Fourth Massachusetts Cavalry to meet the Mayor of the city, from whom General Weitzel received the keys of the public buildings. The Army of the James then marched triumphantly into the Rebel capital, having met with no opposition whatever.

After leaving our works in front of the Rebel entrenchments, our army was greeted with enthusiastic cheers by the populace, who has thus far behaved in a becoming manner, and has shown us every respect.

The colored population was excessively jubilant and danced for very joy at the sight of their sable brethren in arms, the Twenty-fifth Corps, who followed close upon the heels of General Ripley's brigade of the Twenty-fourth Corps in the entree of the Union forces into Richmond.

About daylight this morning our forces were formed in line of battle in front of our works confronting Richmond, and were then moved up by General Weitzel. A few stray shots were fired by the retreating Rebels, injuring no one. Beyond this no opposition was offered us and our troops filed into the Rebel works and up the Osborne and Newmarket Road to the city.

An inspection of the Rebel works disclosed the fact of their having left in great haste. Many of their quarters were left without a thing being taken out of them. Pistols, revolvers, carbines and arms of every description were found in profusion, clothing of every description was in abundance, and in some of the officers' quarters were found their private correspondence, diaries, &c.

While stragglers were pillaging the deserted camps our army continued its march toward the city. The enemy had planted torpedoes in front of Fort Gilmore, and so thickly that it was found necessary to march the column in single file through the fort. They had attached to every torpedo a stick with a piece of red webbing tied on it, to mark the locality of the infernal machines. This precaution they had observed for the safety of their own men. General Weitzel had some days previously been informed of the fact of their having planted the torpedoes and how they were marked.

The General's precaution of not moving until daylight over the ground immediately in front of Fort Gilmore was a very wise one, as, had the torpedoes been exploded, the destruction of life must necessarily have been great.

A couple of hours more brought us into the heart of the Rebel city.

The sight of the burning buildings was truly sorrowful. That part of the city along the river front known as the main business part was one vast sheet of flame.

What with the roaring and dashing and clashing, burning and tumbling buildings, the shouts of our soldiers moving up the main streets to the Capitol, the music of Union bands playing the Star Spangled Banner, the shouts of welcome and the excitement of the people, was a scene of grandeur and magnificence never to be effaced from memory.

The thought of entering the city of Richmond, that city seemingly the objective point of a four years' war, in such a style without a struggle, after many hard-fought battles to possess it, in which thousands of our brave heroes have been slain, was calculated to thrill the hearts of all in the column.

General Weitzel immediately established his headquarters in the State Capitol, in the hall lately occupied by the Virginia House of Delegates, and immediately instituted measures to restore order to the town, as all was a Babel of confusion.

The Rebel rear guard, a small body of cavalry, retreated in the direction of Lynchburg only a few minutes before our advance entered the town. The main body of the enemy commenced to retreat about ten o'clock Sunday evening. Their destination was believed to have been Lynchburg, but whether they will strike for that point, when they come to learn the strait in which Lee, with the main body of his army, has been forced into, is doubtful.

Jefferson Davis remained in the city till dark last night, having, however, sent his family to Charlotte, N. C., sometime during the preceding week.

The inhabitants generally were not informed of the contemplated evacuation until they saw the Confederate troops passing through the town from the east. Then the truth flashed upon them that they were to be left to the mercy of the Yankees.

A number of these, fearful that their past misdeeds would not recommend them to the clemency of the United States Government, hastily left their all to share the fate and fortune of the Rebel army, an army so shattered that it can hardly be dignified by that name.

Libby prison still stands with burning ruins on all sides. It is now filled with Rebel soldiers. The roof of Libby is black with Confederate soldiers, over whom proudly floats that greatest of all flags, the Star Spangled Banner.

Castle Thunder also remains as she did when thousands of our boys were confined there, excepting the contents now are clothed in grey instead of blue.

General Weitzel learned at three o'clock this morning that Richmond was being evacuated, and at daylight moved forward, first taking care to give his men breakfast in the expectation that they might have to fight. He met no opposition, and on entering the city was greeted with a hearty welcome from the mass ol the people. The Mayor went out to meet him and to surrender the city, but missed him on the road. General Weitzel finds much suffering and poverty among the population. The rich as well as the poor are destitute of food. He is about to issue supplies to all who take the oath. The inhabitants now number about twenty thousand, half of them of African descent. It is not true that Jeff. Davis sold his furniture before leaving. It is all in his house. He left at seven o'clock last evening by the Danville Railroad. All the members of Congress escaped. Hunter has gone home. Caron Smith (?) went with the army. Judge Campbell remains in Richmond. General Weitzel took one thousand prisoners, besides the wounded. These number five thousand in nine hospitals. He captured cannon to the number of at least five hundred pieces. Five thousand muskets have been found in one lot. Thirty locomotives and three hundred cars were found. The Petersburg Railroad bridge is totally destroyed, that of the Danville road partially, so that connection with Petersburg cannot easily be made. All the Rebel vessels are destroyed except an unfinished ram, which has her machinery- in her perfect. The Tredegar Works are unharmed. Most of the editors have fled— especially John Mitchell.

The origin of the great fire here was occasioned by the Rebels firing a number of the Confederate storehouses, containing tobacco, and other stores, which they were unable to remove before the evacuation of the city, owing to the confusion existing in all quarters.

No trustworthy estimate can be formed of the amount of property destroyed. The Court House and all the bridges over the James River leading into Manchester were burnt.

The Dispatch and Examiner newspaper offices are also in ruins, and the streets in the vicinity of the fire are littered with the debris of household furniture, &c.

Private and public papers and documents are scattered over the streets, subject to the winds and the rapacity of the pickaninnies who, in innumerable swarms —in danger of falling walls—were diving with their little black hands into every place that suggested a reward for their pains

The colored people were extremely enthusiastic over our arrival and greeted us with the heartiest welcome in a characteristic manner, and "De Lord bless the Yankees" was heard on every side.

The whites thus far have treated us with great cordiality, and on our first entry into the city cheered us vociferously. A few of the loud-mouthed and hasty "Rebs" got themselves into trouble by a too free use of their tongues, and they speedily found themselves confined to close quarters in a room in the building occupied by the Provost-Marshal.

General Weitzel has taken for his private residence the mansion of Jeff. Davis. A portion of his staff are quartered with him, and the remainder in a splendid dwelling a few doors below.

The interior of Davis's house presented the appearance of having been very hastily evacuated by him. Everything is in fine order and good repair. Many of Mrs. Davis's little knick-knacks and ornaments are yet to be found on the mantels and bureaus of her room.

The number of guns captured in the works around the city is roughly estimated at about three hundred. They were all spiked, but otherwise left uninjured.

The powder magazine in Fort Darling and the Rebel rams in the James River below were blown up with a terrific noise. The shock was distinctly felt for miles around.

All the steamers at the wharves—with the exception of the William Allison, Rebel flag-of-truce steamer —were destroyed, together with a new ironclad upon the stocks.

The yard around the State Capitol is literally covered with the household utensils of the burned out families. The Capitol itself has not been injured.

The residents here firmly believe that the Rebellion has received its death-blow, and are rejoicing over their release from the tyranny of Jefferson Davis.

Our soldiers have conducted themselves in a becoming manner, much to the astonishment of the people, who expected that vengeance would be visited upon them.

New York

The Jubilee in Wall Street was one of the most extraordinary demonstrations that the city has ever witnessed. Its spontaneity its vigor and its overwhelming enthusiasm were beyond all precedent. It sprang from accident. Clusters of eager citizens gathered toward noon near the Custom House to exchange congratulations and to spread the glowing intelligence that came in with equal rapidity and profusion. It was not long before all were united in one vast and harmonious assemblage, for the expression of whose exuberant feeling some direct and effective method seemed necessary. Loud calls were made for a number of prominent gentlemen who were seen mingling with the crowd, or standing upon the steps of the Custom House. Without preparation, without organization of any kind, a "meeting" was formed. Spirited and energetic addresses were offered by Moses F. Odell, General Butterfield, Senator Andrews, Wm. M. Evarts, Simon Draper, Prosper M. Wetmore, S. B. Chittenden and George Francis Train. By one o'clock the multitude had swelled to such proportions as to completely block all the thoroughfares in the neighborhood. Business was suspended, not by formal prearrangement, but through natural and irresistible sympathy with the joyous sentiment of the hour. The scene was most inspiring. Wall Street, the center of craft and trade and rigid commerce, turned from its busy purposes to the heartiest, fullest, most genuine thanksgiving that our victories have called forth. There has been nothing like it. At times the masses, unwilling to confine their happy utterances to cheers and outcries, broke into exultant songs, and made the coin-vaults ring with choruses like "Glory, Hallelujah," and "Rally Round the Flag." Nor was the more serious meaning of the day forgotten. With uncovered heads the people joined, fervently and earnestly, in the anthem of "Old Hundred." Voices long unaccustomed to melodious uses lent power and pathos to that chant. It is difficult to describe the strange and touching effect which it produced. The suddenness of the gathering; the time—most absorbing of the financial day; the place—devoted to cold commercial fact, and never yet suspected as the shrine of warm human feeling; the union of the best and most honored of our citizens in the demonstration; and the dignity of sentiment which was everywhere manifested, combined to make the event more impressive, and more memorable than any of the kind that we can call to mind since the opening of the war. It was thrillingly dramatic, not only as a broad picture of popular faith, devotion and energy, but even in the little incidents with which it was crowded. An example will show: One of the speakers, Mr. Train, called attention to the significant and affronting fact that while the Nation's flag was everywhere else gaily flying, the house of August Belmont, directly opposite, was like a house of mourning, without an indication of life or action. In less than five minutes, a flag appeared at the lower window—a very little flag, and excessively new, with the air of very recent purchase all about it, but equal to its duty, and as vehemently welcomed as the biggest of its fellows. And, furthermore, in' less than half an hour, laborers were seen upon the roof, preparing to spread yet another flag, equally new and considerably larger, from the long-neglected staff. The ropes were tangled and were broken, and new ones had to be supplied. The simple process of flag-hoisting seemed to have been so long dormant there as to present unusual embarrassments. But at last the work was done, and the banner rose. It shivered a little at first, as a timid stranger in a hostile society might do, but presently asserted itself with all the boldness and breadth, and flapped exhilarating responses to the cheers of the multitude. This was the culminating incident of the meeting.

Popular enthusiasm felt that it had the right there to expend itself. The force of justice and retribution could no further go.

Washington, D.C.

The news of the fall of Richmond came upon the Capital shortly after breakfast, and while all were awaiting official bulletins that should announce the renewals of the fighting. It ran from mouth to mouth and from street to street, till within ten minutes the whole town was out, and for a wonder Washington was in a state of genuine old-fashioned excitement such as it has not experienced since the memorable second Bull Run battle.

The Treasury Department first caught the infection. General Spinner heard the good news, got out the drummers of the Treasury Guard Regiment, and in a moment had the whole force, nearly two thousand strong, men and women, cheering until the roof seemed in danger. Meanwhile the War Department clerks got waked up, and some of them applied to Secretary Stanton to be excused from duty. His reply was characteristic. *"If the clerks don't know enough to take a holiday for themselves on such an occasion as this, I pity them."*

The Interior Department clerks heard the news almost simultaneously and all rushed into the long corridors that run along the building, raised a cheer that roused that whole section of the town. The Commissioner of Pensions was first called out and made a few remarks; next the Secretary, then the Commissioners of Patents and of the Land Office, and the whole body of clerks united in singing "Rally Round the Flag, Boys." By this time the streets were thronged with clerks, citizens and strangers crowding to the War Department. Mr. Stanton was called out and made a few happy remarks, after which the crowd sang "Rally Round the Flag," and cheered till they were hoarse.

Presently Mr. Stanton appeared again at an upper window, and after prolonged efforts obtained a cessation of the shouts while he read Weitzel's dispatch announcing the occupation of Richmond. After each sentence the cheers burst out afresh, utterly irrepressible. The sentence saying: "The enemy left in great haste," was greeted with tumultuous and derisive laughter, and that saying Richmond was on fire, with cheers louder than ever before. When it was said that efforts were being made to put it out, they cried, "Let it burn! Let it burn!" but when a moment afterward the enthusiasm of the inhabitants at the entrance of our troops was mentioned they burst out again, "All right, put it out! Put it out!"

Philadelphia, Pennsylvania

The ringing of the alarm bells caused a grand turn out of all the firemen, who congregated in front of Independence Hall with their fire engines under steam. After prolonged cheering they formed an impromptu procession, and with bells ringing and steam whistles screaming in full blast, they passed through Third Street, making an uproar of rejoicing such as was never heard here before.

The firemen's procession was about an hour in passing the American Telegraph building. One company had a gun from which they were firing salutes, as they passed along.

A grand salute is now thundering from the roof of The Bulletin Building.

The scene in the vicinity of Third Street tonight is one of great brilliancy and intense excitement. The offices of The Ledger, Inquirer, Press, Evening Bulletin, Telegraph, Sunday Dispatch and Transcript are illuminated. Chestnut Street is crowded with enthusiastic spectators. Fire companies are running their glittering carriages through the streets, and most of their houses and many private residences are illuminated. The general rejoicing is at its height.

Boston, Massachusetts

Bells are pealing, salutes firing and flags flying everywhere, and our citizens are in the highest state of jubilee over the fall of Richmond.

Augusta, Georgia,
Confederate Account

Selma, Alabama, was attacked by the enemy, nine thousand strong, Sunday, April 2. They drove our forces from the entrenchments and turned our left flank on that evening. Our loss in prisoners is very large. The city was captured by the Yankees.

Grant's Army in the Field,
Union Account

The cavalry under Sheridan made an important capture of prisoners, guns and wagons. It appears that Lee's army was moving as rapidly west as his limited transportation and the demoralized condition of his troops would permit, on the road between Amelia Court House and Jetersville.

The cavalry having gained possession of the Danville Railroad some time previous were not long in discovering his whereabouts.

The Fifth Corps being well up in support, and having built entrenchments, preparations for an attack were soon made.

The country here is very uneven, with woods and deep ravines, making it extremely difficult for cavalry to operate to any advantage.

The Second Division, under General Davies, was principally engaged, and the gallant manner in which they charged and drove the enemy is highly spoken of by those who witnessed it.

Gen. Henry E. Davies

But the Rebel infantry came up to the support of their cavalry, forming in the woods and attacking under cover.

Our men were, therefore, forced back on the infantry, but not until one thousand prisoners, six guns, a mile of wagon-trains, together with the drivers, were in possession of the brave Second Division.

Five of the guns were new and of the Armstrong pattern, said to have been a present from the English Government to the Confederacy, and had not yet been used. They are beautiful specimens of manufacture.

The wagons, about two hundred in number, were mostly empty and were burnt after the mules had been cut loose and brought in. Along with the train was a wagon belonging to General Fitzhugh Lee, containing his baggage, &c.

In this engagement, Sheridan took three hundred prisoners, among whom was General Bragg's chief of artillery. The flag of the

Artillery Headquarters of Northern Virginia, with many other trophies, was also captured.

The prisoners taken the past three days foot up fifteen hundred, including a number of officers.

City Point, Virginia, 9:30 O'clock a.m.

To the Hon. Edwin M. Stanton, Secretary of War:

This morning Lieutenant General Grant reports Petersburg evacuated, and he is confident that Richmond also is evacuated. He is pushing forward to cut off, if possible, the retreating Rebel army.

A. Lincoln

Second Dispatch, War Department, Washington, D.C. 10 a.m.

To Major General Dix:

It appears from a dispatch of General Weitzel's, just received by this Department that our forces under his command are in Richmond, having taken it at a quarter past eight o'clock this morning.

Edwin M. Stanton
Secretary of War

Third Dispatch, City Point Virginia 11 a.m

To Edwin M. Stanton, Secretary of War:

General Weitzel telegraphs as follows:

"We took Richmond at a quarter past eight o'clock this morning. I captured many guns. The enemy left in great haste. The city is on fire in one place. Am making every effort to put it out.

"The people receive us with enthusiastic expressions of joy.

"General Grant started early this morning with the army toward the Danville road, to cut off Lee's retreating army, if possible.

"President Lincoln has gone to the front."

T. S. Bowers
Assistant Adjutant General.

Fourth Dispatch, War Department
Washington, D.C. 12 noon

To Major General Dix:

The following official confirmation of the capture of Richmond, and the announcement that the city is on fire, has been received.

E. M. Stanton
Secretary of War

Petersburg, Virginia,
Union Account

The United States colored troops are this morning marching through the streets singing:

> Say, darkeys, hab you seen de massa
> Wid de muffstash on his face,
> Go along de road some time dis mornin',
> Like he gwine to leab de place?
> He seen a smoke way up de ribber,
> Whar de Linkum gunboats lay.
> He took his hat an' leP berry sudden,
> An' I spec'he's run away!
> De massa run, ha! ha!
> De darkey stay,-ho! ho!
> It must be now de kingdom comin',
> An' de yar ob Jubilo.
>
> He six foot one way, two foot tudder,
> An' he weigh t'ree hundred pound,
> His coat so big, he couldn't pay de tailor,
> An' it won't go half way round.
> He drill so much, dey call him Cap'an,
> An' he get so drefful tanned!
> I spec' he try an' fool dem Yankees,
> For to tink he's contraband.
> De massa run, ha! ha!
> De darkey stay, ho! ho!
> It must be now de kingdom comin',
> An' de yar ob Jubilo.
>
> De darkeys feel so berry lonesome,

Libing in de log house on de lawn,
Dey move dar tings to massa's parlor,
For to keep it while he's gone.
Dar's wine an' cider in de kitchen,
An' de darkeys dey'll hab some;
I spose dey'll all be cornfiscated.
When de Linkum sojers come.
De massa run, ha! ha!
De darkey stay, ho! ho!
It must be now de kingdom comin',
An' de yar ob Jubilo.

De oberseer he make us trouble.
An' he dribe us round a spell.
We lock him up in de smoke-house celler,
Wid de key trown in de well.
De whip is lost, de han'-cufF broken,
But de massa'll hab his pay,
He's ole enuff, big enuff, ought to know better
Dan to went an' run away.
De massa run, ha! ha!
De darkey stay, ho! ho!
It must be now de kingdom comin'
An' de yar ob Jubilo.

Selma, Alabama,
Union Account

General Wilson's cavalry column has taken possession of this city. Union "Account. In doing so he captured large quantities of artillery, machinery, &c, &c.

Richmond, Virginia,
Union Account

"At half past eleven o'clock yesterday morning, while seated in his pew at church listening to the lucubrations of the Reverend Doctor Hoge, Jeff. Davis was handed a dispatch from General Lee. Thereupon he instantly arose, and walked hurriedly down the aisle, beneath the questionings of all the eyes in the house. The dispatch was to the effect that Richmond must be evacuated during the coming night. And so his ex-Excellency, the late President of the late Confederacy, went forth from the sanctuary where prophesied the favorite high priest of his realm to pack up his "portable property," in hasty preparation for a journey on the Sabbath day. Like a thief in the night, he stole away with trepidation and fear, and with an agonizing sense of the shortness of time.

As the preacher closed the services the colored sexton handed him a note from his ex-Excellency. The face of the preacher waxed sickly with despair, while that of the sexton glowed with joy too great for concealment. The chagrin of the one was quite as marked as the grin of the other. The former begged his congregation to tarry, and told them in sad utterances that he did not expect to minister to them anymore. His farewell over, he too proceeded furiously to the packing of "portable property"—he also intended to journey on the Sabbath. This Doctor Hoge, it will be remembered, visited England two years ago, ostensibly to procure a supply of Bibles, but really as an emissary of the Rebellion. He was largely feted by the British adherents of the South, and doubtless did much harm. Since his return he has been in the habit of making camp speeches, full of hot unction and perorated with presumptuous appeals to the God of battles. A proslavery fanatic of considerable ability, he has been petted and used by Davis, whose own enormous cunning and wickedness have nothing of the element of fanaticism. The two worthies fled together. *Requie-scat!*"

When Grant began the movement on Petersburg last night General Weitzel was left in command of our line north of the river, with two divisions of his own corps—the Twenty-fifth Colored, and General Devins's Division, the Third of the Twenty-fourth Corps. At three thirty this morning, Captain Bruce, of Devin's staff, being in charge of the picket line, visited the outposts, and his suspicions for some reason aroused, he sent three men to reconnoiter. They penetrated the Rebel line and reported no enemy. These three, like the three children of Israel dispatched by Moses, spied out the land of Canaan. At once advancing his whole picket line by skirmishers, and opportunely falling in with a deserter by whom he was piloted, he, himself, first passed through. The deserter pointed out a tortuous path through three lines of *chevaux de friese* which had been used for egress and ingress of their picket reliefs, and was, unlike the rest of the line, free from thickly planted torpedoes. Ordering his men to deploy widely and continue to advance, Captain Bruce rode rapidly to General Devins, who instantly telegraphed the facts to Weitzel. That energetic officer by daylight was advancing his entire force. By that hour a series of heavy explosions, and the smoke and flames of Richmond burning, put the fact of the evacuation beyond question. Major Stevens, of Weitzel's staff, Lieutenant W. J. Ladd, of Devins's, and Major Brooks, of the Eighth

Vermont, were the first in the city—by virtue of the excellence of their horses. Within that hour Weitzel, Devins, Ripley, Shepley, and other Generals, had come up; the heads of their columns were pushing up parallel streets, and all the prominent points were in our possession. It is said to have been a jolly sight, the colored troops marching in great rapture with long strides and ecstatic shouts, their welcome by their brethren in the city, who, men and women and pickaninnies, embraced them, ran by their sides, cried and laughed, and, in their own extravagant way, thanked the Lord and took courage.

When we entered, the city had been burning three hours. To prevent large quantities of tobacco and other stores from falling into our hands, on the direct order of Breckinridge, millions of private property was subjected to the flames, and one of the fairest cities on the continent ruined. Indeed, it is said that Breckinridge, in person, superintended the great arson, and only left by the last train twenty minutes before we came in.

That the entire city was not destroyed is due entirely to the Union army. The first order issued was for every exertion to be used to stay the conflagration, while regiment after regiment, without orders other than from their own officers, stacked arms, piled knapsacks, and lent willing and tireless energies to save the property of their enemies. Whole squares were tumbling and smoldering to ruin, and when the flames were extinguished, the debris and the smoke, the crumbling walls and the tottering chimneys of a thousand structures, many of them costly, all of them valuable, testified to the relentless cruelty of the Rebel authorities—unpitying even to their friends and their dupes. Included in the destruction are the large mills and warehouses on the river, and the entire business part of the town.

Passing up Main Street, at the left were the crumbling walls and tottering chimneys, and the smoke still rising from the debris of the great fire. At the right, the sidewalk covered with Negroes and poverty-stricken whites, timid women peering from the windows, or bolder ones in untidy garb standing in the doorways, or the doors were closed and the blinds shut—the denizens gone or hiding within.

About nine o'clock this morning, terrific shell explosions, rapid and continuous, added to the terror of the scene, and led to the impression that the city was being shelled by the retreating Confederate army from the Southside ; but the explosions were soon ascertained to proceed from the Government arsenal and laboratory, then in flames.

The Custom House, late Confederate Treasury, passed through the ordeal of fire unscathed, from the fact that the edifice is of granite and fire-proof. The Bank of the Commonwealth presents a granite front, but is a mere shell, as also is the Bank of Virginia. At one time during this morning the Spottswood Hotel was in great danger, the flames leaping toward its location with great rapidity; but a merciful Providence caused a lull in the breeze, and blew the flames out of their track.

One of the pillaging soldiers engaged in robbing the stores on Main Street, was shot from the inside by the proprietor, while he was knocking in the show-glass. A charge of buckshot entered his stomach, and it is believed he died in a short time, but we could not learn what became of his body.

At the Government clothing store, corner of Cary and Pearl Streets, a man, while pillaging clothing, fell through the hatchway and broke his neck.

While hundreds of families have been rendered homeless and houseless by the conflagration, a great many persons who live in sections spared by the flames have accumulated small fortunes by rescuing large quantities of goods from the burning buildings. Clothing, shoes, dry goods of every description, were saved in large quantities, and are now stored away in the houses of those who saved them. Part restitution would be the proper thing in cases where the owners are known.

Confederate bonds, Confederate notes, bank checks, bills, flecked and whitened the streets in every direction —all so worthless that the boys would not pick them up.

The scene at the commissary depot, at the head of the dock, beggared description. Hundreds of Government wagons were loaded with bacon, flour and whisky, and driven off in hot haste to join the retreating army. Negroes with their peculiar "heave oh!" sweated and worked like beavers; but the immense piles of stores did not seem to diminish in the least. Thronged about the depot were hundreds of men, women and children, black and white, provided with capacious bags, baskets, tubs, buckets, tin pans and aprons, cursing, pushing and crowding, awaiting the throwing open of the doors, and the order for each to help himself. When the Government wagons had gotten off all the stores possible, it was found that several hundred barrels of whisky remained in the upper story.

One after another, in hasty procession, the barrels were rolled to the hatchway, the heads knocked out, and a miniature whisky Niagara poured continuously down, pouring into the dock in a current almost strong enough to have swept a man off his feet.

Between two and three hundred barrels were thus poured out—a big drink to the finny inhabitants of the river.

The doors were opened to the populace, and a rush, that almost seemed to carry the building off its foundations, was made, and hundreds of thousands of pounds of splendid bacon, flour, &c, went into the capacious maw of the public.

And here we may remark that while the Confederate Government was making such a poor mouth over the reported failure of supplies—while the people were being starved that the army might be fed, this immense storehouse was bursting with fullness and plenty to come finally to utter wreck and waste.

During the night, stragglers from the retreating army inaugurated a reign of terror and pillage. Jewelry, clothing and liquor stores, and a few private houses, were sacked. The fire revealed immense amounts of provisions—whether the accumulations of the Government or of speculators does not appear, although citizens say the latter. Thousands immediately engaged in the scarcely reprehensible work of removing to their houses family supplies. "The niggers got it all," said a leading citizen, with a wrath he made little attempt to conceal.

Scenes of Destruction at Richmond

Petersburg Virginia

To the celerity of our movement this morning and to the military skill displayed in the maneuvering of the troops, we may confidently attribute the results of this the last campaign in Virginia. There was none of the old-time Antietam and Gettysburg halting after the retreat of Lee became known; no council of war was held to determine the propriety of following up the demoralized foe; but right onward and alongside of the flying foe our columns were pushed and maneuvered with a celerity and skill which has astonished the world.

But a small portion of our army was gratified with an interior view of Petersburg. On ascertaining the line of the enemy's retreat, and discovering that he was rapidly moving westward toward the Danville road, our several columns were pushed as swiftly towards Burkesville for the purpose of intercepting him. Sheridan with his cavalry, the Fifth, and two divisions of the Second Corps, formed our left column, while the remainder of the troops moved along the south side of the Appomattox, by what is known as the River road, to Sutherland's Station, near which the whole army are in bivouac tonight, having as yet encountered no opposition.

Petersburg was occupied by the blue coats at three o'clock this morning. For the first time since the beginning of the war have the Stars and Stripes been allowed to come in without a protest. We are here and propose to stay here, and propose also to plant our proud banner in every city in the Southern States before we get through.

Richmond, Virginia,
Union Account

It is hard to realize the fact that the once great elastic spinal column of the most powerful combination in arms against the Union has been broken and crushed, and that Lee, with his ragged, disheartened and disorganized forces, is flying from our advancing columns, which are rapidly bearing down upon him to complete the work now so nearly finished. And yet, today, from many a dizzy height, our flag floats in the bright sunlight over Richmond and Petersburg; the long lines of earthworks around those cities, a few days ago, bristling with guns and seemingly so impregnable, are silent and tenantless now; our advance is marching on, and today the streets of Richmond and Petersburg are trod by the soldiers of the Union, and, mark it, by men in uniform whose skin nature made dark—men whom the boasted chivalry of the South call *slaves,* whose toil receives only the remuneration of the lash, but who are men nevertheless, and who have made valid their claim to the title by their deeds.

Petersburg, Virginia,
Union Account

This morning at daybreak the Federal troops were all astir; knapsacks were being slung, blankets rolled, and every preparation made for an immediate advance. Portions of our troops had occupied the town two hours before, but the majority was denied the enviable pleasure of breakfasting in the Cockade City. A general falisude was sounding all along our whole line, and, as if it were impossible to indulge sufficiently in other noisy demonstrations, muskets were emptied of their charges to add to the universal din.

Bands were playing "Hail Columbia," "Yankee Doodle," Kingdom Comin'," "We'll all Drink Stone Blind," "Lanigan's Ball," polkas, waltzes, in fact almost everything of a patriotic or an enlivening character. It seemed as if Orpheus himself had gone mad, and was trying to render from all of his creations of lighter music a grand, triumphant and Heaven-swelling chorus in honor of the occasion. Amid this torrent of mellifluous sounds arose from one of the bands that grand old refrain,

"Praise God, from whom all blessings flow,
Praise Him ye people hear below;"

indicating that some, at least, believed it but just and proper to blend thanksgiving with the general jubilation. And thus did the noble old Army of the Potomac and its brethren from above the James celebrate the victory won by their long years of persevering toil.

But few evidences were discovered, on entering the town, of great destruction of life on the Rebel side. They had removed their dead and wounded, to hide from the- eye of our victorious army the full extent of their disaster. Along the Boydtown Road leading to Petersburg was noticed but one poor fellow sacrificed to the devilish ambition of his implacable masters, Davis and Lee. He was dead; but the dark, swarthy countenance almost led one to believe, until he touched his cold and pulseless hand, that life still lingered in his emaciated, half-clad body. He lay in a ditch or gully along the highway, with the water from a pure, perennial spring above trickling musically beneath him; his blanket was neatly rolled and slung across his shoulder; his head was resting upon his arm as if in repose, but the death-glaze upon his eyes told that he slept the sleep that knows no waking. A hideous orifice in the side of the head, surrounded by clotted gore, showed where a fragment of shell had saved him from living to see the overwhelming shame and disgrace which awaits the deluded followers of his former leaders.

The city presents the appearance usually noticeable in every Rebel town falling into our possession. Doors were closed and window blinds shut; but, if I mistake not, I saw many a curious eye intently peering into the street. True, the number of contrabands of all ages and sizes congregated on street corners was legion, and of ancient and crippled whites not a few; but the fairer sex kept close within doors, disdaining to exhibit their peerless charms to our men in blue. Well, the Union boys took it philosophically enough, seeming to care but little for Confederate calico or linsey, and went marching along as if only intent on the capture or dispersion of Lee's defeated army.

The eastern portion of the town exhibits on every side marks of the solid shot and shell thrown by our guns during last summer. The buildings in Bolingbroke Street, which run nearly east and west, are literally perforated in every part. Chimneys have been razed on every building, windows knocked and splintered to pieces, brick walls crumbled and torn, porches carried away—ruin and desolation reign supreme. Almost every house is deserted in this street, but in the center and other portions of the city but little damage seems to have been done by our fire.

A singular rumor was in circulation this noon to the effect that a party of Johnnies still held a certain fort on the line south of the city; that they refused to surrender, and that our forces there had deemed it most judicious to starve them out without shedding the blood always attending an assault. Reports of cannon were occasionally heard during the afternoon in that direction, which seemed to give an air of trustworthiness to the strange rumor; but, nevertheless, no one attached sufficient importance to the story to investigate it. It was explained tonight and proved to have originated in the explosion of shells lying around the works by some of our stragglers, who were strolling about outside the city, and who fired them by means of trains for their own amusement.

From midnight Saturday to Sunday morning a furious cannonading, accompanied by sharp skirmishing, was kept up from the Rebel works in front of the Sixth and Ninth Corps. The enemy had probably discovered our plan, and was endeavoring to thwart our intentions. Their efforts were in vain, however, for before daybreak the Sixth Corps, in compliance with orders, were massing between Forts Fisher and Welch, regardless of the storm of shot and shell, for the final charge. In massing, more were killed and wounded by the fire of the enemy than in the assault which followed, as the rapidity with which the advance was made soon placed our men where the missiles of the Rebels whistled and howled harmlessly over their heads.

Just before daybreak in the morning the Sixth Corps moved on the enemy's works as follows: In this advance the division of General Getty formed in two lines, supported on the right and left respectively by the divisions of Wheaton and Seymour, formed in echelon of brigades, moving left in front to facilitate a flank attack upon the enemy's forts. The advance of the Sixth Corps, in which General Ord's command cooperated, was one of the grandest military spectacles ever witnessed on the battlefield. A bright wall of bayonets firmly grasped by masses of determined men, undaunted by the death-dealing fire from the enemy's forts, which were actually obscured by the volumes of smoke which were vomited forth by a hundred cannon, was a sight, once seen, never to be forgotten. Moving through this murderous fire to the attack, with a line of white smoke puffs telling where the shells of the enemy were bursting, the charging columns still advanced and were soon under the guns of the Rebels, who now almost ceased their fire of artillery and opened with musketry. But the doom of the Rebels was sealed; from all sides our columns were bearing down upon them. Two unsuccessful assaults were made to capture the enemy's forts, when the First Division was formed in front with the Second, and a third charge essayed which proved more successful; Fort Gregg (in which fell the Rebel General A. P. Hill, pierced by three bullets), Battery Forty, and the whole line in front of the Sixth and Twenty-fourth Corps falling into our hands. In carrying the works the Third Division of the Sixth Corps formed to assault the enemy's works on their left flank, taking them without any considerable opposition.

At eleven o'clock the engagement ceased, and the Southside Railroad within three miles of the town was in our possession. The operations of the Ninth Corps, although gratifying, were not equally successful with those of the Sixth and Twenty-fourth. The active participants in the assault of the Ninth Corps were Harriman's Brigade of Wilcox's Division and the divisions of Generals Potter and Hartranft. The main attack was to be made by the two divisions last named, supported on their right by Harriman's Brigade upon the earthworks in front of Forts Hell and Rice, the most formidable of which was Fort Mahone confronting Fort Hell.

Now everyone has heard of Fort Hell—has read of the fierce artillery duels which have occurred between it and its antagonist, Fort Mahone, during the winter. It was this same Fort Mahone, with its labyrinth of moats and abatis, that was assaulted by the left of the Ninth Corps on Sunday morning, and which ultimately fell in our possession after fighting of the most desperate character. At an early hour Wilcox, in obedience to orders, had made a strong demonstration in front of his position on the Appomattox, while on the left Potter and Hartranft had at the same time charged, carried and held Fort Mahone and two other earthworks on its left against the repeated attempts of the enemy to repossess it.

Charge of the 9th Corps on Fort Mahone
Sketched by A. R. Waud, April 3, 1865

At Fort Mahone, the struggle was longer and more determined on both sides. Carried at about eight o'clock in the morning, it was found necessary to abandon its northern face as the enemy had, on being driven out of it, retired a short distance to the rear or inner work, from which they swept with cannon-shot and musketry the locality mentioned. The main part, however, was still in our possession. At about eleven o'clock in the morning the enemy made a most furious sortie to retake it, and for a time our chances of retaining it seemed dubious. The enemy assaulted in overwhelming numbers, and it was plainly evident had received re-enforcements. Fortunately a portion of the Sixth Corps and the provisional Brigade, under the command of Brigadier General C. H. T. Collis, arrived in the nick of time, and, again charging the enemy, they were again driven from the fort, which he made no further attempt to reoccupy during the day.

Previously the Second Corps had carried the works in its front with but trifling opposition, and was wheeling to the north to co-operate in the attack of the Sixth, Ninth and Twenty-fourth Corps. It was too late, however, to participate in the glories of the assault, arriving up the Boydtown road in the afternoon, when the enemy had retired into his inner defenses near the city. The Division of General Miles had been sent to the left to join Sheridan in the morning, and having heard no intelligence from it, the command of General Mott was sent to join it.

Sheridan was somewhere on the left with the Fifth Corps endeavoring to intercept the retreat of the Rebel forces, cut off from Petersburg by the advance of the Sixth and Twenty-fourth Corps. Our line was within a mile and a half of the city, and our left rested west of it, on the Appomattox.

The headquarters of Generals Grant and Meade at night were established at the Ritchie House, on the Boydtown road, three miles from the town, and within easy shelling range of the enemy's batteries. But the enemy was content to rest quietly in his works, sending over a shell occasionally to remind us that he was still there. The battle ended at about eleven o'clock in the morning. From noon until nightfall the enemy exhibited unusual inactivity, and many began making inquiries as to what it boded. Some, with a wise look, believed that Lee was only maneuvering, in order to attack us in some unexpected quarter. Everyone said, "This lull means something!" Most assuredly it did mean something and that something was the retreat of the major part of Lee's forces across the river north of the town. All the afternoon three or four dense columns of smoke were seen ascending from the city, and it was evident that extensive fires were raging.

At dusk a pontoon train, under the guidance of Major Paine, of the Topographical Engineers, at General Meade's headquarters, was sent out to span the Appomattox for the crossing of troops to the west and northwest of the city during the night, from which the inference may reasonably be drawn that Grant knew of the retreat of Lee, or that not aware of it, he was drawing a circle about them from which it would be impossible to escape. At any rate the city was virtually in our possession, and should Lee fail in all of his assaults to break our lines, the retreat of his army would inevitably follow. And then arose the question, "Where will he go?" Officers high in authority said to Richmond, and on referring to that point as no longer tenable, admitted Lee's inability to hold it over a few days at most, but stated that now that he had been thoroughly defeated, he would fight only for effect; that the Rebel authorities would endeavor to make known to the world the fact that they were battling in a holy and righteous cause, and, that should they fail, they would, with their expiring breath, announce the intention of the coming generation to accomplish the work which they had left undone.

Night came, and with it our troops reposed on their laurels. Bright columns of light rose from the Cockade City, and until one o'clock on Sunday morning occasional shots were interchanged between our and the Rebel lines. From that time until morning silence reigned over both lines. At half past four o'clock on the morning of Monday four reports of cavalry from Birney's front were heard, and four shells following one another in rapid succession sped, with a hollow, rushing sound, toward Petersburg. The reports awakened our weary men, and, after an interval of perhaps a minute, loud and prolonged cheers were heard from one end of the line to the other, bands commenced playing patriotic airs, and everyone was wide awake and sensible of the fact that Petersburg had been evacuated.

Colonel Ralph Ely, commanding the Second Brigade of the First Division of the Ninth Corps, is credited with the honor of being the first to enter the city. There are several other claimants to the honor, among them a brigade of the Sixth Corps and the colored division of General Birney, of the Twenty-fifth. The latter claims that at an early hour on the morning of Monday a Rebel deserter came into our lines and reported that the Rebel picket line had just been withdrawn; that he immediately advanced his skirmish line, which entered the town at daybreak, meeting with no opposition, and that Lieutenant West, of his staff, was the first to set free four hundred prisoners, white and colored, from the city jail.

Be this as it may, Colonel Ely, of the Ninth Corps has the official credit of being the first to enter the town, and has therefore received its Provost-Marshalship.

On entering the town the tobacco and cotton warehouses were found smoldering heaps of ruins. They had been fired soon after we gained the Southside road on Sunday, and it was this conflagration which was observable on the afternoon of that day. About eleven thousand dollars worth of cotton and fifteen hundred hogsheads of tobacco were destroyed by the fire kindled by Lee on his exit from the city. Nevertheless, innumerable bales of tobacco were found in the different stores and were appropriated by our soldiers, to whom that article has become as necessary as it is noxious.

In the afternoon, President Lincoln, accompanied by Admiral Porter, arrived in the city from City Point; but so quiet was their arrival and departure that but few knew of their movements until the evening.

At an early hour this morning, the army was again moving westward toward Sutherland's Station in pursuit of Lee's retreating columns. At present, no one seems to know the enemy's exact whereabouts.

Major General George G. Meade
Commanding Officer
Army of the Potomac

Tuesday, April 4, 1865

Richmond, Virginia
Union Account

Today, at about noon, Mr. Lincoln came up from City Point, taking the boat to Varina, and there taking horses to this city. Along with him came Admiral Porter, with a few other persons. The party entered the capital with feelings that can better be imagined than described. It is not known whether the occasion reminded Mr. Lincoln "of a little story," but it is presumed that it did.

This coming of the President seems to point to peace. It is said that he intends to issue a proclamation to the people of the South, calling upon them to return to their allegiance. By this act the President will ignore the existence of the Rebel Government, and appeal to the common sense of the people, who, worn out by a long and bloody war, will no doubt set their rulers aside and make peace on any terms.

It is estimated that there are twenty thousand Union people in the city, who will gladly return to the starry folds of their proper flag. It was only by force of arms that they bowed to the acts of the Rebel Government. To this class will be added the half-way men, who now will of course be good Union citizens.

The Whig appears this morning as a Union paper, with the name of the former proprietor at its head.

The reception of President Lincoln today was enthusiastic in the extreme.

General Weitzel telegraphed the Secretary of War that twenty-eight locomotives, forty-four passenger and baggage cars, and one hundred and sixteen freight cars were captured in this city.

Army of the Potomac in the field,
Union Account

This day was spent by the army in an active pursuit of the enemy. It is a foot race again between the two great bodies for a certain goal. The point for which General Lee is thought to be in march is Danville. Under cover of his left he drew off from his lines on the night of the second, and began a rapid march in the hope of gaining a good start upon us, in which he has failed, for this army is well up with his rear guard, the Second Corps, under General Gordon, which held the left of his lines on the day of the great battle.

By the Cox road the bulk of this army went on Monday, through Petersburg, in pursuit, and the cavalry has been on the heels of the enemy all this day, taking two thousand more men from their ranks, which are fast dwindling away. It is thought that there cannot be more than thirty-five thousand men now with General Lee, and as they go on the men quit the ranks and find their way home.

Our cavalry gives no rest to the broken enemy, and is pressing hard upon the rear of Gordon's Corps (their second). It is from it that most of the prisoners are taken by our cavalry. In many of the houses along the line of march, parties of wounded men are found, who, having been able to march from the late field of battle, were taken along and had to fall out on the way. It is only a very sanguine Rebel who cannot see that all is lost with the lately great army of northern Virginia.

It may not exist as an organized body thirty days longer. If it can reach the force under General Joseph Johnston, a second heavy fight will take place; this time with General Sherman; but the Army of the Potomac would in less than ten hours enter into the fight, and the result to the Rebel forces would be a disaster, which would be final.

The first of May could see the end of this war, for nothing but a heavy line of defenses could enable the enemy to make a stand again, and time to throw up such a line is now wanting. The enemy can only flee from point to point for a short time.

Hill's loss to the enemy is great, for he led their Third Corps with ability, and was perhaps only second to General Lee in importance to the Rebel army. In the late fight his corps was almost ubiquitous. It extended from Hatcher's Run to Battery Gregg, and fought our Twenty-fourth and Sixth Corps. It was in that work that Hill was struck by three balls, which made his death wounds.

Today the cavalry and the leading corps made a long march. The Ninth Corps is some distance in the rear, as it left Petersburg only today, but the rest of the army is well in hand, and the cavalry, under the untiring Sheridan, is doing great service.

There are many reports of extravagant success on our part flying about. One is that twenty thousand of the enemy have been forced to lay down their arms, but this is at least premature. It is the old story of bagging. The army is doing well, but has not made such short work of the enemy as that.

Burkesville may be the point at which another great fight will take place. It is sixty miles from Petersburg, and the army has not made more than about half that distance up to this evening.

Washington, D.C.

Mrs. Lincoln received a dispatch Washington, D. C, from the President today, dated as follows:

"From Jefferson Davis's late residence at Richmond."

Correspondents from City Point state that Lee has divided the remnant of his army, and is retreating in two small columns. Our prisoners at noon on the third exceeded twenty-five thousand. The Rebel destruction of property on their retreat literally beggars description. Stragglers and deserters are even in excess of what was anticipated.

New York

This morning's Tribune contains the following editorial:

RICHMOND OURS!

The fall of Richmond and Petersburg so closely following the victories of Saturday and Sunday, has gladdened the hearts of the loyal millions as no other event has done or had power to do. Newbern, Nashville, New Orleans, Memphis, Norfolk, Vicksburg, Chattanooga, Knoxville, Atlanta, Savannah, Charleston, Columbia, Wilmington, Fayetteville, were each important, and its capture was hailed with satisfaction; but even Charleston the cradle of Secession, was not so generally esteemed the cockade of the Rebellion as Richmond, the seat of the Confederate Government, but lately deserted by its Congress, and till yesterday the focus of all that was left of its authority and prestige. "Richmond is Ours!" as it was yesterday flashed to Madawaska and to Oregon, awakened more shouts of exultation than if it had been telegraphed that Lee had surrendered his army.

For Richmond has been long an eyesore to the Republic. The sudden and secret plunge of Virginia into the abyss of treason—the instant rush upon the National Army and Navy Yard within her borders— the sudden transformation of the entire State into an active volcano of hostility to the National existence —the violence and terrorism wherewith Unionism was instantly suppressed from the Atlantic to the crests of the Alleghenies—the perils wherewith the National Capital was suddenly environed—above all, the long and wearying efforts to plant the Old Flag once more on the battlements of the Rebel Metropolis—the precious lives sacrificed in those persistent efforts—all contributed to heighten the joy wherewith Unionists yesterday grasped each other's hands and shouted "Richmond is Ours!"

It might have been ours long ago. It could have been taken with little loss by the tens of thousands whom General Scott persistently held idle and useless around Washington throughout May and June, 1861. It might easily have been taken by McClellan in the spring of 1862, had that illustrious professor of the art *"How Not To Do It"* really and zealously tried. It might have been taken, but was not, for God's time had not yet come. At last, that time *has* come, and millions joyfully echo "Richmond is ours!"

City Point, Virginia,
Union Account

On Sunday night before the evacuation of Richmond, the Rebels blew up their forts and rams in the James River, the explosion of which was terrific, resembling an earthquake, and was heard for miles around. Our gunboats have moved up the James River, and are now engaged in removing the obstructions. General Weitzel, upon entering Richmond, was directed by General Grant to allow no one to leave the city, or permit any one to enter, who was not connected with the army or had authority to do so. Petersburg was occupied by our troops on Monday morning. The Rebels fired Petersburg in several places before evacuating the town, but the fire was speedily extinguished. Over five thousand prisoners have already been received at City Point, and others are constantly arriving. In fact there were so many prisoners there that a sufficient number of troops could not be spared to guard them, and consequently detachments of sailors and marines were taken from the gunboats and placed in charge of them. The entire number of prisoners captured by our troops up to yesterday was estimated at thirteen thousand by well-informed officers. Our wounded are being sent in to City Point as rapidly as possible and hospital boats are there taking them on board for shipment to Baltimore and Washington. The Rebel deserters in the Bull Pen at City Point appeared to receive the news of the fall of Richmond with as great enthusiasm as our own troops, and gave cheer after cheer.

Sheridan's Army in the Field

We are now on the Danville Railroad south of Amelia Court House. Sheridan has urged Meade to hurry forward the Second and Sixth Corps, by the River road. If the troops can get here in time, we have hopes of capturing the whole of Lee's army.

We are moving with our left wing under command of General Ord by the Burkesville road.

We hear that Lee is at Amelia Court House from men of that army who have become disgusted and are going home, generally unarmed.

Richmond, Virginia,
Union Account

A pontoon bridge now spans the James River, connecting Richmond with Manchester. The only trace on the river of the Petersburg Railroad Bridge are the huge stone piers that were left when the bridge was fired on the night of the second instant.

Sutherland Station, Virginia,
Union Account

General Grant has sent the following telegram:

"General Sheridan picked up twelve hundred prisoners today, and from three to five hundred more have been gathered by our troops. The majority of the arms that were left in the hands of Lee's Army are now scattered between Richmond and where his troops now are. The country is full of stragglers. The line of retreat is marked with artillery, ammunition, burned or charred wagons, caissons, ambulances, &c."

Augusta, Georgia,
Confederate Account

Five hundred Yankee prisoners from Sherman's army were last week brought into Charlotte, N. C. The Charlotte Democrat is informed that some of these prisoners, when told that they would be immediately exchanged, remarked that *"If that was known in their army, Sherman would not have enough men to take him to Washington."*

Baltimore, Maryland,
Union Account

A daring act of piracy was perpetrated today at Fairhaven, Herring Bay, about fifty miles below this city, the steamer Harriet Deford, being seized by a company of Rebel soldiers in disguise. The Deford had scarcely left Fairhaven wharf before a dozen or more of newly received passengers threw off their overcoats, and drawing revolvers, revealed to the astonished gaze of the passengers the uniform of Rebel soldiers.

The passengers, about seventy in number, thirty being ladies, were ordered to the saloon, and guards placed over them, while the balance of the pirates proceeded to take command of the steamer. Captain and officers were forced into obedience at the muzzle of the pirates' revolvers. One of the pirates assumed control of the wheel, the pilot and engineer being compelled to proceed to sea.

Mr. A. Donnell, clerk of the Deford, believing that he had met the leader of the outlaws on a former occasion, accosted him as Captain Fitzhugh, when the latter acknowledged the recognition, and said he was Captain of the Fifth Virginia cavalry, and acting under orders of superior officers.

Under the persuasive eloquence of a revolver, the clerk handed over to the pirates nearly twelve hundred dollars belonging to the owners of the steamer and different firms in this city, which Fitzhugh carefully fobbed.

When about a mile from Fairhaven, Fitzhugh compelled the engineer to sound the steam whistle three times, in answer to which signal three boats, containing thirty-two men, put off from each side of the river and stood for the steamer. The crews of these boats having been taken aboard, the steamer was headed down Chesapeake Bay.

On the way down Captain Leage, Captain Dayton, officer in charge of steamer, and several old gentlemen, with ladies and children, were placed on board of the schooner Hiawatha, bound for this city. The balance of male passengers, engineer, firemen and twenty colored freedmen were retained as prisoners. The Deford was valued at fifty thousand dollars, and had a cargo of tobacco, potatoes, grain, furs, &c, valued at eighty thousand dollars.

Fitzhugh would not permit his men to rob passengers. The captured steamer is a fast sailer, having repeatedly made fourteen knots per hour. The intention of the pirates could not be learned, but it is supposed they will endeavor to run outside of the Capes, transfer the cargo to a larger vessel, burn the Deford, and proceed to Nassau.

In Front of Mobile, Alabama,
Union Account

The looked-for artillery attack on the Rebel Spanish Fort was instituted this evening. All of our guns, both field and siege pieces, numbering upward of one hundred, were engaged for two hours in a terrific bombardment of the fort. An assault was not attempted. The Rebels threw their missiles with spirit and showed no signs of giving up.

Spanish Fort contains at least four thousand Rebel troops and three generals. No body of troops can possibly escape from it without being captured.

The enemy's gun boats make no attempt to approach the fort. Battery Smith, manned with thirty-pound Parrott guns, controls the bay in front and keeps the Rebel boats at a distance.

Mobile, Alabama,
Confederate Account

Reliable news reaches us today that the Federals captured Selma yesterday with a great deal of Government property, twenty-three pieces of artillery, ammunition and all of our valuable machinery.

Danville, Virginia,
Confederate Account

The evacuation of Richmond commenced Sunday afternoon. President Davis and Cabinet arrived here Monday. Very few persons were able to leave Richmond, except Government officials, in consequence of the suddenness of the movement.

No telegraph communication beyond the Junction. The Richmond arsenal has been removed. All the valuables of the Richmond banks were brought away and also the specie belonging to the Government.

The last passenger said he saw a lot of low class foreigners burning the mills and warehouses and plundering stores as he left Richmond.

The enemy had not occupied the city at last account, which was on the night of the second inst.

Army of the Potomac, Union Account

This morning came and found Army of the Potomac, every one as anxious to continue the pursuit as ever. Lee was on the march for the Danville Road, and had possibly reached it already, and delay on our part would have been criminal. Let it be understood that at this time Grant was south of, and marching parallel with Lee; and that, on the possession of the railroad mentioned, were based all our hopes of effectually preventing the escape of the enemy. Accordingly, our columns were again in motion early this morning, one pushing down the Southside Railroad to Wilson's Station, and another moving up the Namozine Road toward Amelia Court House. Considerable skirmishing in front of the last mentioned column occurred during its advance, but the enemy was continually forced back upon his main body with the loss of guns and prisoners.

Montgomery, Alabama, Confederate Account

General Forrest estimated the Yankees in Selma at nine thousand mounted infantry. Our force in Sunday's fight was Armstrong's and Roddy's brigades, some militia and seventeen pieces of artillery. The enemy turned our left, captured our wagons, artillery and a number of prisoners, and occupied Selma.

It is reported they burned only Government buildings in Selma.

The Yankees say they are going to Mobile.

Some accounts say our forces burnt the cotton and Government stores.

Forrest is all right, and in the proper place. Not much excitement.

No official information of the enemy leaving Selma.

The Dispatch newspaper is the only one saved.

The Kentucky brigade lost heavily at Plantersville. Plenty of rumors. No immediate danger apprehended here.

Goldsboro, North Carolina, Union Account

It is not the intention to allow this fine, campaigning weather to pass unimproved. Every effort is being made for an advance. Cavalry scouts report Rebel infantry pickets at Moseley Hall, twelve miles northeast of us. This indicates an attempt to interfere with our railroad communication. They can't hope to succeed, as our guards are strong.

A flag of truce, from the Rebel General Hampton, made its appearance yesterday in front of General Cox's line. The dispatches were received by Captain Knapp, of the One Hundred and Fourth Ohio, and sent to General Schofield. Hampton, it is understood, wants an exchange of prisoners now on hand. An answer has not yet been given him.

A walk through the streets of Goldsboro today would convince you that the name "Yankee"—which the Rebels seem determined shall cling to us—is well applied. Every corner and crossing is crowded with soldiers peddling tobacco, cigars, stationery, canned milk, or some other article. Everyone is as earnestly at work as though his livelihood depended on success.

The query is where are the buyers? All the capitalists-seem to be dealers. The paymasters have not been seen for months, and yet there is sufficient of "the medium" here to keep up a lively business. Another thing that is not explained is, where do these dealers get their supplies? There is mystery even here as to how some things are done, and that mystery we cannot solve.

Confederate Capitol Building, Richmond, Virginia

Wednesday, April 5, 1865

Jeffersville, Virginia,
Union Account

To Lieutenant General U. S. Grant: I send you the enclosed letter, * which will give you an idea of the condition of the enemy and their whereabouts. I sent General Davie's brigade this morning around on my left flank. He captured at Fame's cross roads five pieces of artillery, about two hundred wagons, and eight or nine battle flags, and a number of prisoners. The Second Army Corps is now coming up. I wish you were here yourself. I feel confident of capturing the army of Northern Virginia if we exert ourselves. I see no escape for Lee. I will put all my cavalry out on our left flank except McKenzie, who is now on the right.

*This letter is omitted.

P. H. Sheridan,
Major General

Goldsboro, North Carolina, Union Account

Without intending to convey any information to the enemy, It is a matter of pride to see the numbers and material of which this army is composed. There is now a right, left, and center army, commanded respectively by Generals Howard, Slocum and Schofield, and if they should have the opportunity afforded them of again meeting the enemy 'in the field in a pitched battle, will strike a blow which will use up the last vestige of Johnston's army, now thoroughly demoralized by fear of Sherman's victorious legions.

With the exception of slight picket firing there has been no change in the monotony of camp life, and we would have no idea of our proximity to an enemy.

Sherman's army has been thoroughly re-clothed and prepared for the coming campaign, and before this reaches you our army will be on the march.

Refugees arriving inside our lines report the evacuation of Raleigh. It is impossible to know how much credence is to be placed in this rumor, but it is not altogether improbable that Johnston may have moved his command further north, in order to try to make a junction with Lee.

News reaches us that a band Charleston, s. c, of guerillas made a dash upon

Charleston, South Carolina,
Union Account

Summerville today, captured a few Negroes and threatened to shoot all the whites who have taken the oath.

Augusta, Georgia,
Confederate Account

Alabama is over-run by Yankee cavalry, under Wilson and other commanders, moving toward Mobile. McCook's forces burned Red Mountain Iron Works and the town of Eltoton. They have tapped the telegraph in several places, sending dispatches to our officers. Two columns of Yankees are also reported advancing from Columbus, Miss.

Army of the Potomac,
Union Account

This afternoon Sheridan and the Fifth Corps had, by dint of hard marching, reached the Danville Road near Jettersville, and had already thrown up temporary works to dispute the passage of the enemy at this point.

Later in the day the force was strengthened by the arrival of the Second and Sixth Corps, which were placed in a position supporting Sheridan and the Fifth Corps. Our tactics proved the accuracy of the Lieutenant General's calculations. Lee, having crossed the Appomattox at Devil's Bend, was with his army in the vicinity of Amelia Court House, and had counted on his ability to reach Danville, his objective point, via the road of the same name, and on discovering the formidable force in his front, and the utter impossibility of penetrating our lines, changed his direction from southwest to west, with the intention of reaching Lynchburg, or possibly of heading us off, crossing the Southside west of Burkesville, and by a rapid detour, striking the Danville road south of the junction.

But whether his objective point is Lynchburg or whether he still adheres to his original intention of reaching Danville, it matters not; subsequent events proves his inability to reach either, and leaves him a prisoner cut off from Richmond, Lynchburg and Danville, in the region around Appomattox Court House, with no alternative but absolute surrender.

While the cavalry with the infantry force named was marching toward Jettersville to seize the railroad at that point, the column of Ord was moving rapidly down the Southside to Burkesville where it bivouacked tonight, while our right wing is thrown into position across the Danville road at Jettersville.

The position of both armies on tonight may be explained by saying that the enemy held one side, the west, of a triangle formed by the junction of the Southside and Danville railroads. Ord's column is at Burkesville, Sheridan with the Second, Fifth and Sixth Corps is higher up on the Danville road at Jettersville, while Lee with the remnant of his army is still further up in the vicinity of Amelia Court House. Sheridan has by a series of heavy attacks demonstrated the fact of Lee's presence at the point mentioned, and has telegraphed to Grant this evening expressing the opinion that, if pressed, the enemy would surrender.

Burkesville, Virginia, 10 O'clock p.m., Union Account

Honorable Edwin M. Stanton, Secretary of War:

Lieutenant General Grant received the following dispatch at half past six o'clock in the evening while on his way to this point, and at once proceeded to General Sheridan's headquarters.

General Grant desired me to transmit the dispatch to you on the opening of the telegraph at this place, and to say that the Sixth Corps without doubt reached General Sheridan's position within an hour or two after the dispatch was written. Two divisions of the Twenty-fourth Corps will encamp here tonight, and one division of the Twenty-fifth Army Corps at Black's and White Station, Southside railroad.

S. Williams,
Brigadier General

Danville, Va., Evacuation of Richmond, Confederate Account

Richmond and Petersburg have fallen; they have gone down in a blaze of glory, and with a record unstained by one blot of shame. All that the enemy have gained, has been purchased at a terrible price in blood, while our own army, although suffering severely, is still strong, intact, and ready for its future work.

Of the events of the last five days I can give you but a cursory view, and even this is obscured by the yet fresh smoke of the battle.

Grant commenced his grand movement as early as Tuesday, the 28th. It was not unanticipated. Our only doubt was as to the exact point at which he would make his main or decisive demonstration. He felt our lines at different localities along their entire length. Hence General Lee was compelled so to distribute his forces as to be prepared to repel the principal assault with the least possible delay.

On the Tuesday in question the enemy advanced oh the south side to within one mile of the Boydtown Plank Road, threw up entrenchments and built a large fort in the vicinity of the Lewis house. During the night, his skirmishers pushed forward a few hundred yards further. Wednesday, we fought this column with varying success, and night drooped on a drawn battle. At Hatcher's Run, during the afternoon, there was also heavy fighting, in which the enemy lost heavily. Thursday, heavy skirmishing and movement of troops. Friday, the efforts were resumed and with greater determination. The Federal cavalry swept around our works towards the railroads, but were met by General Fitz Lee and repulsed. The Yankee infantry, upwards of forty thousand strong, were massed near Burgess' Mill, and here battle was joined in earnest. Of its results I know nothing definite, save that the enemy gained no substantial advantage, and suffered greatly. We captured between four and six hundred prisoners.

On Saturday and Sunday, the fighting was fearful—the shocks of conflict the most terrible of the war, and the casualties on both sides immense. Our entrenchments, in many places, were held by a thin line only, but this stood nobly to its post, throughout Saturday. On Sunday, however, Grant resumed his old vocation of "Butcher." Finding that he could make little or no impression in the ordinary way, he massed his troops several columns deep against a portion of the line on the right, and then driving them relentlessly forward succeeded at last after frightful sacrifice of life in obtaining possession of a section of the works. It was not in the power of any men, however brave, to have withstood these desperate assaults without greater support—Longstreet had not yet come up, although hurrying from another part of the field. Meanwhile the Federals were rolling forward and recoiling like waves —those behind impelling those before—until a lodgment was effected, the works mounted, a flanking position and enfilade fire secured, and the battle substantially won.

Our grape and canister mowed the enemy down by hundreds, our rifles told with unerring precision, and the ground was literally carpeted with the dead and wounded, but sheer physical brute force proved at last superior to everything else, and the defenses were taken.

We know nothing yet of the military movements of the day in detail. But every statement that reaches us confirms the fact that our officers and soldiers fought like heroes.

General A. P. Hill is said to have been killed or mortally wounded. He was passing through the woods and came upon two Yankees, whose surrender he demanded, but instead of yielding one of them drew sight and shot him through the body. Whether he was killed outright or not, we don't know. It is thought by some that he is in the hands of the enemy and probably still alive. General Gordon is reported mortally wounded. He was one of the lions of the day. General Pickett is said to have been killed. These reports may all prove premature, and I recommend that they be received with caution. Our total losses are estimated at from eight to fifteen thousand, of whom a considerable portion are prisoners. That of the enemy can only be guessed at; but officers who were engaged at the front and saw something of the slaughter, state that it cannot be less than from forty to fifty thousand.

The scene in Richmond, on the reception of the news, beggars all description. While preparations for an evacuation had been in progress several weeks, the suddenness of the movement took everyone by surprise. The President was at church; officials were resting in comparative quiet, waiting the dispatches of General Lee: citizens were confident and hopeful. No one anticipated disaster. When, however, the truth was foreshadowed, such hurrying to and fro, such gathering of goods, disposition of effects, and endeavors to leave the city, as took place has had no parallel during the war. The streets were thronged by an excited populace. The departments were alive with swarms of officials packing and removing the public records. The torch was freely applied by order of the Government to all species of public property. In some instances the patriotic owners set fire to their own premises—lobby's prison, tobacco warehouses and flour mills, whole acres of "Virginia weed," commissary stores and buildings, the Laboratory and Arsenal, in brief everything that could afford sustenance to the Yankee army, or incite pillage was given to the flames. During Sunday night many of the stores were broken open and robbed of their contents; and others were thrown open to the poor and needy.

Before sunrise flames and smoke were coiling above and around the sacrificial pile in every direction, and I recalled amid the bursting bombs, the rush and roar of conflagration, the movement of trains, and a thousand other incidents of the hour, the siege of Sebastopol in the Crimea. Our Malakoff had fallen, our noble fleet of gunboats were either sunk or blown up as on that memorable occasion, and our men might have been seen, with the lurid light of their burning capital glimmering on their faces, retreating slowly from the place. Take it all in all; it was one of the most fearful sights I have ever contemplated. Imagination can scarcely fill the picture.

On Monday, up to the hour of my departure, the excitement still continued and the work of destruction progressed. The superb railroad bridge across the James was burned and other similar structures above and below it. Little railroad rolling stock, if any, remained. The last train left on Monday morning.

At what hour the enemy entered I am not now informed. But as their advance was within seven miles, I presume a column must have marched up during the day. An officer who escaped from Richmond in a canoe, says that when he left, a Yankee officer was addressing a crowd from the Washington monument.

So far as we have advices, they show good spirits still prevailing in the army and a general determination not to succumb to the temporary difficulties by which they have been enshrouded. People are generally beginning to regard the event as one necessary to our final success. We hope for the best.

Richmond, Virginia,
Union Account

Rapidly is Richmond assuming prominence as a point of Federal occupation. Today the James River at Rocketts shows that our vessels have successfully passed the torpedoes long since placed by the enemy in the river, to be exploded in case of an attempted advance on Richmond by the Federal gun-boats. Our navy has already cleared the greater portion of these obstructions from the channel of the river, and our water communication is now open. The United States hospital transport Hero of Jersey arrived today under charge of Surgeon John F. Pratt, and is now at the wharf, flying the stars and stripes, giving to Rocketts the appearance of being again a port of the United States.

Montgomery, Alabama,
Confederate Account

All apprehension of an immediate advance of the enemy on this city has passed away. The excitement incident to first reports has subsided, and, although business has not been resumed, a much quieter state of feeling pervades the public mind, and were the enemy to come today, a pretty stout resistance would be made.

General Buford, who is in command of our local defenses, leaves with his command this morning, in obedience to orders received from General Forrest last night.

The enemy's force is estimated at six thousand. They have made no positive attempt to advance in any direction, but seem to rest quietly in the midst of their recent successes. Forrest and his command are at Marion Junction, and it does not seem possible, from the combination now making, for a single man of the enemy to escape.

Thursday, April 6, 1865

The Cincinnati Commercial of this morning says: "Old Abe" is in luck. He has Jeff Davis's Arabian "hoss," puts his knees under Jeff Davis's mahogany, occupies Jeff Davis's house, possibly sleeps in Jeff Davis's bed, and, if reports be true, came very nigh having possession of Jeff Davis's wife, and even Jeff himself.

Goldsboro, North Carolina,
Union Account

The capture of Richmond and the great victory of General Grant were telegraphed here this morning from Newbern, and the joy and enthusiasm which the good news creates in Sherman's army is beyond description. The Union citizens in Raleigh have also celebrated the event in spite of the Rebels who are now powerless to prevent such loyal manifestations of joy, which refugees say are also being openly displayed in different parts of the State. Here, at Newbern and at other points in this department, bells were rung and guns fired.

Carl Shurz has just arrived at Newbern, and it is rumored that he is on the way to Raleigh.

No movement for the return of North Carolina to the Union will probably be made until Raleigh is occupied by our troops, though it is now the general desire of the people throughout the State.

A portion of General Sherman's army was under orders to move prior to the reception of the news that Richmond was captured. It was generally believed both in and outside of our lines that Sherman would move from this point to assist Grant in the capture of the Rebel capital.

Some curious cattle of African breed, imported by General Wade Hampton, consisting of a bull, cow and calf, captured on his plantation near Columbia, S. C., were brought here and delivered over to General Meigs, who has forwarded them to New York to be placed in Central Park. On the same plantation was captured a band of minstrels, consisting of thirteen slaves, among whom were two white brothers, all of whom now travel with General Logan, their deliverer, for the amusement of himself and friends.

The delay in reopening the port of Newbern causes much anxiety there. All the avenues from Beaufort to Newbern are still used exclusively for the public service, and not a pound of food can go to the relief of the inhabitants until that port is reopened, for which its authorities petitioned over a year ago.

Columbia, South Carolina

Washington, D.C.

Hancock's column is moving up the Shenandoah Valley toward Lynchburg. Should Lee manage to survive Grant's blows in front, Hancock will strike his rear. The Eighth Corps is ready to meet the enemy, and we are now on the war path.

The Navy Department has received information of the destruction of *the* extensive Rebel salt works on Buro Neck, in McIntosh County, Georgia, by an expedition from the United States steamer Ladona.

The War Department has been perfectly inundated with applications for passes to visit Richmond, from parties having friends or property there, curiosity seekers and tobacco or cotton speculators. It is stated that passes have been forged by parties assuming the character of representatives of the press. To such an extent has the Government transportation been monopolized that on the fifth, Secretary Stanton issued orders that no more passes are to be granted persons not in the military service.

Today's City Point boat brought up the band of the Fourteenth Virginia. They numbered twenty-seven pieces, and deserted to us last Sunday. They have been playing "Yankee Doodle," "Star Spangled Banner" and the like in our streets to their own and our citizens' extreme delight.

One hundred and eighty-five Rebel officers captured the last few days, came up in the same boat. They confess the fate of the Confederacy as hopeless.

The hospital steamer, State of Maine, arrived at Alexandria this evening with six hundred wounded Union soldiers. Two other vessels similarly freighted have arrived here today.

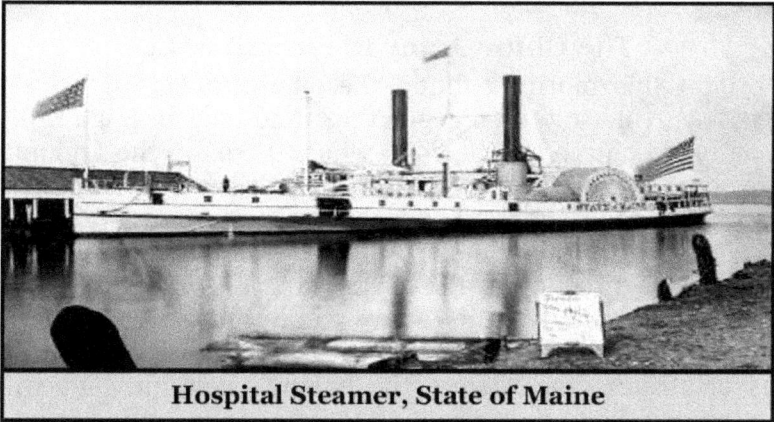

Hospital Steamer, State of Maine

Extensive hospitals are to be erected upon Craney Island, near Old Point, for the vast number of Rebel sick and wounded who have fallen into our hands.

General Hoffman, Commissary General of Prisoners, has gone to City Point to see to the disposal of the thousands of Rebel prisoners in our hands. The sudden and enormous acquisition causes much embarrassment.

New York

The steamers Decatur and Jersey Blue arrived at Fortress Monroe on April 2d, from Newbern, North Carolina, with an aggregate of eight hundred Rebel prisoners and about two hundred refugees. The condition of these refugees is of the most distressing nature, many of them being encumbered with numerous children, barefooted, ragged and half-starved. They were taken charge of by the Provost-Marshal and will be sent north in a few days.

A gentleman, recently arrived from Richmond, states that the best informed there believe that Davis has fled to Georgia, and that he will attempt a re-establishment of his government at Augusta, which possesses strong natural defenses and has been elaborately fortified. As a singular coincidence, it may be stated the elder Mr. Blair made this prediction weeks ago.

Letters received by the Sanitary Commission from Wilmington state that three thousand paroled Union prisoners have arrived there, and that sanitary supplies in abundance were at hand.

The New York, from Fortress Monroe, arrived at this port yesterday with one thousand three hundred prisoners. The Weybosset also arrived from Wilmington with one hundred refugees and seven hundred and fifty Rebel prisoners.

The Union Army in Pursuit of Lee

Daylight this morning found the enemy on his way westward toward Farmville, and then began the grand race for High Bridge, on the Southside railroad at the point where it crosses the Appomattox.

Previous to the discovery of the enemy's whereabouts, however, our forces on the right were advanced several miles in the direction of Amelia Court House; but, on finding that the enemy had gone westward, the direction of the cavalry and Second and Sixth Corps was immediately changed to the west in hot pursuit of General Lee. The Fifth continued its march northward toward Painesville, in hopes of striking the rear of the enemy's column, but, with the exception of a large number of stragglers, met nothing to resist its progress, and subsequently wheeled to the left, connecting with the Second and Sixth Corps late in the day in the vicinity of High Bridge.

Meanwhile we were not ignorant of the enemy's intention to cross at High Bridge, and from Ord's column at Burkesville, had been sent out a detachment consisting of the Fifty-fourth Pennsylvania, One Hundred and Twenty-third Ohio, and two squadrons of the Fourth Massachusetts Cavalry, the whole under command of Brevet Brigadier General Reed, Chief of Staff to General Ord, with orders to hold the bridge against the enemy if possible, and if not to destroy it by fire.

The expedition met with a sad fate, and, after making a desperate and heroic stand near the bridge against the overwhelming numbers of the enemy, who afterward completely encircled them, was almost literally cut to pieces or made prisoners. In the encounter General Reed was killed, shot it is said by the Rebel General Dearing, whom he engaged in a hand-to-hand conflict. The contest was a short and unequal one. General Reed, whose sword-arm had been disabled by a wound through the shoulder, received at Gettysburg, was shot by his antagonist while refusing to surrender. Three charges were then made by Colonel Washburn, commanding the cavalry detachment, in an endeavor to cut his way through the enemy toward the bridge, but only with the result before stated—the capture of the whole of his detachment.

Second and Sixth Corps in Pursuit of Lee

This morning we find the Second moving on the enemy's rear toward Deatonsville. On its left, and advancing on a line parallel with it, was the Sixth Corps, while still on the left of Wright dashed the indomitable Sheridan, his horses on' the gallop, and his men at short intervals amusing themselves with murderous dashes upon the flank of the thoroughly demoralized Rebels, in which prisoners, guns, colors and wagons were remorselessly gobbled.

The Second had in the meantime, struck the enemy at Ferguson's Bridge, across a small stream east of Deatonsville, and, after a brief but sharp encounter forced him back, crossed, and was again in pursuit, toward Sailor's Creek, moving *in line of battle* for nearly twelve miles through a country broken up into deep wooded ravines, and making in that distance five distinct charges against as many determined stands of the enemy, and in every instance compelling his retirement with severe loss.

Shielding his rear as much as possible, the enemy continued his rapid retreat toward High Bridge. Intervening was Sailor's Creek, a tributary of the Appomattox, which he must cross on his way to the last named stream. But the forces of Sheridan, Wright, and Humphrey were bearing rapidly down upon him, and, late in the afternoon, the Second Corps, forming the right of our pursuing columns, came up with his rear at Sailor's Creek, where, to cover the passage of his artillery and wagons, he made a desperate stand on a high bluff east of the stream.

Finding the enemy prepared to hold their crossing at Sailor's Creek, the First and Third Divisions of the Second Corps were immediately formed for the purpose of dislodging the enemy from his position, and, if possible, of capturing his train, which was then crossing. The assault was highly successful. The enemy was driven from his position, and a large number of prisoners, together with two hundred and twenty-five wagons, fifty ambulances, and eleven colors captured, and all with but slight loss on our side.

Meanwhile the Sixth Corps and Sheridan were engaging the enemy on the left of the Second Corps toward the Southside railroad, and at nightfall had succeeded, in the capture of six or seven thousand prisoners, among them seven general officers of the Rebel army, including Ewell, commanding a corps. In this brilliant affair the cavalry had operated on the left, or, on the right flank of the enemy, who was then endeavoring to cross the Southside railroad near Rice's Station, on his way to Danville, the Sixth Corps in the center, and the Second on the right. The Fifth, which, as before stated, had in the morning moved north towards Painesville, was meanwhile returning to the position of the Second and Sixth, but it reached it too late to participate in the engagement mentioned. During today General Hayes, commanding the Second Division of Humphrey's Corps, was summarily relieved from command for tardiness of movement, and succeeded by General Barlow, formerly of the First Division, who had reported for duty. General Smyth in the interim had commanded the division previous to the arrival of Barlow.

Exhausted by their arduous labors of today, the Second and Sixth Corps bivouacked near Sailor's Creek tonight, while Sheridan, with the Fifth Corps, which had, after the fight at Sailor's Creek, swept round to the left, is again westward toward Appomattox Court House, toward which point it has been ascertained the enemy was retreating.

Ord's command, which this morning was at Burkesville, has pushed up the railroad toward Lynchburg, and, on arriving at Rice's Station met the advance of the enemy, who was still persisting in his attempt to reach the Danville railroad, but who, on finding our forces again intervening, changed his course from south to northwest toward Appomattox Court House, with the hope of there passing our advance and gaining the coveted railroad.

Here again, Lee had counted without his host as subsequent events demonstrated. Tonight our pursuing army rests from Sailor's Creek on the right to Prince Edward's Court House on the left, to which point a detachment of Sheridan's cavalry has already been sent simultaneously with the advance of Ord's column up the railroad to Rice's Station.

Gen. Edward Ord

Friday, April 7, 1865

Sixth Army Corps in Pursuit of Lee, Union Account

The Appomattox here is a mere shallow creek running over a sandy bed. Three bridges spanned it, one being the railroad bridge, a second the Cumberland, and the third the Buffalo. All these were destroyed by the enemy after they had crossed. They passed at eight in the morning with a long wagon train. On our coming in sight of the Appomattox, we found the railroad bridge on fire and the other two destroyed.

The Second Corps soon passed the stream, covered by a strong skirmish line. Very little artillery was used, not more than twenty shots being fired.

The ground about the Appomattox here is hilly, and offered good positions for our batteries, which could have swept the other bank of the stream if the enemy had made a stand there.

Farmville is a small town, divided by the Appomattox, and has perhaps two thousand inhabitants: Its site is a rather picturesque one, on the slopes of the little stream. It has a thriving look, but was found by our foragers to be very poor in food. The people took their change of situation very quietly, and, for the most part, stayed in doors. The place is about fifty miles from Lynchburg.

The Rebel army is said by the people to be very much reduced— not to number half of ours. It cannot have more than thirty-five thousand men left, and in guns it must be very deficient. By the heavy "bag" made by us yesterday—the first really large body of prisoners taken by us at one time—General Lee has also lost some of his best Generals, Ewell being one of them.

Our advance has been quite rapid, and has given no time to the enemy to recover the heavy blows dealt at them. The cavalry and Second and Fifth Corps lie on the other side of the Appomattox, while the Sixth is in bivouac on the hills this side (east) of the stream. The Ninth and Twenty-fourth Corps and a Division (the Second) of the Twenty-fifth are in the rear. The army is well in hand, and in fine spirits.

The roads are much broken about a mile back from the Appomattox, and the rain today rendered them nearly impassable; but the weather so far has favored us. Today the scene along the line of march was the same old Virginia one of rain, mud, and a long line of wagons splashing through a broken road, drawn by mules covered with mud from hoof to the tips of their long ears.

The line of march today was through a hilly but fresh country, many of the farms being in a state of good cultivation, and small stacks of corn were found on most of them, though the half of last year's crops had been taken by the Rebel Government as a tax. In most of the houses the women remained and some of the old men. As to the young men they were "in the army," that is, in the Rebel army. Very little live stock was to be seen, and the lowing of a cow made our foragers prick up their ears, so to speak.

On the east side of the Appomattox, about half a mile from this point, and on a fine plantation of ground, is the Venable House. There General Joseph E. Johnston was born, and the family has given several men to the army, one of whom is Major Venable, on General Lee's staff. The house was an object of interest to us as we passed.

Sheridan is far in the front, sweeping on with untiring vigor, the Murat of our army. His cavalry pick lip prisoners in parties. In the course of the day some five hundred prisoners were taken, many of whom were very glad to get out of their bondage.

There has been a good deal of pillage done by our men, and the consequence is that some of them have been found shot, or throat cut, in the woods. This is the fate of pillagers in the country of an excited enemy. The Provost-Marshals did much to put a stop to marauding. I saw two of them drub with the flat of their sabers a squad of these fellows, who ran off as fast as their legs could carry them.

The enemy has only six hours' start of us, and we are gaining in this grand foot race.

In Pursuit of Lee, in the Field

The following correspondence of today between Generals Grant and Lee will explain itself:

To General R. E. Lee, Commanding C. S. A.,

General: The result of the last week must convince you of the hopelessness of further resistance on the part of the Army of Northern Virginia in this struggle. I feel that it is so, and regard it as my duty to shift from myself the responsibility of any further effusion of blood, by asking of you the surrender of that portion of the Confederate Southern Army, known as the Army of Northern Virginia.

Very respectfully, your obedient servant,

U. S. Grant, Lieutenant General,
Commanding Armies of the United States.

To Lieutenant General U. S. Grant,
Commanding Armies of the United States.

General: I have received your note of this date. Though not entirely of the opinion you express of the hopelessness of further resistance on the part of the Army of Northern Virginia, I reciprocate your desire to avoid useless effusion of blood, and therefore before considering your proposition ask the terms you will offer on condition of its surrender.

R. E. Lee, General.

Goldsboro, North Carolina,
Union Account

Johnston is reported retreating toward Virginia, attempting to join Lee. Sherman is after him.

New York, New York

The Tribune's editorial on the position of Grant's army is as follows:

Grant's Advance. One of Sheridan's electrical, and yet practical, business-like, and soldierly dispatches came over the wires yesterday afternoon and announced him at Jettersville, on the Danville road, twelve miles northeast of Burkesville, on the 5th of April at five o'clock in the afternoon. At the same time, two infantry corps, the Second and Sixth, were close up to him, and would reach Jettersville within an hour. General Grant with Ord's command was then at Burkesville, and General Grant himself forthwith started to join Sheridan, who besought his chief to come up, saying that he saw no escape for Lee's army if matters were vigorously pushed. Seeing affairs in this light, Grant instantly started to take command in person.

The march from Petersburg to Burkesville will rank among the swiftest and most remarkable of the war. It is fifty-three miles and was done in about two days and a half. Grant distributed his forces into three columns, as above indicated, and he himself entered Burkesville without any sort of opposition. Lee has not ventured to re-cross the Appomattox since the evacuation of Petersburg. He has not been able to make any sort of an attempt to get to Burkesville, and yet Burkesville is the very first place to which he must have meant and expected to go on leaving Richmond. Losing it, he is cut off from Johnston, and has no more hope of getting to Danville than to New York. With the dispirited remnant of his army he is shut up in that irregular belt of territory between the James and the Appomattox, and his position, more even than the condition of his army, justifies the opinion of Sheridan that he has no chance of escape. The Appomattox bends far to the north, where the Danville road crosses it, and its course so lengthens Lee's march, that if he does not get on the south bank of the river, he is hopelessly out-marched by Grant's pursuing columns, and may be cut off from Lynchburg as he has been from Danville. It is passing strange that a soldier of Lee's reputation should be so completely outmaneuvered as he seems to have been during the last week.

Something might be pardoned to Sheridan's enthusiasm if he over-estimated the chances of surrounding or dispersing the army of Lee. But on the coolest survey of the field, of the line of retreat forced upon Lee, and of the positions of the different columns, we cannot impeach the soundness of his judgment, nor doubt that Lee's best hope of retreat is gone. It is Grant who is now operating on interior lines, and who takes the chords of the arcs which Lee has to describe. And the soldiers of Grant are marching with that elate step which follows and foretokens victory, while Lee's beaten forces are haggard and sluggard with the despair of defeat. So with Sheridan we "see no escape for Lee," or none but in the daily increasing distance between the advancing columns of Grant and their base of supplies at Petersburg. We do not know how much of the Southside road was torn up, nor how soon the cars can be sent to Burkesville, but every energy will be bent to get that line in order, and then for aught we can see, Grant can go ahead indefinitely.

And even were it necessary to stop at Burkesville, the possession of that intersection of the two railroads is a victory. The separation of Lee and Johnston is another victory. The enforced retreat of the former to Lynchburg—if he could even get there—is another. Every dispatch from the front is more hopeful than the last, and it is likely enough that today will bring news to supersede all these speculations, and announce positively that Lee is cut off and hemmed in, and brought to bay with nothing to do but surrender to an overwhelming force.

Talladega, Alabama,
Union Account

Texas has very materially increased in both population and wealth since the beginning of the war; and is today as earnest for the prosecution of the war, and as much opposed to reconstruction as she was in 1861. Texas will never again be a State, or province, or dependency of the United States. Whatever may be the destiny of the seceding States of Cis-Mississippi, the States of the Trans-Mississippi, especially Texas, will remain free, separate, and independent States.

Augusta, Georgia,
Confederate Account

Prices at Auction — Messrs. W. A. Ramsay & Company, on Wednesday last, at the auction sale at the late residence of Mrs. Thomas Gardiner, obtained the prices annexed: One china dinner set, three hundred and eighty-one pieces, $5,100; one green china set, eighty pieces, $1,550; one white china set, ninety-five pieces, $5,000; celery glasses, $18 to $22 each; punch glasses, $19 each; champagne glasses, $12 to $12 1/2 each; wine glasses, $20 to $22 1/2 each; cordial glasses, $25 each; decanters, $120 to $150 each; celery stands, $105 each; glass pitchers, $62 to $255 each; ice cream bowls, $300 each; finger bowls, $8vto $18 each; vases, $190 to $475 each; gas fixtures, $80 to $300 each; tumblers, $25 to $50 each; jelly glasses, $13 each; bed room sets, crockery, $425 to $850 each; china egg cups, $4 to $7 each; doll heads, $100 each; one baby house, furnished, $1,500; one tapestry carpet, $7,000; one medallion carpet, $10,500; one brocatelle set parlor furniture, $15,000; one rosewood set, bedroom furniture, $17,000; one rosewood piano, $28,000.

Grant's Army in Pursuit of Lee

This morning dawned and found the enemy again on the wing toward Farmville and Appomattox Court House. Again the pursuit was resumed and again we struck the rear of the enemy at High Bridge, where the Southside railroad crosses the Appomattox. The river at this point is about one hundred feet in width, and is spanned by two bridges, one the railroad structure elaborately constructed and of great height, and the other an ordinary bridge for the passage of vehicles. Both were fired on the crossing of the Rebels and four spans of the High Bridge destroyed before our advance, consisting of Barlow's Division, were able to extinguish it.

To insure the complete destruction of these bridges, Mahone's Division had remained behind on the other side, where, forming in battle line, it prepared to dispute our further pursuit.

A sharp engagement ensued from either side of the stream on the arrival of Barlow, and the enemy still doggedly holding his position, a light battery of Miles's Division was brought up and posted on the eastern bank of the river, its fire soon compelling the retirement of the Rebel Mahone.

The crossing of the Second Corps was then made, and, covered by skirmishers, we again advanced toward Farmville. In the advance the brigade of General Smyth led the van, and from the High Bridge to Farmville were constantly engaging the enemy, who as his chances of escape grew fainter fought the more desperately, and only retired when charged impetuously.

It was about three miles from Farmville, where, with the flush of victory on his cheek, and the shout of triumph still ringing on his lips, that General Smyth fell mortally wounded, while leading in person his skirmish line against the enemy.

In a number of important engagements General Smyth, during the absence of General Gibbon, commanded the Second Division of the Second Corps, and always so creditably as to win from his admirer, the gallant Hancock, deserving of the highest praise. If there was any formidable position to be stormed in which daring and skill were requisite, General Smyth with his brigade was always selected for the undertaking. Dashing and soldier-like in appearance, he never failed to secure the entire confidence of his men, and when with true Irish impetuosity he lifted his cap and at the head of his column swept with a cheer down, Sheridan-like, upon the enemy, his purpose was sure to be accomplished.

He was shot in the mouth by one of the enemy's sharpshooters—a branch of the service, by the way, which has inflicted upon us more loss in general officers than the remainder of the Rebel Army. The ball, passing through the mouth, lodged in the spinal column, paralyzing the whole body and rendering him almost insensible to suffering. He retained his consciousness until his death, early on Sunday morning; and, on inquiring of the Surgeon as to his chances for recovery, and receiving no definite answer, he said, "Don't hesitate, Doctor, but speak candidly, for I am no coward and not afraid to die!"

But to resume, Barlow still led the advance with the Second Division toward Farmville, through which, after making several obstinate stands, the enemy retreated, leaving at every step guns, wagons, and camp equipage in his wake. General Humphrey, meanwhile, with the First and Third Divisions of his corps, was pushing forward on the right toward Lynchburg; in the direction of which it soon became evident the enemy were retiring. At three p. m., Barlow was ordered to rejoin the main body of Humphrey's command, soon after which the First and Third were directed to again demonstrate against the enemy.

A charge of the First Brigade of Miles's Division is represented as having been unusually gallant, although unsuccessful, as the main body of the enemy was struck northwest of Farmville. Darkness then came on and put an end to further operations. The captures of the corps during the day were five hundred prisoners, nineteen guns, a number of colors, besides wagons and ambulances in great numbers.

Gen. Thomas Alfred Smyth
Killed by a Confederate Sniper

Saturday, April 8, 1865

New York, New York

By the arrival of the Merrimac at this Port we have important intelligence from Mobile. General Canby had landed on the eastern shore of Mobile Bay, and laid siege to Spanish Fort, which is the main defense of the city at that point. The Rebel General Maury was in command at the Fort. Our skirmishers had advanced to within eighty yards of the Fort, while three or four of our batteries were stationed within three or four hundred yards. The Fort was invested by the Thirteenth and Sixteenth Army Corps, and from the 26th to the 30th ult. heavy skirmishing and artillery firing had occurred. The Union killed and wounded in the two corps up to the 31st was estimated at about eight hundred. Two of our ironclads, the monitors Milwaukee and Osage, were blown up in Mobile Bay on the 28th and 29th ult. by Rebel torpedoes, killing four men and wounding seven. It is thought that the vessels may be raised, as they sunk in shallow water. The water and land for miles around Mobile were filled with torpedoes. On shore several casualties had occurred from them, and many had been dug up by the troops. The navy was actively co-operating with the army. A fleet of Rebel ironclads was lying on Blakely river, below the city, and a battle between them and our fleet was hourly expected. It was believed at Dauphin Island on the 31st ult. that the fight had already taken place, as heavy firing in the direction of Spanish Fort was heard throughout the day. General Steele's column from Pensacola had arrived at Blakely, six miles from Spanish Fort, opened communication with General Canby, and commenced hostilities on the 29th. He had captured one Brigadier General, twenty-two other officers, four hundred men, four hundred and fifty horses, and two wagon trains.

Memphis, Tennessee,
Union Account

The Bulletin this evening says a report prevails, and is well authenticated, that Selma, Alabama, was captured and burned a few days ago by the cavalry force of General Thomas's command.

Sixth Army Corps in Pursuit of Lee,
Union Account

Today the army left the Appomattox, moving in three columns by as many roads which converge at Appomattox Court House, on the way to Lynchburg.

The cavalry and Fifth Corps took a road to the left of the old stage road. The Twenty-fourth Corps went by another road to the right of them, and the Second and Sixth Corps took the old stage road. This was the one followed by the enemy.

The plan of movement is for the cavalry and Fifth and Twenty-fourth Corps to head off the enemy from any route to Danville, which General Lee still seems to seek, and to force him to go toward Lynchburg, which is said to be now in the hands of General Stoneman.

The action about the Appomattox yesterday was more serious than I was led to suppose. The First Brigade of the First Division, Second Corps, commanded by Colonel G. W. Scott, lost heavily, and this gallant officer was himself struck by a spent ball.

During this day the Sixth Corps met with no enemy, and the Second Corps was equally free in its march. The two corps marched about sixteen miles over a good road.

The line of march passed through a finer and fresher country than any part we have seen yet. As we go west the farms appear better cultivated, and less devoid of stock. There was the same pillage to be seen today as on the march to the Appomattox, and the number of stragglers was shameful. They showed an utter disregard for discipline; yet there was no excuse for all this marauding, for the men had drawn three days' rations.

Tonight I learn that the cavalry have taken fourteen more guns and one thousand two hundred to one thousand five hundred prisoners. This loss must leave General Lee with less than thirty thousand men, and very little artillery. A few more days of such work, and the enemy will be undone.

Tomorrow the Sixth Corps will effect a junction with the Second, and the two will move on together toward Lynchburg, on the heels of the enemy, while the cavalry and Fifth and Twenty-fourth Corps moving by a road to the left, will turn them from any route that leads to Danville.

Appomatox Court House, Virginia

The following correspondence. was held today between Generals Grant and Lee:

To General R. E. Lee,
Commanding C. S. A.

General: Your note of last evening in reply to mine of the same date, asking the conditions on which I will accept the surrender of the Army of Northern Virginia is just received. In reply I would say that peace being my first desire, there is but one condition that I insist upon, viz: That the men surrendered shall be disqualified for taking up arms again against the Government of the United States until properly exchanged. I will meet you, or designate officers to meet any officers you may name for the same purpose, at any point agreeable to you, for the purpose of arranging definitely the terms, upon which the surrender of the Army of Northern Virginia will be received. Very respectfully, your obedient servant.

U. S.Grant, Lieutenant General
Commanding Armies of the United States.

To Lieutenant General Grant,
Commanding Armies of the United States,

General: I received at a late hour your note of today in answer to mine of yesterday. I did not intend to propose the surrender of the Army of Northern Virginia, but to ask the terms of your proposition. To be frank, I do not think the emergency has arisen to call for the surrender. But as the restoration of peace should be the sole object of all, I desire to know whether your proposals would tend to that end. I cannot therefore meet you with a view to surrender the Army of Northern Virginia, but so far as your proposition may affect the Confederate States forces under my command and tend to the restoration of peace, I should be pleased to meet you at ten o'clock tomorrow morning, on the old stage road to Richmond, between the picket lines of the two armies. Very respectfully, your obedient servant,

R. E. Lee,
General C. S. A.

Richmond, Virginia,
Union Account

The Second Division of the Twenty-fourth Army Corps was today reviewed by General Devins. It was witnessed by nearly the whole population of Richmond, and passed off in a creditable manner.

The First and Third Divisions of this corps under General Ord are chasing Lee in his flight from Petersburg. They are no doubt in the direction of Lynchburg today, and are having a different kind of review from what the Second Division has passed for today.

All the hospitals of Richmond have been taken possession of by the military authorities and are used for the care and comfort equally of the Union and Confederate sick and wounded. A number of Confederate surgeons left in the city have been paroled to attend to the Confederate sick and wounded. More than half of General Pickett's Division has been brought in or captured, and the country between Richmond and Amelia County is said to be full of Confederate soldiers, nearly all of them Virginians, making their way to their homes. The Castle is used as a receptacle for citizen prisoners, of whom quite a number are gathered there.

Grant's Army in Pursuit of Lee

It was found this morning that Lee had again disappeared from our immediate front, and it was soon discovered that he was moving northwest to reach the road running southwest across the Southside railway from Appomattox Court House, and again with the apparent desire of "heading us-off" and ultimately reaching the Danville railroad. Again, and for the last time, did we successfully prevent the consummation of his desperate plan for escape.

The command of General Ord had during the night received orders to move rapidly up the railroad to Appomattox Court House, while Sheridan was to lead the advance on its right, having the same objective point. The Second and Sixth Corps were ordered to march northward, taking up a position east of the Court House, and thus almost completely encircling the remnant of Lee's army.

Richmond, Virginia

The theatres have opened and are lighted with tallow candles. There is not much to be seen, but the singing is enjoyable. Imagine a Richmond theatre, one week ago, and then the following as was sung on its stage tonight:

> To Richmond town the Yankee came
> To whip the southern Rebel;
> There old Bob Lee did make a stand
> And got whipped like the devil;
> Their handbills they distributed,
> Their heads were full of fun;
> Of course they say the ball commenced
> With round-shot, grape and bum (bomb
>
> Chorus—Let 'em bum—let 'em bum-
> The way is always clear:

And while they are bumming
We'll take 'em in the rear.

Now talk about your horses fast,
Or take a two mile heater.
But if you turn a Rebel loose
He's much the fastest creeter.
Now, we would to the Rebels say,
To one and all fair warning—
If once the Yankees catches them
The Lord have mercy on 'em

Now, here's a health to General Grant!
Who all his words fulfills
And always to the Rebels gives
His lead and iron pills:
And when Phil Sheridan catches them
Oh Lord! how bad they fare;
He flanks them on the right and left,
And bags them in the rear.

'Twas neck and neck on either side;
And neither thought the best,
The Yankees and the Rebels, then
Were fighting breast to breast;
'Twas then Bob Lee rode up his lines,
And rising in his saddle,
He waved his sword and gave command
To right face and skedaddle.

While this was being sung there were sufficient Yankees present to show that it was appreciated, which was done in anything but a silent manner.

Montgomery, Alabama, Confederate Account

"The force which advanced upon Selma was nine thousand mounted infantry, to oppose which Forrest had but seventeen hundred men. The enemy, owing to the bad conduct of Roddy's men, made a rapid advance in overpowering numbers, but were met on the breastworks by Forrest, who there manfully fought them, hand to hand, face to face, but unavailingly. About seven hundred of Forrest's men were captured.

Selma is now garrisoned by nine thousand Yankees.

Augusta, Georgia,
Confederate Account

There are persons amongst us (multitudinous unfortunately) whose souls are too small to comprehend the vastness of a struggle for freedom, too selfish to appreciate the necessity of a sacrifice, and too ignorant to fathom the depth of manhood through which the strong heart labors for the rights of man. After every reverse to our arms, these dreary and ephemeral creatures are whipped and subjugated, nor do they hesitate to confess their craven fears and seek to impregnate others with them. Such men are the fungi, the barnacles which cluster about the Ship of State, only for its evil. We would to Heaven that such men were well out of a country which they secretly despise, or openly calumniate; and rid thereby of a cause which they are too shallow to understand, and too pusillanimous to uphold. A rotten apple amongst a barrel of sound ones is not more pernicious in its effects than a rotten heart in a true community.

A great many men who, at this juncture avow themselves conquered, were, four years ago, blatant about the principles which they now malign.

Are not these principles the same now as formerly? Are they not to noble natures ten thousand times dearer in this hour of trial, sanctified by the blood of the brave and the dolor of the poor, than when our eagles soared triumphantly over the battlefield and our starry banner flamed along the coast? It is the part of magnanimity to persevere unflinchingly and hold that thing or principle the more closely because it has suffered calamity. If such, however, be the action of a great soul, the reverse is equally true of *ignes fatui,* called souls, which abandon everything at the first blush of alarm and help the panic which they have dismally contributed to engender.

We are almost inclined to believe that such men are not of the porcelain clay from which the glorious heroes of the world were fashioned; but rather of the wreck which remained from the creation of their superiors. We deem that such monstrosities are worthy neither of heaven nor earth.

For ourselves we embraced this cause in the beginning, because we deemed it right. We have clung to it since, through good and evil report, because the coming times brought confirmation of its rectitude. With the blessing of God—that God who promises his rest and liberty only to those who persevere to the end—we shall continue to maintain our ancient sentiments to the last.

We loved our country when its flag nodded under the triumph-gates; we will not desert that country in the day of disaster. A land may be subjugated in a material sense, but the soul of a man, just and tenacious of his purpose, will walk abroad, in spite of tyrants and their machinations.

In the same proportions as our territory contracts our love of it expands. Like the Sibylline leaves, it becomes the more precious for the partial loss.

Fortress Monroe, Virginia, Union Account

Parties have arrived from Danville within our lines, who report that the fugitive insurgent, Jeff. Davis, arrived at Danville on the afternoon of the third, covered with dust and perspiration. His only baggage consisted of three dilapidated trunks, which looked hardly fit for a journey to Mexico. Jeff was accompanied by two or three members of his cabinet, and the whole party seemed to be in an extremely demoralized condition. Breckenridge, the Rebel Secretary of War, had not turned up, and was not heard from although diligent inquiries were being made for him.

15-inch Rodman Gun at Fortress Monroe
Wt. 49,909 lbs. Charge Wt. 40lbs. Shot Wt. 400 lbs. Shell Wt. 352 lbs.
Maximum Range 5018 Yards with shell and 30 degree setting

Sunday, April 9, 1865

War Department,
Washington, D. C. 9:30 O'clock p.m.

Lieutenant General Grant:

Thanks be to Almighty God for the great victory with which He has this day crowned you and the gallant armies under your command. The thanks of this department, and of the Government, and of the people of the United States—their reverence and honor have been deserved—will be rendered to you and the brave and gallant officers and soldiers of your army for all time.

Edwin M. Stanton,
Secretary of War

10 O'clock p.m. Ordered: That a salute of two hundred guns be fired at the headquarters of every army department, and at every post and arsenal in the United States, and at the Military Academy at West Point, on the day of the receipt of this order, in commemoration of the surrender of General R. E. Lee and the Army of Northern Virginia to Lieutenant General Grant, and the army under his command; report of the receipt and execution of this order to be made to the Adjutant General, Washington,

Edwin M. Stanton,
Secretary of War

Appomattox Court House, Virginia

It has come. Here it is:

General R. E. Lee,
Commanding C. S. A.

General: Your note of yesterday is received. As I have no authority to treat on this subject of peace, the meeting proposed for ten o'clock this morning, could lead to no good. I will state, however, General, that I am equally anxious for peace with yourself; and the whole North entertain the same feeling. The terms upon which peace can be had are well understood. By the South laying down their arms they will hasten that most desirable event, save thousands of human lives, and hundreds of millions of property not yet destroyed Sincerely hoping that all our difficulties may be settled without the loss of another life, I subscribe myself, very respectfully, your obedient servant,

U. S. Grant,
Lieutenant General U. S. A.

To Lieutenant General Grant,
Commanding United States Armies

General: I received your note this morning on the picket line, whither I had come to meet you and ascertain definitely what terms were embraced in your proposition of yesterday with reference to the surrender of this army. I now request an interview in accordance with the offer contained in your letter of yesterday for that purpose. Very respectfully, your obedient servant,

R. E. Lee,
General

In answer to this communication General Grant replied that, at the time of receiving the note, he was on the Farmville and Lynchburg road, four miles west of Walter's Church, but that he would immediately go to the front for the purpose of meeting General Lee. The following additional correspondence transpired previous to the surrender:

General R. E. Lee,
Commanding C. S. A.:

In accordance with the substance of my letter to you of the 6th inst., I propose to receive the surrender of the Army of Northern Virginia, on the following terms, to-wit: Rolls of all the officers and men to be made in duplicate, one copy to be given to an officer designated by me, the other to be retained by such officers as you may designate. The officers to give their individual paroles not to take arms against the Government of the United States until properly exchanged, and each company or regimental commander sign a like parole for the men of their commands, the arms, artillery, and public property to be parked and stacked and turned over to the officers appointed by me to receive them. This will not embrace the side-arms of the officers, nor their private horses or baggage. This done, each officer and man will be allowed to return to their homes, not to be disturbed by United States authority so long as they observe their parole and the laws in force where they may reside. Very respectfully,

U. S. Grant,
Lieutenant General

Lieutenant General U. S. Grant,
Commanding U. S. A.

General: I have received your letter of this date, containing the terms of surrender of the Army of Northern Virginia, as proposed by you. As they are substantially the same as those expressed in your letter of the 8th inst., they are accepted. I will proceed to designate the proper officers to carry the stipulations into effect. Very respectfully, your obedient servant,

R. E. Lee,
General

Goldsboro, North Carolina, Union Account

General Slocum assumes command of the New Army of Georgia.

The trains are all loaded, the troops clothed, and the armies prepared for a movement. No opposition is looked for until the crossing of the Neuse River, at Smithfield, is attempted.

We have orders from General Sherman to be prepared for rapid marches, so that speedy results may follow. The Rebel army in his front will be promptly dealt with.

Johnston's Army is reported as at same place as for the past few days. It is expected that Johnston will endeavor to hold Raleigh as long as possible.

The glad tidings from the, of the James, came at an opportune moment. The army is rested from its long and wearisome labors, and with such cheering news as "Richmond is ours," they begin the new campaign—now of a far different nature—with more confidence of a speedy triumph. Nothing could have exceeded the wild enthusiasm with which the news was received. It was announced to the troops in' an "extra," printed in hand bill form, containing the dispatches to General Sherman. It was at first received with doubt. "Too good to be true", the boys would say. The official announcement, however, cleared all doubt, and as the real magnitude of the victory was finally realized, the excitement reached its height. Each one manifested his joy as best suited him. All kinds of enjoyment was the go. Some found their hidden bottle and dished out its contents; some mounted their gay steeds and galloped up and down the dusty streets, no matter how lame his *"muleship"* was, while some filled their canteens, bottles and boxes with powder and fired a salute. The bands played; the flags proudly floated in the breeze; a genuine hand shaking was had and a wild time was had in rejoicing over the fall of the Rebel Capital.

Army of the Potomac, Appomattox C. H., Va.
Union Account

After a march of about twelve miles, the column of the army moving by the old stage road to Lynchburg came to this point.

The Second and Sixth Corps formed the column, and the Second was in front, with its First Division leading. At this point a flag of truce was seen in front of the skirmish line, and General Miles, in command of the division, sent one of his staff, Captain J. D. Cook, A. D. C., to meet it. On going out, this officer found Colonel Taylor, General Lee's Chief of Staff, with a written communication for General Meade. Captain Cook took in the note, which made a request that this army would suspend hostilities until General Lee could fully consider the terms offered him yesterday by General Grant. To this the Commanding General replied, that he was not authorized to grant a suspension of hostilities, but that he would give two hours for General Lee to accede to the terms, and if at the end of that time he did not do so, this army would continue its advance. The two hours were passed by us in agreeable suspense. At the end of that time the order was given to advance, and the Second Corps was hardly ten minutes in motion when a staff officer of the enemy came in with a note from General Grant, sent by General Sheridan, directing the Commanding General of this army to suspend hostilities until further orders, and adding that General Grant would be with him in half an hour. On receipt of this, General Meade gave the necessary order, and the army came to a halt.

At two-thirty in the afternoon General Grant arrived and held a conference with General Lee, the result of which was that the latter agreed to surrender the remainder of his army, now reduced to about twenty thousand men, as prisoners of war, to be paroled and sent home not to serve until duly exchanged, and signed articles to that effect.

From the staff officer who came in we learn that General Lee ordered all their trains and the carriages of such guns as they did not intend to use—everything, in fact, that could not be carried on horseback—to be burned last night, in order that they might be free to cut their way through our cavalry. This they tried to do today, but met the Fifth Corps, which was with the cavalry, on a road to our left. Finding himself thus met, General Lee abandoned his intention, which might have been successful if there had been only cavalry to fight at the point where he expected to find only cavalry.

Colonel Taylor, the Chief of Staff of General Lee, in chatting with Captain Cook, said that the General, though calm, was in low spirits at the straits to which he saw his army reduced; and that for the two last days he was in rear of his main column, not more than ten minutes ride from our advance, so closely did he watch the movements of this army.

The officers and men of the Rebel army were anxious to hear what was to be done with General Lee, and showed great concern for him, saying that they did not care for themselves.

There can be only one view of our operations, and it is that they have been short, sharp and decisive. They have been a fine combination against the enemy, which has been well executed. To our strong force of cavalry and the untiring activity of General Sheridan may be ascribed the decisive success that our arms have met with; but it must be added that the action of the Sixth Corps, on the 2d instant, in taking the Southside Railroad, and the support of the Second, Fifth and Twenty-fourth Corps, have contributed greatly to the results. All our corps commanders have done well, but Generals Sheridan and Wright have, owing to circumstances, been able to strike more vital blows at the enemy than those of the other officers.

In eleven short days these great results have been gained. Who would have thought it? From our great numerical superiority, I thought the campaign would be over in thirty days, and in one of my letters, mentioned the first of May as the time it would likely come to an end; but the time has been even shorter.

A copy of the articles of surrender is not to be had at headquarters tonight, but one will no doubt be officially published tomorrow.

Tomorrow the formal surrender of the remainder of General Lee's army will take place, when one of the most striking scenes of the war will be witnessed by this army. No event in the history of the United States can compare with it in importance, and the gladness of a people thus saved from the danger of half ruin will be great.

Our feelings are in a state of gladness that can hardly be imagined. Men see in the capture of the greatest army of the enemy an end to their hardships and a return to their homes. All the bands are filling the air with sounds of jubilee, and cheer after cheer comes from the ranks of the brigades as they file into their bivouac grounds for the night.

Mobile, Alabama, Union Account

Spanish Fort and Fort Blakely were captured today. We secured seven hundred prisoners at Fort Blakely and five thousand at Spanish Fort, with a large amount of guns and ordnance stores. Our troops have entered Mobile and are this evening in full possession. General Smith's forces led the advance into Mobile.

Mobile, the last remaining Rebel stronghold east of the Mississippi River, has fallen and is in the quiet possession of our troops. From the 3d to the 9th of April—Selma on the 3d, Richmond on the 3d, and Mobile today—what a week of victories the past week has been, will never be forgotten.

At five o'clock yesterday—Saturday afternoon—all of our land batteries opened on Spanish Fort and Fort Blakely with our Parrott guns, the shells of which did great work against the sand-works and their beleaguered defenders. A heavy and constant fire was kept going until about seven o'clock in the evening when the signal for advance was given. Two brigades of the Third Division, sixteen corps, which occupied our extreme right, made a gallant charge on the Rebel works and captured three hundred yards of them, then clambered on the inside and secured three hundred and fifty prisoners—the greater part of two Confederate regiments. As it was now dark, we entrenched ourselves and lay upon our arms. Many of the Rebels had bestowed themselves so deep in their caves of sand, or bomb-proofs, that they were taken completely by surprise. A Rebel officer said, "The first thing we knew was, that the Yankees were dragging us out of our quarters and beds, saying, surrender, boys, at once." This surprise soon had its effect, and at one o'clock this morning the whole fort surrendered. We secured in this surrender twenty-five commissioned officers and five hundred and twenty-seven enlisted men.

Ninth Army Corps, Petersburg, Virginia, Union Account

This city is quiet and fast assuming a business activity. This Corps is guarding the railroad as far through as Burkesville. We are anxiously waiting for news from Grant.

Washington, D.C.

Three companies of Mosby's guerillas disbanded on Wednesday last at Culpepper Court House, and dispersed for their homes. Mosby has less than three hundred men left, mostly operating on a neck of land running down Cynia Creek and Fredericksburg.

Sandusky, Ohio,

The old flag was raised and lustily cheered by the oath-takers block No. 1, of the Rebel prison on the island. While the oath-takers cheered the flag, the dyed-in-the-wool Rebel hissed it.

If this hissing element was turned loose in our midst and resort to such doings, the lamp posts of Sandusky would be kept ornamented for a few hours at least.

Sheridan's Cavalry, Appomattox C. H., Virginia, Union Account

The position of affairs just before the surrender was as follows:

Sheridan's Cavalry had struck the Rebel column on the main Lynchburg Road and cut it in two, west of the Appomattox Court House, and, together with his infantry support, was now facing east and driving the rear portion of the column (which was the main portion) back the way it had come, while the Second and Sixth Corps, which had been following it up on the same road, now lay as a lion in the path of retreat. In other words, the main portion of the Rebel column, with General Lee in the midst of it, was completely cut off, surrounded and hemmed in. There was no chance of escape. The column had been driven from the Danville to the Lynchburg Road, and now its course on the latter was stopped. There was no other road for it to take. Twenty-five thousand men— nearly one-half of whom had already thrown away their arms in their demoralization—were at the mercy of twice or three times as many victorious muskets and sabers!

While the Second and Sixth Corps were pounding the column forward with their artillery, and Sheridan's Cavalry and the Twenty-fourth and Fifth Corps were driving it back with all arms, like sheep in a slaughter pen. The Rebel General Gordon, who was in the beleaguered column, sent forward to General Sheridan's lines a flag of truce, proposing a surrender of the entire command and asking an armistice until the terms of capitulation could be agreed upon. The order was immediately passed along General Sheridan's lines to cease firing, which was promptly obeyed, followed by the cheers of the troops who understood the reason for the order.

Our skirmish line going east had now been advanced to within a quarter of a mile of the Court House, and the armies were within full view of each other, General Sheridan's forces resting on a circle of cleared hills immediately west of the Court House, and the head of the Rebel column, well closed up, lying in a valley about a mile to the eastward. Orders were issued to both sides for the troops to remain in the same position as they were, when the flag-of-truce was sent forward and the firing ceased. On the reception of the flag-of-truce and accompanying message by General Sheridan, he sent an aid to accompany General Gordon, at his request, to the Court House, to talk over the matter of surrender. Soon General Gordon arrived, accompanied by the Rebel General Wilcox, and they were met in the village by Generals Sheridan and Ord; these were also joined by General Longstreet, who soon afterward came up.

The result of this interview was a reference of the matter of a surrender to Generals Grant and Lee, both of whom, it was understood, were within reaching distance, consequently a messenger was sent by General Sheridan down the Lynchburg road to the rear of the Rebel column, near which General Grant had his headquarters (in the saddle) and in the course of an hour or so the General arrived, in response to the message, at General Sheridan's headquarters in a dooryard in the west end of the village. Lieutenant Colonel Price, of General Sheridan's staff, was then dispatched into the Rebel lines to escort General Lee to the village, to be met on intermediate or neutral ground by General Grant. In a short time General Lee, accompanied by Colonel Price and two or three of his own aids, rode up to the residence of Major McLean, alighted and went in. To make sure of his identity I asked an aid of General Long, who was on a visit to General Sheridan at the time, what officer that was.

"That," said he, *"is the greatest man the country ever produced, General Robert E. Lee."*

That General was soon joined by General Grant, with two or three of his staff, at Major McLean's, the two being introduced by

Colonel Price. After an exchange of the usual civilities, General Lee opened the negotiations by saying:

"Well, General, you have got us in a tight place, and to save the useless effusion of blood, I propose to surrender this command on such honorable conditions as you, as a magnanimous General may prescribe."

"You are right, General," replied General Grant, *"in expecting magnanimous terms, magnanimity and liberality, I am happy to say, is the policy of the Government I represent. As you ask nothing, I take the more pleasure in tendering the most liberal terms in my power. I therefore propose the surrender of all officers and men as prisoners of war, subject to exchange or parole, and, of course an unconditional surrender of all public property, such as trains, supplies, arms, ordnance and other munitions of war. If I could have the assurance of General Lee that it would be safe for us, I would gladly parole every officer and man on the spot and allow him to go to his home."*

General Lee—*"I think I can safely promise that no officer or private of the Army of Northern Virginia would knowingly and willfully violate his parole of honor."*

General Grant—*"To what forces does this surrender extend?"*

General Lee—*"I can only surrender that portion of the Confederate forces now in your power; I cannot speak for the remainder at present."*

General Grant—*"Well, that is all we can ask at this time. I understand the surrender to embrace all the men and material of the Army of Northern Virginia now in transit in this column?"*

General Lee—*"You are right. I will recall the advance of the column, which I consider in your power."*

General Grant—*"Well, I propose to take immediate possession of all the public property, and parole all the officers and men on the spot, the officers to retain their side-arms and private horses."*

General Lee—*"That is all we can ask!"*

The terms of capitulation were accordingly drawn up on this basis, at the dictation of General Grant, by one of his aids, and after some further exchange of social civilities, the interview terminated, General Lee, with his white hair and beard flowing in the soft April wind, mounting his fine grey horse and riding back to camp, and General Grant repairing to his new headquarters on the west side of the town.

General Lee looks well, though somewhat anxious and careworn, and a good deal whiter about the head and face, they say, than he was four years ago. It is understood that on being paroled he will immediately start for Richmond, where his family is.

After the surrender General Gordon addressed his troops, intimating to them that the war was about over, and advising them on being paroled to repair to their homes and become good citizens again of the old Union. This advice was received with the most vociferous cheering by the Rebel soldiers. They even went so far as to fire a salute in honor of the surrender and no more fighting.

The Rebel arms and trains, and various munitions of war, have been taken possession of this afternoon by infantry detachments from the Fifth and Twenty-fourth Corps, and the paroling will be attended to tomorrow. The number of prisoners is estimated at about twenty-five thousand, with two thousand supply wagons, two hundred artillery guns and twelve thousand stand of small arms, a great many of these having been thrown away.

Goldsboro, North Carolina,
Union Account

This army, the Rebels speak of us as Sherman's "Bummers." Possibly the name does not belong to us. The name was given us by the enemy because our boys would walk around the country and try to pass the time pleasantly. Had they not kept out of our way and had they stood up like men and fought, our men would not have had time to do any "bumming."

The title of "bummers" was given at the early part of the late campaign to such men as were in the habit of foraging on their own account, independent of the details made for foraging on every day's march. The "bummers'" first object was to get "transportation" for his proposed "pick up" which will account for the presence of so many coaches, buggies, &c, in this army. After having "borrowed" rolling stock, he must also have freight, so he solicits it generally from that same locality, and carries a few "cluckers" with other "presents" into camp, and for this is called a "bummer." If there is anything wrong about this the enemy should keep us so busy that our boys would have no time for "bumming."

Augusta, Georgia,
Confederate Account

We learn from a reliable source that our Trans-Mississippi army is not only very large, but likewise very efficient. The complaint which has existed, heretofore, with regard to its supineness, will soon be dissipated. Movements are in progress which will electrify the country.

General Kirby Smith, very far from being the speculator he has been reported, is so poor that he had to sell his favorite battle horse; the one he rode at Manassas and Richmond. He works incessantly and, though, not advanced in years, has become much worn and grey. His proper sphere is the field, and there he will soon be we trust.

The Yankees have a post at Morganza, commanded by General (Judge) Davis, the renegade Texan of Corpus Christi. Captain Collins, a true hearted son of the Lone Star State, who was promoted from the ranks at Perryville for distinguished gallantry, keeps the garrison in perpetual terror with his band of scouts. Collins is the Mosby of Louisiana. With a small force he has neutralized and decimated a large garrison.

At one time Davis threatened to burn the house of every person that fed Collins and his men. As soon as our partisan heard of this, he communicated with the renegade general and told him if this threat was ever executed, he would hang ten Yankees for every dwelling destroyed and five more for every lady insulted. As Collins had managed to pick up a number of "blue bellies" and was known to be a man of his word, the people around Morganza and the Bayou Fordoche remain unmolested.

Governor Allen is universally beloved. With him as the State Executive and Dick Taylor military chief, the army of the Trans-Mississippi would not long remain torpid.

Gen. Edmund J. Davis

Monday, April 10, 1865

Vicksburg, Tennessee,
Union Account

We are reliably informed that, Alabama, is added, to the line of Federal occupancy. It is said that Forrest, by the skin of his teeth, only succeeded in getting away.

It is beyond dispute that Wilson's boys are doing their share of the work. Their ambition has led them through the roughest of roads without fear, and their work will prove this.

Wilson's cavalry dismounted and made their charge of the 2d inst., against Forrest, one of the most determined of the war. They carried everything before them.

With the capture of Selma, also comes the news of the surrender or capture of Montgomery. Did you ever hear of so many good things as are coming our way this April? I guess not.

Norfolk, Virginia,
Union Account

An expedition composed principally of the First New York Mounted Rifles, left Norfolk on the 1st inst., for reconnoitering purposes up the Chowan River, with the intention, if possible, of reaching Weldon, N. C. The expedition was under the command of Colonel Tanner, of the First Mounted Rifles, and resulted in entire success. The cavalry struck the Seaboard and Roanoke Railroad and demolished the track for a considerable extent. While thus engaged, they were attacked by a force of six hundred Rebels, and after a severe fight succeeded in repulsing them. The cavalry then fell back to Murfreesborough where the booty was delivered to the gunboats. Among the captures were one hundred bales of superior cotton, a large amount of tobacco and snuff, and thirty prisoners. Parties of the cavalry scouted to within a few miles of Weldon, and from the prisoners taken it was learned that the town was strongly fortified, and garrisoned by a force of one thousand Rebels, with several batteries of artillery. The expedition returned last Saturday night. This expedition—said to be the largest sent into northern North Carolina— accomplished a great deal of good in ascertaining the exact locality of the Rebel forces in that section of the State.

Knoxville, Tennessee,
Union Account

A scout of Union troops, sent out from Fort Donelson, in command of Lieutenant Colonel Brott, met a gang of guerillas in the vicinity of the Cumberland River, between Clarksville and the fort, and a brisk engagement ensued. A number of the outlaws took refuge in an old mill, and, thus sheltered, kept our troops at bay. One of the guerillas, Hardis Wiley, was shot and killed. Two others belonging to the band refused to surrender, when the mill was fired for the purpose of driving them from their shelter. The outlaws were firm, and boldly stood their ground. The building burned rapidly, and the two desperate men were consumed in the flames.

Chattanooga, Tennessee,
Union Account

Today, at ten o'clock, the gratifying news that Lee has surrendered was received at General Steedman's headquarters, creating the wildest excitement. As the news spread the men gathered in crowds and rent the air with the most vociferous cheers. The Twenty-ninth Indiana was ordered to "fall in" without arms, and then followed a regimental "three times three" that would have done your heart good to hear. At noon the forts that crown the crests of the hills about town, fired a salute of one hundred guns, the whistles of the locomotives and machine shops screamed, while everybody feels good.

Lee's Surrender, Appomattox C. H., Va.
Confederate Account

A bright, clear, beautiful day, Lee's surrender, but it opened gloomily. Our army had reached Appomattox Court House, on the road to Lynchburg. Thomas, with his army, had arrived before us and effected a junction with Grant; cavalry, infantry and artillery completely surrounded our little command. We had from five to eight thousand prisoners, and only eight thousand effective men with muskets, all told. The supply of ammunition was nearly exhausted. In this emergency General Lee determined to cut his way through. Orders were given for a grand charge, and our troops massed accordingly.

General Grimes' division led the charge, followed successively by two others. The engagement commenced shortly after sunrise, and was continued until our men had broke through the Federal lines, driven them nearly a mile and a half and captured several pieces of artillery, and some hundreds of prisoners. The old spirit of fight was un-subdued. Meanwhile a heavy force of cavalry threatened our flanks. For some reason General Lee issued orders to the troops to cease firing and withdraw.

Subsequently an officer, said to be General Custer of the Yankee cavalry, entered our lines with a flag of truce. Whether his appearance was in response to a request from General Lee, or he was the bearer of a formal demand for the surrender initiated by General Grant, we are not informed. At this time, our army was in line of battle on or near the Appomattox road, the skirmishers thrown out, while two hundred and fifty yards from those, on an eminence, was a large body of Federal cavalry.

Soon after the return of General Custer to his lines, General Grant, accompanied by his staff, rode to the headquarters of General Lee, which were under an apple tree near the road. The interview is described as exceedingly impressive. After the salutatory formalities, which were doubtless brief and business-like, General Lee tendered his sword to Grant in token of surrender. That officer, however, with a courtesy for which we must accord him due respect, declined to receive it, or receiving it declined to retain it, and accompanied its return with substantially the following remarks:

"General Lee, keep that sword. You have won it by your gallantry. You have not been whipped, but overpowered, and I cannot receive it as a token of surrender from so brave a man."

The reply of General Lee we do not know. But Grant and himself are said to have been deeply affected by the occasion, and to have shed tears. The scene occurred between ten and eleven o'clock in the forenoon. When the sad event became known to the army, officers and men gave way to their emotions and some among the veterans wept like children. A considerable number swore that they never would surrender and made their way to the woods. Generals Gary of South Carolina and Rosser of Virginia, with a few followers, cut their way out and escaped. But the bulk of the army, the men who for four years have done battle so nobly for the cause, together with leaders like Longstreet, Gordon, Kershaw, and others whose names are forever distinguished, were obliged to accept the proffered terms.

These were—capitulation with all the honors of war— officers to retain their side-arms and personal property and the men their baggage. Each one was thereupon paroled and allowed to go his way.

During Sunday and Monday a large number of Federal soldiers and officers visited our camps and looked curiously on our commands, but there was nothing like exultation, no shouting for joy and no word uttered that could add to the mortification already sustained. On the contrary every symptom of respect was manifested, and the Southern army was praised for the noble and brave manner in which it had defended our cause

The force of the Yankee army is estimated at two hundred thousand men. Our own, at the time of surrender, embraced not more than eight thousand effective infantry and two thousand cavalry, but it is said that the total number paroled was about twenty-three thousand of all arms and conditions.

All the Federals spoke of General Lee in unbounded praise. The remark was frequently made "he would receive as many cheers in going down our lines as General Grant himself."

It is understood that Generals Lee, Longstreet and other officers are now on parole in the city of Richmond.

The following is a true copy of General Lee's Address to his army, issued after the surrender to General Grant at Appomattox C. H., on Sunday, April 9th, 1865:

Headquarters
Army of Northern Va.
April 10th, 1865.
General Orders No. 9

After four years of arduous service, marked by unsurpassed courage and fortitude, the Army of Northern Virginia has been compelled to yield to overwhelming numbers and resources.

I need not tell the brave survivors of so many hard fought battles who have remained steadfast to the last, that I have consented to this result from no distrust of them. But feeling that valor and devotion could accomplish nothing that could compensate for the loss that would have attended the continuance of the contest, I determined to avoid the useless sacrifice of those whose past services have endeared them to their countrymen.

By the terms of the agreement officers and men can return to their homes and remain until exchanged. You will take with you the satisfaction that proceeds from the consciousness of duty faithfully performed, and I earnestly pray that a merciful God will extend to you His blessing and protection.

With unceasing admiration of your constancy and devotion to your country and a grateful remembrance of your kind and generous consideration for myself, I bid you an affectionate farewell.

R. E. Lee,

General

Below is a special order embracing General Grant's order for the passage of paroled soldiers to their homes and also the form of pass given them:

Headquarters Army of N. V.
April 10th, 1865.
Special Order No. ___

All officers and men of the Confederate service paroled at Appomattox C. H., Va., who, to reach their homes are compelled to pass, through the lines of the Union armies, will be allowed to do so, and to pass free on all Government transports and military railroads.

By command of Lieutenant General Grant,
E. S. Parker, Lieutenant Colonel A. A. G.
By command of R. E. Lee,
C. L. Venabee, A. A. G.

Tuesday, April 11, 1865

Fifth Army Corps near
Appomattox Court House, Virginia

The process of paroling Lee's Army is slowly progressing. The Confederate officers are hard at work in furnishing individual paroles for those lately under their command. As fast as the Confederate soldier gets his parole, that quick does he start for home.

Appomattox Court House, Virginia,
Union Account

On the surrender of Lee it was estimated that his army consisted of about thirty thousand men. It will therefore astonish the country to learn that of paroled prisoners we probably received at the surrender not more than eight thousand. The question naturally arises, what became of the remaining twenty-two thousand? Rebel officers aver that on learning of Lee's intention to surrender, thousands, among them the Rebel cavalry, left, either for their homes or to join the army of Johnston before being paroled, and that these men will doubtless soon be found in the fighting ranks of the Rebel armies elsewhere.

After the surrender, the Fifth Corps was ordered to remain for the purpose of superintending the removal of the surrendered property. Sheridan and the command of General Ord marched for Danville, while the Second and Sixth returned to Burkesville for supplies.

The Ninth Corps took no part in the pursuit of Lee's army from Petersburg, but remained behind for the purpose of guarding the railroad at Burkesville.

Lee, it is said, attributes the capture of his army to his endeavors to save his wagon train, which greatly delayed his progress. Had he abandoned it he might possibly have reached the Danville Road before us, and escaped with his army southward. He will doubtless learn wisdom by experience.

Near the Appomattox, and at the point where Sheridan and Wright achieved their brilliant success of Friday, lay the ruins of army wagons, ambulances, forges, caissons, and the *debris* generally of the Rebel army. On the white canvas cover of an army wagon some wag, possibly a good-natured Johnny, had written in glaring capitals, "WE'UNS HAVE FOUND THE LASTt DITCH." From the scene presented in the gorge referred to one might very easily believe that it was the long vaunted "last ditch" of the expiring "Confederacy."

Lynchburg, Virginia

The keys of this city are today in the hands of Griffin's scouting party, and will be given to General MacKenzie upon his arrival, which is momentarily expected. The citizens show signs of satisfaction over the result and are courteous. The streets are filled with Confederate soldiers who are anxiously awaiting the result of the change. We hope that Sherman is meeting with success. We are now ready to digest good news from him, which, with Johnston bagged, must close up the deal.

Columbus, Georgia,
Confederate Account

The following prices are today's market values: Tobacco, common, $4.22 to $7.10; cigars per thousand, $200; one sole leather trunk, $610; powder, $20; one Negro woman, thirty five years old, and four children, $5,500; four per cent, certificates, 33c; cotton, 60c; diamond rings, $1,500 to $2,400; cane syrup, per gallon, $16 to $17.50; salt, $2.60 to $2.75; Irish potatoes, $15 to $16; gold watches, $800 to $3,300; oranges, 55c.; horse, $2,000.

Lynchburg, Virginia,
Union Account

The capture of this important place this morning without opposition, shows plainly what other places in this section may allow. The people here—or the majority of them— are glad that the "Old Flag" has come back.

So important a town as this in our hands is another great loss to the enemy. Here, the center of three railroads, and the depository of vast supplies is given over to a squad of men under the command of a lieutenant. The base of guerilla warfare that has been promised to exist for twenty years to come is now under Federal authority, and another page written in the history of Southern expectations.

Lynchburg is now where it will possibly stay; another of those cities belonging to the United States exclusively.

Wednesday, April 12, 1865

Richmond, Virginia

Mrs. General Lee is seriously indisposed. A Negro guard was placed in front of the home she is occupying, but on it being represented that the color of the guards was an insult to Mrs. Lee, they were withdrawn and white guards substituted.

Fairfax Station, Virginia

Colonel Gamble, commanding the Union forces at this point, received a message from the Rebel General Mosby, in which he says he does not care about Lee's surrender, and that he is determined to fight so long as he has a man left.

Fifth Army Corps near
Appomattox Court House, Virginia

General Longstreet's entire corps Fifth Amy corps marched from their camps and formed in line in front of the First Division of this corps and stacked their arms, flags, &c, when they slowly and sorrowfully returned to their camp. It is a sight that cannot be pictured properly to those who have not witnessed it.

General Longstreet wore a smile on his face while General Gordon's expression was very different. General Pendleton disliked to give up Lee's artillery, but did so.

Mobile, Alabama

The Stars and Stripes were hoisted on Batteries Porter and Mackintosh at half past ten this morning. The most prominent church steeple also had our flag placed on it at half past two o'clock. General Granger's forces are now in full possession of this city.

The Rebels commenced evacuating on the 10th and continued until yesterday when they had all left.

Salisbury, North Carolina,
Union Account

Stoneman's command, at ten o'clock this morning, captured this place, and with it eight stand of colors, nineteen pieces of artillery, eleven hundred and sixty-five prisoners, one thousand stand of arms and accoutrements, one million rounds of small ammunition, together with clothing, bacon, salt, sugar, rice, wheat, &c.

The greater part of these supplies came from Raleigh. We destroyed on our way, an equipped arsenal, six depots, two engines and trains, and several bridges.

We lost few killed in the engagement this morning.

Thomas's Army, Washington, D.C.

News now comes that General Thomas has captured Selma and Montgomery, Alabama, and has defeated and captured Forrest's and Roddy's entire command. When will these good things end? A few more days and there will not be a grease spot left of the Rebel armies.

Washington, D.C.

General Lee has obtained permission to visit Weldon, North Carolina. His army is still at the point where it surrendered. The work of preparing the Rebel rolls duplicates of which have to be made, and the turning over the property of the army is progressing as fast as possible. In a few days every detail necessary to complete the surrender will be concluded. The army will then be permitted to disperse, according to the terms agreed upon. General Lee and the officers surrendered by him are overwhelmed with gratitude for the generosity displayed by Lieutenant General Grant.

Lee surrendered less than eight thousand fighting men to Grant. Less than five thousand muskets were surrendered. It is the opinion of many patriots at Washington that the morale of our success only should be celebrated, and that with exceeding modesty. Grant had one hundred and twenty-three thousand men under his command. General Lee confessed to General Grant that Johnston's entire force would not number more than ten thousand.

Savannah, Georgia

Jeff. Davis is reported at Macon, Georgia, on the 10th. It is also stated that he has one hundred and sixty thousand dollars in gold on deposit in Havana.

Augusta, Georgia, Confederate Account

If this Revolution has produced some of the meanest and most groveling of mankind, it has held an even balance by the example of some of the most exalted and aspiring souls—the true lords of the creation. The grub worms who prosper now, bloated with profit—a profit that has been sternly but veraciously denominated the sweat of the poor and the blood of the brave—these earth bugs, we say, shall be blotted from the records of the book of memory, or recollected only with infamy, while the anointed names of a thousand heroes shine in perpetual splendor.

Out of the mass of those who have done well and gloriously a few arise who possess individual traits of superiority, which are calculated to elevate them above their fellows and make them memorable.

We do not allude, at the present writing, to the Titans of our time who have had the world for an applauding audience. Their fame is secure. We would select a humbler worker in the vineyard of liberty, and one who has recently yielded for his country the sacrifice of life. Who can read of the death of Marcus Jerome Clarke—the romantic "Sue Munday"—without a thrill of horror and admiration—horror at his murder; admiration for his courage and demeanor. "I DIE BEFORE MY MANHOOD, AND YET I HAVE BEEN A MAN TO MY COUNTRY!" Such is the language of a noble spirit, and such the sentiment which should animate the bosom of every Confederate youth. What a stigma does such language fix upon those lusty lads and brawny men who seek every avenue of escape from service and are not ashamed to deny their masculinity by cowardly evasion and finesse. You, skulker in the swamps, can you read the words of this young man unmoved? You, sleek young fellow, with herculean shoulders and iron thews, how can you caper about at concerts and crawl in bomb-proofs, while the country bleeds and such men as Jerome Clarke die because of paucity of numbers in the ranks? Read that last utterance of sublime faith and patriotism with which the young Kentuckian bade farewell to the hopes of youth and the vanities of the world. Strive to emulate his magnificent career. BE A MAN to the country which the Lord your God has given you, and the imps of Satan shall not wrest it away.

Thursday, April 13, 1865

Raleigh, North Carolina

Evidently one of our opponents has had what they call "His fill of it." The following letter picked up on our entrance here states the case, and does it in a very pointed manner. The letter is given exactly as it was written:

"deers sister libby: i hev conkludid that the dam fulishnes uv tryin to lick shurmin Had better be stoped. we hav bin gettin nuthin but hell & lots uv it ever sinse we saw the dam yankys & i am tirde uv it. shurmin has a lots of pimps that dont care a dam what they doo. and its no use tryin to whip em. if we dont git hell when shurmin starts agin i miss my gess. if i cood git home ide tri dam hard to git thare. my old horse is plaid out or ide trie to go now. maibee ile start to nite fur ime dam tired uv this war fur nuthin. if the dam yankees Havent got thair yit its a dam wunder. Thair thicker an lise on a hen and a dam site ornraier. youre brother jim."

This morning at about nine o'clock Kilpatrick's cavalry entered the city, and were soon after followed by the First Division of the Fourteenth Corps, commanded by General C. C. Walcutt. A Provost-guard was immediately placed at every house to prevent stragglers from molesting the citizens, who have since remarked that there has been more quiet and order since the advent of our troops than there was when Johnston's command were here.

Wheeler's men have treated the people shamefully, breaking into houses and stores and robbing everybody, friend and foe alike. The people all through the country, as well as those in this town, represent them as acting more like a band of robbers than, an organized body of troops.

After the city had been formally surrendered, and while Kilpatrick was marching through the town, an officer belonging to Wheeler's command, who, with some of his men, were engaged in plundering a store near the Market House, rushed into the street and fired his revolver at Kilpatrick, who was riding at the head of the column; the ball fortunately missed Kilpatrick, but wounded one of his staff. Chase was instantly made, and the ruffian captured. In less than ten minutes he was swinging by his neck from a tree.

The march from Goldsboro was a very severe one in consequence of the rain and naturally bad roads over which the army was obliged to pass.

The pioneer corps and large details from different regiments were worked day and night, corduroying the roads for nearly half the distance marched.

The Fifteenth and Seventeenth Corps, commanded respectively by General Blair and Logan, and which are commonly known as the right wing of the Army of the Tennessee, under General Howard, took the extreme right on the march to Raleigh, which, in consequence of the circuitous route traveled, amounted to nearly sixty-four miles. This march was accomplished in three days and a half, an almost incredible short time when it is taken into consideration that the roads had to be made for full one-half the distance, amid a drenching rain storm which to any ordinary army would have made the roads impassable; but Sherman's veteran and victorious troops have learned how to overcome almost every obstacle to success, and they accordingly accomplished this march in the short time stated. The same march could not have been made in the same time by any other army in the world.

With the exception of some slight cavalry skirmishing this wing of the army has had no enemy to contend with or to impede their progress since they left Goldsboro.

Those few of Wheeler's men, not amounting to over fifty or one hundred, who kept in our front were easily driven and kept at a respectful distance from our advance, which consisted of the Seventh Illinois Mounted Infantry of Major General Course's Division of the Fifteenth Corps.

Charleston, South Carolina

The news that "Lee has surrendered" reached here this evening. Many are so intoxicated with delight that they are wild.

Patriotic songs are heard all over the city. Little sleep can be expected for tonight. Even the residents are joining in the jubilee. Charleston is, this evening, doing her share in the jollification.

Washington, D.C.

There is truth in the report that recruiting and drafting has ceased. Orders were issued today to that effect from the War Department. War will soon have become a thing to look back upon, and the horror will never be fully known.

With every hour comes news from all sections, announcing the success of our army and the rapid destruction of opposition. Every loyal man, no matter if he is in affliction, wears an expression of satisfaction over the result of April so far. The end is near at hand, thank God.

Raleigh, North Carolina,
Union Account

The Capital of North Carolina was entered and occupied this morning by the Union troops, and the Stars and Stripes wave from the ample dome of the State House. The First Division of the Fourteenth Corps, General Walcutt, was the first infantry command to enter the city. In accordance with General Sherman's order, the citizens were notified that they could all have a guard by applying for it. On entering the city about half past two o'clock in the afternoon, I found a guard at every door, and a Sabbath-like quiet pervading the place. Kilpatrick's cavalry came in early in the morning, as the cavalry of General Wheeler—the rear guard of Johnston's army—withdrew. The latter ransacked and robbed a large number of stores during the last night of their stay. They held high carnivals, got drunk, insulted the citizens, and kept up a reign of terror during the last days' occupation of the city. It was unsafe for ladies to walk the streets, and they kept shut up in their houses. General Johnston, whose troops proper were kept under the strictest discipline, had withdrawn.

The greatest panic prevailed among a portion of the people on account of the exaggerated stories which had been circulated concerning the outrages they might expect from our troops. Their surprise and gratification at the good order and perfect quiet which prevailed upon the entry of the army, knew no bounds. It was an immense relief to the people. One of Wheeler's Cavalry who remained among the last, against the remonstrance of the citizens, fired upon some of Kilpatrick's men as they rode up toward the capital. He attempted to escape, but was shot in the mouth, his horse fell, and he was captured and hung. The act of firing upon our men after the surrender of the city, was in violation of all propriety, and fully justified the fate which he met. General Johnston's army, consisting of twenty thousand infantry in a very good condition, and a large body of cavalry, some reports say ten thousand, in poor condition, evacuated Raleigh on yesterday morning, marching toward Hillsborough.

The army of General Sherman, divided into three grand columns, and a column of Kilpatrick's cavalry, advanced from Goldsboro by three or four different roads. General Slocum had the left; General Schofield, with General Cox's Twenty-third Army Corps, the center, and the Army of the Tennessee, General Howard, the right. General Terry with the Tenth Corps, part of Schofield's command, kept up the south side of the Neuse to unite with the other portion of General Schofield's army, near Smithfield. Before we had reached the latter place, it became known to General Sherman that Johnston would fall back from Raleigh. The army was accordingly pushed forward as fast as possible. When General Sherman arrived at Clayton's depot, he was met by a deputation from Raleigh, sent forward by Governor Vance, to make terms of surrender, and to secure protection.

The wish to secure his own person from arrest, and to perpetuate his lease of power, and that of the Legislature elect was evidently another—perhaps the chief object of the mission. The party was of the highest respectability, consisting of ex-Governor Graham, and ex-Governor Swain, President of the University. General Sherman received them with great politeness, and listened with attention to their remarks. The interview was brief and cordial, and, at its close, General Sherman assured them of full protection, on condition that his troops should not be molested or fired upon during their further march into the city. The assurance was given by the Commission that the city would be evacuated by General Johnston, and no opposition made to our advance.

Hereupon General Sherman issued the following order, which was promulgated to the troops through the different commanders the same evening:

Headquarters
Military Division of the Mississippi, In the Field,
Gauley's Store, N. C., April 12th, 1865.

All officers and soldiers of the army are commanded to respect and protect the Government of North Carolina, and all officers and agents of the State Government, the Mayor and citizens of Raleigh—provided no hostile act is committed against the officers and men of this army.

W. T. Sherman,
Major General Commanding

It is understood that Governor Vance instructed his Commissioners to ask of General Sherman an armistice to enable him to convene the Legislature to take steps for bringing the State back into the Union. Vance, who has been very violent and made a rabid speech to the troops only five days ago, left last evening on horseback, as was supposed, in company with Captain Guthrie, late of the navy. A delegation has been sent after the fugitive Governor to get him back.

General Kilpatrick's Cavalry, which had been skirmishing with the cavalry of the enemy during the previous day on the Smithfield road, were met a mile out of the city by the Mayor, Wm. H. Harrison, who was accompanied by the Honorable Kenneth Rayner. The latter addressed General Kilpatrick, speaking for the Mayor and the citizens of Raleigh. He desired to surrender the city, and requested protection for the citizens, the women and children, and for the two asylums near the city, viz: the Insane and the Deaf and Dumb. The Presidents, or a delegation from the government of both these institutions were present. General Kilpatrick assured them of protection, and he and his staff then rode forward, entering the city at the eastward, while Wheeler's Cavalry retired in the opposite direction. At about eight o'clock in the morning they rode to the capitol, and the Fifth Ohio Cavalry, ascending to the top, planted the American flag upon the State House dome. Some of Wheeler's men, against the earnest entreaties of the citizens, remained to get a final shot at the Yankees. The result was that one of them got a halter for his pains, and no sympathy from the citizens.

Adjutant James, the Rebel Provost-Marshal, who was suspected of conniving at the act, was arrested.

General Schofield and staff arrived at General Sherman's headquarters about half past two o'clock in the afternoon. During the evening there was a meeting of the Generals and prominent Union citizens at headquarters.

The city is perfectly quiet. Scarcely a soldier is to be seen—only the guards; the stores are all closed, and the main streets seem like Sunday. General Slocum and staff soon followed and General Sherman and staff arrived and took quarters at the Governor's mansion between nine and ten o'clock in the morning. The Governor was not at home to receive him, having urgent business at Hillsborough. General Sherman, however, made himself quite at home, as he had previously done at the mansions of other Southern Governors. A splendid American flag hung over the main entrance, fronting Fayetteville Street.

The Central or Gasten Depot was set on fire by some of the Rebel troops before leaving, and together with a large quantity of corn, which was stored in the building, destroyed. The object was supposed to be the destruction of the corn to keep it out of our hands. A portion of it had previously been distributed among indigent families. I learn that a pretty clean sweep has been made of the corn throughout this region by Johnston's troops.

Prominent Rebel citizens here had information that Jeff. Davis had been heard of on his way to Cheraw, South Carolina. More recent news, however, locates him at or near Hillsborough, where he will probably put himself under the wing of Johnston's army from the Yankee raiders who are now thronging all the main roads of western North Carolina.

Jeff, telegraphed to Johnston that the news from Lee was of the most disastrous character; that he could not depend upon that army, and must make the best defense he could unaided by it.

Hardee, before leaving Raleigh, remarked that if General Lee had surrendered, and he had no doubt of it, any further slaughter of men in battle was only murder. He is believed to express General Johnston's opinion on this point; and intelligent North Carolinians expect to see a surrender of Johnston's army within a few days.

It is reported that there was a large amount of specie accumulated at Danville—the proceeds of the late tax on gold and silver—with which it is expected Jeff, Jew Benjamin and their associates in treason will try to smuggle *with themselves* out of the country.

Great anxiety prevails everywhere among the people. The State is thoroughly impoverished, and distress and starvation must overtake them unless an immediate cessation of hostilities affords the opportunity to plant a crop during the present spring. Days, even hours, are now more precious than gold to those who must depend upon this year's crop for support of themselves and families.

Washington, D.C.

General Grant is here, in consultation with the President. His headquarters are hereafter to be in Washington. He goes to Philadelphia tomorrow.

Lee visits Johnston to stay bloodshed. He is truly penitent. Ewell is on his parole at the Metropolitan.

General Lee was at City Point yesterday, but was expected to proceed to Richmond today. He will be present at the convening of the Rebel Virginia Legislature, and urge the immediate passage of a resolution restoring the Old Dominion to the Union.

Greenville, East Tennessee, Fourth Army Corps Headquarters

General Stanley has issued the following order:

"The glorious success of the National armies under Lieutenant General Grant, being no longer a matter of any doubt, the army under his command having killed, wounded, captured and forced the capitulation of the entire principal army of the Rebels, including their Commander-in-chief, tomorrow, which is the day appointed by the War Department for the raising of the old flag over Fort Sumter, where it was first insulted and pulled down by insolent traitors, will be kept as a holiday and a day of thanksgiving in this corps. A salute of one hundred guns will be fired at twelve o'clock noon, under the direction of Major Goodspeed, chief of artillery. All military duty excepting necessary police and guard duty will be suspended. It is recommended that chaplains of regiments hold services in their respective places of worship, to render thanks to Almighty God for his goodness and mercy in preserving us as a nation and giving us the great victory over our enemies. Let us in our thankfulness; remember in tears the many brave men who have fallen at our sides in this great and terrible war. Who among us has not lost a brother, a relative, or a dear comrade? Let us reflect, and we may profit by so doing, that great national, as great personal sin, must be atoned for by great punishment."

Friday, April 14, 1865

Raleigh, North Carolina

Sherman's Bummers have a new song that is expressive of the present feeling of his army:

Tune:—" When Johnny Comes Marching Home."

Old Tecumseh is in the lead,
Oh, Ho,. Oh! Ho!
Help from Grant he does not need,
Ah, Ha! Ah, Ha!
For now he's giving the Johnnies enough,
To try the quality of their stuff.
The times they're having are mighty tough.
While Sherman's boys they're trying to bluff,
Oh, Ho! Oh, Ho! Ah, Ha!

We've been flying around from town to town,
Oh, Ho! Oh, Ho!
We've found no one that could do us up brown,
Ah, Ha! Ah, Ha!
We're on the wing and going along
Not caring a cuss for Johnston's throng
For while he's pounding his worn out gong,
We're dropping right in. as it were, headlong,
Oh, Ho! Oh, Ho! Ah, Ha!

Another week, and where will we be.
Oh, Ho! Oh, Ho!
On our march from bv the sea?
Ah, Ha! Ah, Ha!
Perhaps Old Johnston with his bad licked crowd.
Will be screaming to Cump, in a voice real loud
"Come on old Yank, we're done up proud.
Take away that gang, you've got us cowed."
Oh, Ho! Oh, Ho! Ah, Ha!

Now we're in Old North Caroline,
Oh, Ho! Oh, Ho!
Chewing things that are sublime,
Ah, Ha! Ah, Ha!

Our bellies are full of chicken breast,
Our Boys are taking in the best,
While Old Tecump is taking a rest,
Before he again drops on the pest,
Oh, Ho! Oh, Ho! Ah, Ha!

It's bound to come in a few days.
Oh, Ho! Oh, Ho!
Even if the Johnnies don't like our ways,
Ah. Ha! Ah Ha!
If they don't come up to General Cump.
And offer to give it up in a lump.
We'll give them another Yankee thump
That will surely settle every chump,
Oh, Ho! Oh, Ho! Ah, Ha!

Fortress Monroe, Virginia

The Steamer George Leary, which has arrived from City Point, this afternoon, brings down a rumor that Johnston has surrendered to Sherman. It lacks confirmation.

Charleston, South Carolina

Major Anderson, before a distinguished assemblage, hoisted the Stars and Stripes on Fort Sumter, today. The flag had an evergreen wreath attached. The occupants of the stage all joined in taking hold of the halyards, and helped hoist the beautiful banner, while the enthusiasm was unbounded. There was a simultaneous rising, and cheering, and waving of hats which lasted fully fifteen minutes.

General Anderson then introduced the Rev. Henry Ward Beecher who made the leading address.

Raising the Old Flag over Fort Sumter

Raleigh, North Carolina

Today the anniversary of the capture of Fort Sumter, the right wing of Sherman's army made its triumphant march into the capital of North Carolina, to the intense delight of a goodly number of loyal citizens, who never favored Secession, and who would at any time during the present Rebellion have gladly sought refuge under the folds of the old flag, if they could have done so with safety to themselves and families.

Two days ago a committee of gentlemen proceeded to General Sherman's headquarters at Clayton Station, on the Goldsboro railroad, and surrendered the city. They were: Ex-Governor L. Swain and William A. Graham, with Dr. Warren, Surgeon General of the State, on Governor Vance's Staff, acting as Secretary. General Sherman received the committee very kindly, accepting the surrender of the city and promising to afford every protection to citizens and their property.

New York, New York

This morning's Tribune has New York, N.Y., the following editorial on the situation:

The path of Peace opens pleasantly before us. There may be thorns in the way as we advance, obstacles to be removed, pitfalls and snares to be avoided, but we look back to the dread road we have traveled for four long and weary and painful years, and the road before us smiles only with Summer sunshine. It is natural for man to indulge in hope, and hope is not always illusive. That the war is over is a mighty fact. The courage, the endurance, the patriotism, the self-sacrifice that have stood the test of this gigantic struggle have borne the heaviest burden that can be laid upon the heart and the character of a nation, and whatever else may be before us we accept the future with a cheerfulness that needs no abatement, with a joy that should be dimmed with no gloomy anticipations. There are ships that will encounter the toughest storms and rot to pieces in the calms that succeed them. But ours is not one of these. The storm caught us with our rigging unbraced, our sails flapping, our decks in disorder, our yards unmanned, our rudder unshipped. A ship put in order to encounter peril amid such multiplied dangers, and that then rode out the tempest, is too stanch and too well-conditioned to fear any wind that blows or any swell it can upheave. With flag and pennant streaming gaily out upon the breeze, she takes a new departure upon a smiling sea.

It is a moment only for rejoicing. The hours of despondency— how many we have passed through!—the fears that courage, or strength, or resources might fail us, have passed away. The good fight has been fought; the Right has triumphed. We are a Nation, no longer divided against itself, but one, indivisible, united, Free. The darkness, the gloom, the doubts, the fears, have gone forever, and the hearts of all the people sing together for joy. Even those that are stricken with a sorrow that can never be forgotten, smitten with bereavements for which there can be no earthly cure— even these will rejoice with a tenderer joy inasmuch as the gifts they have laid upon the country's altar are above all price.

The war is over. The house is to be set in order, but the cause of disorder exists no longer. Within the week the President has issued two Proclamations giving notice to the world that we are not now a distracted household, that the nations are to conduct themselves accordingly, and cannot again be permitted to take advantage of our disturbed condition. Today we publish an order from the War Department, that the draft and recruiting are to be stopped; that no more arms and ammunition are to be purchased; that the expenses of the military establishment are to be reduced; that military restrictions upon trade and commerce are to be removed; that the Government, in short, no longer needs to call upon the country for men and means to carry on the War, for the gates of the temple are swinging on their hinges, and will close presently, firmly and silently! The dispensation is over; the new era begun! The throes, the pains, the tortures of birth are finished. A new world is born, and the Sun of Peace rises in splendor to send abroad over the land its rays of warmth and light! Never before had nation so much cause for devout Thanksgiving; never before had a people so much reason for unrestrained congratulation and the very extravagance of joy.

Richmond, Virginia

There is but one army left to April 14, 1865. those of the Rebellion, large enough to be kept together for even a few weeks. While it is reported that Johnston's Army amounts to fully forty thousand men, but little truth is given this report, as we hear, every day of desertions by the hundreds, and that the news of Lee's surrender has so completely disheartened Johnston's command as that it will not be possible to hold them together. If Johnston is determined on meeting Sherman, with a respectable army, it must be done very soon. The result of a contact would surely paint a picture for Johnston that is in keeping with the one Lee now looks upon. If Johnston retreats, which is about the only thing he ever did, he will have to abandon Raleigh; then to take up a march in this direction he would run against more than he could possibly handle, and if he chooses to go in a westerly direction he will find Stoneman's forces far from asleep. Now what will he do is the question? His army at this time is an absurdity, and the sooner Johnston comes to realize this fact, the earlier will peace be declared.

Washington, D.C.

Information has been received at General Grant's headquarters, from scouts, that General Stoneman has arrived with his command upon the railroad below Danville, and between Danville and Greensborough. He will doubtless capture Greensborough, and cut the railroads around it, rendering Johnston's escape from Sherman impossible. It is highly probable that Johnston will be compelled to surrender to Sherman as Lee has to Grant. If he attempts to fight

Sherman, he will be annihilated, and it is impossible for him to get away from him. General Carl Schurz has arrived in Goldsboro, with orders to report to General Sherman for duty.

Special advices from Goldsboro to April 10, state that positive information had been received at Goldsboro that Johnston's army was within fifteen miles northeast of that place.

President Lincoln's Assassination, Washington, D.C.

President Lincoln and wife, with other friends, this evening visited Ford's Theater for the purpose of witnessing the performance of "The American Cousin". The President and Mrs. Lincoln did not start for the theater until a quarter after eight o'clock. Speaker Colfax was at the White House at the time, and the President stated to him that he was going, although Mrs. Lincoln had not been well, because the papers had announced that General Grant and they were to be present, and, as General Grant had gone north, he did not wish the audience to be disappointed. He went with apparent reluctance, and urged Mr. Colfax to go with him, but that gentleman had made other engagements, and with Mr. Ashmun, of Massachusetts, bid him good night.

President Abraham Lincoln

John Wilkes Booth

The theater was densely crowded, and everybody seemed delighted with the scene before them. During the third act, and while there was a temporary pause for one of the actors to enter, a sharp report of a pistol was heard, which merely attracted attention, but suggested nothing serious, until a man rushed to the front of the President's box, waving a long dagger in his right hand, and exclaiming, *Sic semper tyrannis,"* and immediately leaped from the box, which was on the second tier, to the stage beneath, and ran across to the opposite side, making his escape amid the bewilderment of the audience, from the rear of the theater, and mounting a horse, fled.

The screams of Mrs. Lincoln first disclosed the fact to the audience that the President had been shot, when all present rose to their feet, rushing toward the stage, many exclaiming, "Hang him, hang him!"

The excitement was of the wildest possible description, and of course there was an abrupt termination to the theatrical performance.

There was a rush toward the President's box, when cries were heard, "Stand back and give him air." "Has any one stimulants?" On a hasty examination, it was found that the President had been shot through the head, above and back of the temporal bone, and that some of the brains were oozing out.

He was removed to a private house opposite to the theater, and the Surgeon General of the army and other surgeons sent for to attend to his condition.

On an examination of the private box, blood was discovered on the back of the cushioned rocking chair on which the President had been sitting, also on the partition and on the floor. A common single-barreled pocket-pistol was found on the carpet.

A military guard was placed in front of the private residence to which the President had been conveyed. An immense crowd was in front of it, all deeply anxious to learn the condition of the President. The shock to the community was terrible.

At midnight the Cabinet, together with Sumner, Colfax and Farnsworth, Judge Curtis, Governor Oglesby, General Meigs, Colonel Hay and a few personal friends, with Surgeon General Barnes and his immediate assistants, were around his bedside.

The President was in a state of syncope, totally insensible, and breathing slowly. The blood oozed from the wound at the back of his head. The surgeons exhausted every possible effort of medical skill, but all hope was gone.

The assassin is said to have gained entrance to the President's box by sending in his card, requesting an interview. In the President's party were Mrs. Lincoln, Miss Harris, daughter of Senator Harris, and Captain Rathbone, of Albany. Immediately upon opening the door he advanced toward Mr. Lincoln with a six-barrel revolver in his right hand, a bowie-knife in his left. The President, who was intent on the play, did not notice his intrusion; and the gentleman who was seated beside him arose to inquire the reason of his entry.

Before he had time to ask the assassin what he wanted he fired one charge from his revolver which took effect in the back of the President's head. The ball passed through and came out at the right temple. Capt. Rathbone attempted to arrest the murderer, and in trying to do so, received a stab in his arm.

So sudden was the affair that for some moments after its occurrence the audience supposed that it was a part of the play, and were only undeceived when it was announced from the stage by the manager that the President of the United States had been shot.

The shock fell upon the audience like a thunderbolt, and loud cries were immediately made to capture or kill the assassin. The scene which ensued cannot be described. Men and women rushed for the doors crying and shouting for vengeance on the murderer.

The murderous emissary of the Slave Power escaped easily and rapidly from the theater, and mounted a horse and fled. The President, insensible, was carried out and taken to a house opposite the theater.

Mrs. Lincoln fainted in the box and was borne out after her husband. The mass of the evidence is that J. Wilkes Booth committed the crime.

William H. Seward

Washington D.C. 11:30 p.m.

When the excitement at the theater was at its height, reports were circulated that Secretary Seward had also been assassinated.

On reaching this gentleman's residence, a crowd and a military guard were found at the door, and on entering, it was ascertained that the reports were based on truth.

Everybody there was so excited that scarcely an intelligible word could be gathered, but the facts are substantially as follows:

About ten o'clock a man rang the bell, and the call having been answered by a colored servant, he said he had come from Dr. Verdi, Secretary Seward's family physician, with a prescription, at the same time holding in his hand a small piece of folded paper, and saying, in answer to the refusal, that he must see the Secretary, as he was entrusted with particular directions concerning the medicine.

He still insisted on going up, although repeatedly informed that no one could enter the chamber. The man pushed the servant aside, and walked heavily toward the Secretary's room, and was then met by Mr. Frederick Seward, making the same representation which he did to the servant. What further passed in colloquy is not known; but the man struck him on the head with a "billy," severely injuring the skull and felling him almost senseless. The assassin then rushed into the chamber and attacked Major Seward, Paymaster of the United States Army, and Mr. Hensell, a messenger of the State Department, and two male nurses, disabling them all. He then rushed upon the Secretary, who was lying in bed in the same room, and inflicted three stabs in the neck, but severing, it is thought and hoped, no arteries, though he bled profusely. The assassin, then ran down stairs, mounted his horse at the door, and rode off before an alarm could be sounded, and in the same manner as the assassin of the President.

It is believed that the injuries of the Secretary are not fatal, nor those of either of the other, although both the Secretary and the Assistant Secretary are very seriously injured.

Secretaries Stanton and Welles, and other prominent officers of the Government called at Secretary Seward's house to inquire into his condition, and there heard of the assassination of the President. They then proceeded to the house where he was lying, exhibiting, of course, intense anxiety and solicitude. An immense crowd was gathered in front of the President's house, and a strong guard was also stationed there, many persons evidently supposing he would be brought to his home.

The entire city tonight presents a scene of the wildest excitement, accompanied by violent expressions of indignation, and the profoundest sorrow; many shed tears. The military authorities have dispatched mounted patrols in every direction, in order, if possible, to arrest the assassins. The whole Metropolitan police force is likewise vigilant for the same purpose.

The attacks, both at the theater and at Secretary Seward's house, took place at about the same hour— ten o'clock—thus showing a preconcerted plan to assassinate those gentlemen. Some evidences of the guilt of the party who attacked the President are in the possession of the police.

Lewis Payne
Seward's Attacker

Sherman's Army near Raleigh, North Carolina, Union Account

We have received some news today from the forces co-operating with this army against Johnston, which if true is very important, and indicates the speedy envelopment of the last Rebel army of note in a strategic net, the meshes of which it will be impossible to break. Stoneman, we learn, has succeeded in cutting the railroad behind Johnston, between Greensborough and Salisbury. This, if true, will sadly embarrass the Rebel host in its plans of retreat. Another report which is very generally credited, and is probably true, states *Sheridan to be within one day's* march of Johnston, with a large body of cavalry. Retreat as fast as the Rebel Chieftain may, he cannot escape scathless, and probably cannot elude us at all. In this present position it would certainly be the part of a wise man to make a virtue of necessity, and surrender at once his army. He could doubtless obtain as favorable terms as were granted to General Lee, and to pursue the war further is simply to prosecute murder. It is strongly hoped in the army that Johnston will take this view of affairs and will prevent further bloodshed by a manly submission to irrevocable fate. If he does not, however, a rapid pursuit of his flying forces will be made, and when brought to a stand he will be annihilated, for our soldiers are not in a humor to trifle, and would feel very savage at a useless prolongation of the war, and the consequent sacrifice of lives and happiness.

The allurements of an easy life in a capital city have speedily vanquished from the minds of all who entertained hopes of realizing it, for no intermission has been permitted in movements of the army. The Fourteenth Corps marched out of town early this morning. The Fifteenth was reviewed by General Sherman, and tomorrow will go on its way after Johnston. The Seventeenth is to be reviewed this afternoon and at daylight tomorrow will go on its way in chase of the enemy, and at daylight tomorrow the Twentieth Corps will leave its camp and be reviewed on its march through the city by Sherman. The town is to be garrisoned by a brigade of the Twenty-third Corps, which General Schofield has detailed for that purpose. It is supposed that the General will remain in the city in person for a time and act as Military Governor until another is regularly appointed to that position. North Carolina is to be permanently occupied as a Union State, and Raleigh is to be converted into a vast depot of supplies. The railroad to Goldsboro is so nearly completed that a train is confidently expected to reach here from Newbern tomorrow morning.

Raleigh possesses many features of interest to the observer of public institutions. The most prominent of these to the generality of people, is of course the State Capitol. This is a fine structure, as State Capitols generally are. It confronts one end of the main street and gives to that thoroughfare an aristocratic appearance. From the dome one obtains a very fine view of the surrounding country, which contains some excellent scenery.

At the other end of Fayetteville (the main) Street stands the Executive Mansion. This is occupied by General Sherman, and thus it happens that from the same building whence issued the fiery pronunciamentos of Vance, in aid of the Rebellion, proceed the calm, clear orders of Sherman for its dismemberment.

Another interesting building is the Deaf, Dumb and Blind Asylum, which I visited today. It is a handsomely-designed edifice. The pupils are given a thorough course of instruction in the trades, bookbinding, printing, broom-making, and shoe-makings, and when they leave the institution, are competent to earn a livelihood in ordinary times. Music is also a prominent branch of instruction, and several of the young ladies are fine performers. Among the unfortunate inmates is Miss Lamb, a sister of the gallant Colonel Lamb, who fought the Fort Fisher fight so gallantly. She is a pretty, interesting girl of about fourteen, and seems to be very intelligent.

At the Insane Asylum, which in point of size is next to the Capitol building, is a curious individual who has amused a large body of soldiers from the windows ever since the occupation of the town. He has a fine sweet melodious voice and employs it in singing comic songs and making speeches to his audience. From all appearance he is as sensible as any man in the Confederacy. He speaks fluently and uses choice language. His own story is that having been once out of his mind he was sent to the asylum, and since his recovery has been kept in confinement there because he was a Union man. He is certainly the greatest curiosity I have seen in the town, and his history, if it could be known, would no doubt be highly interesting.

The Standard and Progress are to be continued, and will probably issue their first number under Union auspices tomorrow. Both will be published by their former editors.

Saturday, April 15, 1865

Brooklyn, New York

Mrs. John Tyler, the widow of the ex-President, is, as is well known, a native of this State, and now resides near Factoryville, Staten Island. She has never disguised her sympathy with the Rebels, but, on the contrary, has permitted no opportunity to escape her of proclaiming it, even in church, protesting, by rising from her knees, against the prayers for the President of the United States. It being well known that the Rebel flag was draped over her parlor mantle-piece, this evening several young gentlemen—none of them over eighteen years of age—considering that if, at such a time as this, the flag was not voluntarily put out of sight Mrs. Tyler should be reminded that some decent respect was due to public opinion, waited upon her for that purpose. Two of them, sons of neighbors and well known to her, entered the parlor, when one of them said:

"Madam, I beg pardon for disturbing you, but we have called to ask for the Secession flag you have in your possession."

"There is no such flag here," replied Mrs. Tyler.

"I beg pardon again," said the young gentleman, courteously, "but such a flag, if I am not mistaken, hangs over your parlor mantle-piece."

Mrs. Tyler again denied that she had any such flag, but added: "You can look for yourself."

The young man did look for himself, and found the flag where he expected. Deliberately mounting a chair, he carefully took it down folded it up and stepping back into the other room once more apologized for the necessity of his intrusion, and bowed himself out with his companion. There was no attempt to interfere with the bold striplings by the three or four grown men who were present. One of them, indeed, left the room and went up stairs with the intention, the visitors supposed, of getting a weapon. The spokesman, on observing it, only shifted a short policeman's club he carried, from the left to the right hand coat pocket.

Some hours later a nephew of Mrs. Tyler's called upon the father of the young man who had walked off with the flag under his arm, and asked that the "French flag" which the son had taken might be returned. Of course the father knew nothing about it, as the son had not taken him into his counsels, who, he preferred, should be free from all responsibility for his acts. The flag could only be called French because it is a tricolor, while its field with seven stars conclusively settled its character. It was lodged in a place of safety.

New York, New York

The Rebel General Ewell passed through the city early this morning, on his way to Fort Warren.

While breakfasting at the Soldiers' Rest, on Fourth Avenue, he was told of the assassination of Mr. Lincoln, and not only expressed his deep regret, but seemed to be painfully affected by the intelligence.

Washington, D.C.

General Sherman is reported in treaty with Joe Johnston for the surrender of his army, and simultaneously we hear of Jeff. Davis as on the wing westward and having his quarters at Macon instead of Danville, whence he issued that last proclamation which announced his "re-occupation" of Virginia. Both accounts are probably true. Johnston is a soldier and knows that his work as a soldier is done— that further resistance is not war—that he has no military resource but to follow the example of his general-in-chief. Besides which, it is understood that Lee went to Danville to advise Johnston to give up the- contest. If he acted in good faith it is natural we should hear of Johnston's surrender and Davis's flight. Safe to say that the latter will never trust himself within reach of the defenders of the Republic.

New York, New York

The capture of Mobile is one of those events which a few weeks ago would have been welcomed with joyful enthusiasm all over the North, and which only a few days since would have seemed an important success, and filled the streets with flags. But today, what is Mobile to us, or what military triumph shall lift up the hearts that are bowed down with the weight of a national sorrow? Yet even at this moment the possession of the last seaport save one of the Rebellious States, is a victory of value. If the fall of Mobile has no other effect, it will accelerate the return of Alabama to the Union, since Mobile holds to that State the same position as Savannah to Georgia, Charleston to South Carolina, and Wilmington to North Carolina.

President Lincoln's Death
10 o'clock a.m.

At twenty minutes after seven the President breathed his last, closing his eyes as if falling to sleep, and his countenance assuming an expression of perfect serenity.

There were no indications of pain, and it was not known that he was dead until the gradually decreasing respiration ceased altogether.

Surrounding the death bed of the President were Secretaries Stanton, Welles and Usher, Attorney-General Speed, Postmaster-General Dennison, M. B. Field, Assistant Secretary of the Treasury, Judge Otto, Assistant Secretary of the Interior, General Halleck, General Meigs, Senator Sumner, R. F. Andrews of New York, General Todd of Dakota, John Hay, Private Secretary, Governor Oglesby of Illinois, General Farnsworth, Mrs. and Miss Kenney, Miss Harris, Captain Robert Lincoln, son of the President, and Doctors E. W. Abbott, R. K. Stone, C. D. Gatch, Neal Hall and Mr. Lieberman. Secretary McCulloch remained with the President until about five o'clock, and Chief Justice Chase, after several hours' attendance during the night, returned early this morning.

Immediately after the President's death, a Cabinet meeting was called by Secretary Stanton, and held in the room in which the corpse lay. Secretaries Stanton, Welles and Usher, Postmaster General Dennison and Attorney General Speed were present. The results of the conference are unknown.

The President's body was removed from the private residence opposite Ford's Theater to the Executive Mansion this morning at half past nine o'clock, in a hearse wrapped in the American flag. It was escorted by a small guard of cavalry, General Augur and other military officers following on foot.

A dense crowd accompanied the remains to the White House, where a military guard excluded the crowd, allowing none but persons of the household and personal friends of the deceased to enter the premises, Senator Yates and Representative Farnsworth being among the number admitted.

The body has been embalmed, with a view to its removal to Illinois.

Flags over the Departments and throughout the city are at half mast. Scarcely any business is being transacted anywhere, either on private or public account.

Our citizens, without any preconcert whatever, are draping their premises with festoons of mourning.

The bells are tolling mournfully. All is the deepest gloom and sadness. Strong men weep in the streets. The grief is wide spread and deep, and in strange contrast to the joy so lately manifested over our recent military victories.

This is indeed a day of gloom.

The Government Departments are closed by order, and will be draped with the usual emblems of mourning.

The roads leading to and from the city are guarded by the military, and the utmost circumspection is observed as to all attempting to enter or leave the city.

Washington, D.C.

An autopsy was held at eleven o'clock this morning of the President's body by Surgeon General Barnes, aided by a number of assistants. On examination, the ball, which, as has been stated, entered the back of the head, near the base of the brain was found to have taken a direct course toward the right eye, the orbital bone of which it struck, and rebounding lodged several inches from the surface.

The ball was found to have been flattened, and resembled in shape the canteen commonly carried by the soldiers. The orifice in the back of the head is perfectly round and the skull un-fractured, so close was the murderer when he fired the fatal shot. The circular piece of skull was taken from the head one and a half inches from the orifice.

The piece, together with the Derringer pistol left behind by the assassin and the bullet, were duly sealed and deposited in the War Department.

The corpse of the late President was laid out in the room known as the "guests' room," northwest wing of the White House. It was dressed in the suit of black clothes worn by him at his late inauguration. A placid smile rests upon his features, and the deceased seems to be in a calm sleep. White flowers were placed upon the pillow and over the breast.

The corpse of the President was to be laid out in state in the east room on Tuesday, in order to give the public an opportunity to see once more the features of him they loved so well.

The catafalque upon which the body will rest is to be placed in the south part of the east room, and is somewhat similar in style to that used on the occasion of the death of President Harrison. Steps will be placed at the side to enable the public to mount to a position to get a perfect view of the face. The catafalque will be lined with fluted white satin, and on the outside it will be covered with black cloth and black velvet.

The funeral car, which is being prepared for the occasion, is to be a magnificent affair. It is to be built on a hearse body. The extreme length will be fourteen feet. The body of the car will be covered with black cloth, from which will hang large festoons of cloth on the sides and ends, gathered and fastened by large rosettes of white and black satin over bows of white and black velvet. The bed of the car on which the coffin will rest will be eight feet from the ground, in order to give a full view of the coffin, and over this will rise a canopy, the supports of which will be draped with black cloth and velvet. The top of the car will be decorated with plumes. The car will be drawn by six or eight horses, each led by a groom.

It was ascertained, some weeks ago, from personal friends of the late President, that he had received several private letters warning him that an attempt would probably be made upon his life. But to this he did not seem to attach much if any importance. It has always been thought that he was not sufficiently careful of his individual safety on his last visit to Virginia.

It is known that on frequent occasions he would start from the Executive Mansion for his summer country residence at the Soldiers' Home without the usual cavalry escort, which often hurried and overtook him before he had proceeded far. It has always been understood that this escort was accepted by him only on the importunity of his friends as a matter of precaution.

The President before retiring to bed would, when important military events were progressing, visit the War Department, generally alone, passing over the dark intervening ground even at late hours on repeated occasions; and after the warning letters had been received, several close and intimate friends, armed for any emergency, were careful that he should not continue his visits without their company. For himself the President seemed to have no fears.

Washington, D.C.
9:40 o'clock a.m.

Major General Augur, commanding the Department of Washington, has offered a reward of ten thousand dollars to the party or parties arresting the murderer of the President, and the assassin of the Secretary of State and his son.

It is now ascertained with reasonable certainty that two assassins were engaged in the horrible crime, Wilkes Booth being the one that shot the President and the other a companion of his whose name is not known, but whose description is so clear that he can hardly escape. It appears from a letter found in Booth's trunk that the murder was planned before the 4th of March, but fell through then because the accomplice backed out until "Richmond could be heard from."

The Rebel assassin is described by the colored porter on duty at the entrance door of the house as a man in light pantaloons, and dark frock coat, buttoned up, about the size, to use his own words, of Mr. George E. Baker.

He represented that he was sent by Doctor Verdi with a prescription of medicine for Secretary Seward, which he was told to deliver personally, with the doctor's instructions how it should be taken. The party declined to admit him, a parley ensued, and full five, minutes passed before the assassin effected admission into the house.

With a directness of walk which would indicate knowledge of the house, he went straight up to the Secretary's bedroom and entered it.

The character of physician was instantly thrown off, and that of a determined murderer put on. There were four persons in the room: Major Augustus Seward, Miss Fanny Seward, the Secretary's daughter, a hired man nurse, and the chief messenger of the State Department, also acting as nurse.

The Secretary lay in bed on his back; the assassin jumped on the bed and endeavored to cut the throat of his victim.

He inflicted three different wounds upon it. While engaged in it the man nurse had flung himself upon his bed and thrown his arms around him and striven to pull him off the bed.

The murderer instantly reversed the action of his knife, and stabbed and cut quickly over his shoulder, and drove the nurse off his back. He then sprang from the bed and engaged in a fight for escape with all that opposed him.

He stabbed the chief messenger dangerously in the breast, stabbed Major Seward in the arm and beat him over the head and face with a heavy pistol and disabled him, and attacked Frederick Seward, who had entered the room from an adjoining chamber, and gave him a scalp wound with his knife, which, strange to say, commenced at the forehead, passed over the top of the head, and extended part way down the back of the head, and then struck him, either with the pistol or a slung-shot, a heavy blow, which knocked him down insensible.

The way of escape was clear; the assassin ran downstairs, mounted his horse and rode rapidly away.

The Secretary's throat has three distinct gashes; no artery has been severed, and although much effusion of blood has taken place, and a terrible shock given to his enfeebled system, hopes are entertained of his recovery.

Frederick Seward sustained a fracture of the skull. Portions of bone have been removed from the wound. The unfavorable symptoms of stupefaction and vomiting ensued upon the injury, and have characterized his condition during the night.

Major Seward is about this morning, one arm in a sling and his head and face bandaged.

The department messenger is considered to be dangerously wounded. The hired nurse's wounds, although numerous, are not serious.

The assassin is said to have been traced by the horse he rode, and which was hired from a livery stable here, to the Long Bridge, and over into Virginia. Both the man and his crime are the slave power.

New York, New York

The gloomiest day in our national history dawned upon us this morning, and dark days have not been infrequent during the last five years. The astounding news that President Lincoln had been basely assassinated by a desperate Rebel, while sitting, oblivious of danger, in a theater at Washington on Friday night, and that an assault, with similar deadly intent, had been made a few minutes later upon Secretary Seward, while lying helpless on his bed, shocked, mortified and exasperated the entire Northern people on Saturday. At first there were many who, in spite of telegraphic information to the contrary, hoped that the injuries of the President would not prove fatal. But a few hours later came the darker intelligence that the blow of the assassin had been sure—that our wise, good, noble, generous President was indeed no more.

The excitement everywhere was intense. There was but one expression of sentiment—that of the deepest sorrow at the loss of a wise chieftain and excellent man, mingled with horror, indignation and exasperation against his assassin, as well as against all the leaders of this accursed Rebellion, who are, of course, more or less directly implicated in the foul murder. A general gloom seemed to pervade the entire community. Not only genuine loyalists, who had loved and honored the murdered chieftain, but thousands who had never given him a hearty support, were horror-stricken and incensed. We did not see a smiling face as we walked down Broadway, but everywhere could read in the bent brows and firm pressed lips of the moving throng regret, indignation and vengeance.

At an early hour in the morning the hundreds of flags and streamers, which on the previous day fluttered so victoriously in the sunshine as indicative of a nation's jubilation, were slowly and sadly disappearing, one by one, only to reappear again dismally hung with sable streamers, as significant of the awful cloud which had so swiftly gathered in the sky (but yesterday so bright and blue!) and descended upon the Nation. Before noon every banner bore the ominous black accompaniments; the fronts of most of our public buildings and many private residences were also draped in the same melancholy livery; the flags on the shipping were all lowered to half-mast, and the sorrow deepened as it grew apace.

The same feeling was probably manifested in every locality to which the mournful intelligence could be transmitted by telegraph.

In Brooklyn, Jersey City, Newark and other towns and cities in the vicinity, the sentiment is identical. If the expressions of sorrow are profound and lamentable, the curses against the assassin and his abettors are no less loud and deep.

"No more compromise! No more forgiveness!" is the one earnest expression upon thousands of quivering lips. "We have but one thing for all the Rebel leaders now—a dog's death by the gallows-tree! It shall be war to the knife hereafter."

On the receipt of the intelligence of the President's assassination in this city, Mayor Gunther immediately issued a proclamation recommending the suspension of business, and that public mourning for our departed Chief Magistrate be observed. The Common Council met, passed resolutions expressive of sorrow at the National bereavement, directed that their chambers and the public buildings and offices be draped in mourning for thirty days, and adjourned, without transacting any business. The Board of Supervisors passed resolutions testifying their sorrow and respect, and likewise immediately adjourned. In all the Courts similar proceedings occurred.

Dispatches narrating the thrilling events at Washington were received in this city from the State Department and immediately forwarded to the American Minister at London via steamer from Portland.

Collector issued an order closing the Custom House, except for the clearance of vessels, and announcing to the employees that it would be in order to wear crape upon the left arm for thirty days, as an emblem of respect of the deceased President.

Major General Peck issued an order from the headquarters of the Department of the East, directing guns to be fired every half hour at each camp and post on the day following the receipt of the order, and that the National colors be hoisted daily from sunrise to sunset at half-mast until after the occurrence of the funeral obsequies.

The Chamber of Commerce and Produce Exchange met and passed resolutions condemnatory of the outrage which had stricken down the official head of the Republic, pledging their undivided support to his Constitutional successor, and tendering their warmest sympathy in their bereavement and affliction to the families of the late President and of the Secretary of State. Both Boards adjourned without transacting any business, as did also the Stock Exchange, the Petroleum and other Boards.

Philadelphia, Pennsylvania,
Booth's Letter

This letter was in the possession of John S. Clarke, a brother-in-law of Booth. It was handed to Honorable William Millward, United States Marshal, after the news of the assassination of President Lincoln. The envelope was sealed and held "for safe keeping," and was opened when it was heard that J. Wilkes Booth was the assassin:

_____, _____, 1864

My Dear Sir:

You may use this as you think best. But as *some* may wish to know *when, who* and *why,* and as I know not *how* to direct, I give it (in the words of your master),

"To WHOM IT MAY CONCERN:"

Right or wrong, God judge me, not man. For, be my motive good, or bad, of one thing I am sure, the lasting condemnation of the North.

I love peace more than life. Have loved the Union beyond expression. For four years have I waited, hoped and prayed for the dark clouds to break, and for a restoration of our former sunshine. To wait longer would be a crime. All hope for peace is dead. My prayers have proved as idle as my hopes. God's will be done. I go to see and share the bitter end.

I have ever held the South were right. The very nomination of Abraham Lincoln, four years ago, spoke plainly, war—war upon Southern rights and institutions. His election proved it. "Await an overt act." Yes, till you are bound and plundered. What folly! The South was wise. Who thinks of argument or patience when the finger of his enemy presses on the trigger? In a *foreign war* I, too, could say, "Country, right or wrong." But in a struggle *such as ours* (where the brother tries to pierce the brother's heart), for God's sake, choose the right. When a country like this spurns *justice* from her side she forfeits the allegiance of every honest freeman, and should leave him, untrammeled by any fealty so ever, to act as his conscience may approve.

People of the North, to hate tyranny, to love liberty and justice, to strike at wrong and oppression, was the teaching of our fathers. The study of our early history will not let *me* forget it, and may it never.

This country was formed for the *white,* not for the black man. And looking upon *African Slavery* from the same stand-point held by the noble framers of our Constitution, I, for one, have ever considered *it* one of the greatest blessings (both for themselves and us) that God ever bestowed upon a favored nation. Witness heretofore our wealth and power; witness their elevation and enlightenment above their race elsewhere. I have lived among it the most of my life, and have seen *less* harsh treatment from master to man than I have beheld in the North from father to son. Yet, Heaven knows, *no one* would be willing to do *more* for the Negro race than I, could I but see a way to *still better their* condition.

But Lincoln's policy is only preparing the way for their total annihilation. The South *are not, nor have they been fighting* for the continuance of Slavery. The first Battle of Bull Run did away with that idea. Their causes *since for war* have been as *noble* and *greater far than those that urged our fathers on. Even* should we allow they were wrong at the beginning of this contest, *cruelty and injustice* have made the wrong become the *right,* and they stand *now* (before the wonder and admiration of the world) as a noble band of patriotic heroes. Hereafter, reading of *their deeds,* Thermopylae will be forgotten.

When I aided in the capture and execution of John Brown, (who was a murderer on our Western border, and who was fairly *tried* and *convicted,* before an impartial judge and jury, of treason, and who, by the way, has since been made a god), I was proud of my little share in the transaction, for I deemed it my duty and that I was helping our common country to perform an act of justice. But what was a crime in poor John Brown is now considered (by themselves) as the greatest and only virtue of the whole Republican Party. Strange transmigration! *Vice* to become a *virtue,* simply because *more* indulge in it.

I thought then, *as now,* that the abolitionists *were the only traitors* in the land, and that the entire party deserved the same fate of poor old Brown, not because they wish to abolish slavery, but on account of the means they have ever endeavored to use to effect that abolition. If Brown were living I doubt whether he *himself* would set slavery against the Union. Most or many in the North do, and openly curse the Union, if the south is to return and retain a *single right* guaranteed to them by every tie which we once *revered as sacred*, the South can make no choice. It is either extermination or slavery for *themselves* (worse than death) to draw from. I know *my* choice.

I have also studied hard to discover upon what grounds the right of a State to secede has been denied, when our very name, United States, and the Declaration of Independence, *both* provide for secession. But there is no time for words. I write in haste. I know how foolish I shall be deemed for undertaking such a step as this, where, on the one side, I have many friends and everything to make me happy, where my profession *alone* has gained me an income of *more than* twenty thousand dollars a year, and where my great personal ambition in my profession has such a great field for labor. On the other hand, the South has never bestowed upon me one kind word; a place now where I have no friends, except beneath the sod; a place where I must either become a private soldier or a beggar. To give up all the *former* for the *latter,* besides my mother and sisters whom I love so dearly (although they so widely differ with me in opinion), seems insane; but God is my judge. I love *justice* more than I do a country that disowns it; more than fame and wealth; more (Heaven pardon me if wrong) than a happy home. I have never been upon a battlefield; but O, my countrymen, could you all but see the *reality* or effects of this horrid war, as I have seen them (in *every State,* save Virginia), I know you would think like me, and would pray the Almighty to create in the Northern mind a sense of *right* and *justice* (even should it possess no seasoning of mercy), and that He would dry up this sea of blood between us, which is daily growing wider. Alas! Poor country, is she to meet her threatened doom? Four years ago I would have given a thousand lives to see her remain (as I had always known her) powerful and unbroken. And even now I would hold my life as naught to see her what she was. O my friends, if the fearful scenes of the past four years had never been enacted, or if what has been had been but a frightful dream, from which we could now awake, with what overflowing hearts could we bless our God and pray for His continued favor.

How I have loved the *old flag* an never now be known. A few years since and the entire world could boast of *none* so pure and spotless. But I have of late been seeing and hearing of the *bloody deeds* which she has *been made the emblem,* and would shudder to think how changed she had grown. O how I have longed to see her break from the mist of blood and death that circles round her folds, spoiling her beauty and tarnishing her honor. But no; day by day has she been dragged deeper and deeper into cruelty and oppression, till now (in my eyes) her once bright red stripes look like *bloody gashes* on the face of Heaven. I look now upon my early admiration of her glories as a dream. My love (as things stand today) is for the South alone. Nor do I deem it a dishonor in attempting to make for her a prisoner of this man, to whom she owes so much of misery. If success attends me, I go penniless to her side. They say she has found *that* "last ditch" which the North have so long derided, and been endeavoring to force her in, forgetting they are our brothers, and that it's impolite to goad an enemy to madness. Should I reach her in safety and find it true, I will proudly beg permission to triumph or die in that same "ditch" by her side.

A Confederate, doing duty upon his own responsibility,

J. Wilkes Booth

Sunday, April 16, 1865

Washington, D.C.

Yesterday morning Attorney General Speed waited upon the Honorable Andrew Johnson, Vice President of the United States, and officially informed him of the sudden and unexpected decease of President Lincoln, and stated that an early hour might be appointed for the inauguration of his successor. The following is a copy of communication referred to:

Washington City, April 15, 1865

To Andrew Johnson, Vice President of the United States

Sir:

Abraham Lincoln, President of the United States, was shot by an assassin last evening at Ford's Theater, in this city, and died at the hour of 7:22 o'clock. At about the same time at which the President was shot, an assassin entered the sick chamber of the Honorable W. H. Seward, Secretary of State, and stabbed him in several places in the throat, neck and face, severely if not mortally wounding him. Other members of the Secretary's family were dangerously wounded by the assassin while making his escape. By the death of President Lincoln the office of President has devolved, under the Constitution, upon you. The emergency of the Government demands that you should immediately qualify according to the requirements of the Constitution and enter upon the duties of President of the United States. If you will please make known your pleasure, such arrangements as you deem proper will be made.

Your obedient servants,

       Hugh McCulloch, Secretary of the Treasury
Edwin M. Stanton, Secretary of War
      Gideon Welles, Secretary of the Navy
      William Dennison, Postmaster General
      J. P. Usher, Secretary of the Interior
      James Speed, Attorney General

Mr. Johnson requested that the ceremonies take place at his rooms at the Kirkwood House, in this city, at ten o'clock in the morning.

The Hon. Salmon P. Chase, Chief Justice of the United States, was notified of the fact, and desired to be in attendance to administer the oath of office.

At the above named hour the following gentlemen assembled in the Vice President's room to participate in the ceremony: The Hon. Salmon P. Chase, the Hon. Hugh McCulloch, Secretary of the Treasury; Mr. Attorney General Speed, F. P. Blair, Sr., the Hon. Montgomery Blair, Senator Foot, of Vermont, Yates, of Illinois, Ramsey, of Minnesota, Stewart, of Nevada, Hale, of New Hampshire, and General Farnsworth, of Illinois.

After the presentation of the above letter, the Chief Justice administered the following oath to Mr. Johnson:

"I do solemnly swear that I will faithfully execute the office of President of the United States, and will, to the best of my ability, preserve, protect and defend the Constitution of the United States,"

After receiving the oath and being declared President of the *United States, Mr. Johnson remarked:*

"Gentlemen, I must be permitted to say that I have been almost overwhelmed by the announcement of the sad event which has so recently occurred. I feel incompetent to perform duties so important and responsible as those which have been so unexpectedly thrown upon me. As to an indication of my policy which may be pursued by me in the administration of the Government, I have to say that that must be left for development as the administration progresses. The message or declaration must be made by the acts as they transpire. The only assurance that I can now give of the future is reference to the past. The course which I have taken in the past in connection with this Rebellion must be regarded as a guarantee of the future. My past public life, which has been long and laborious, has been founded, as I in good conscience believe upon a great principal of right, which lies at the basis of all things. The best energies of my life have been spent in endeavoring to establish and perpetuate the principles of free government, and I believe that the Government, in passing through its present perils, will settle down upon principles consonant with popular rights, more permanent and enduring than heretofore. I must be permitted to say, if I understand the feelings of my own heart, I have long labored to ameliorate and elevate the condition of the great mass of the American people. Toil and an honest advocacy of the great principles of free government have been my

lot. The duties have been mine—the consequences are God's. This has been the foundation of my political creed. I feel that in the end the Government will triumph, and that these great principles will be permanently established. In conclusion, gentlemen, let me say that I want your encouragement and countenance. I shall ask and rely upon you and others in carrying the Government through its present perils. I feel in making this request that it will be heartily responded to by you and all other patriots and lovers of the rights and interests of a free people."

At the conclusion of the above remarks the President received the kind wishes of the friends by whom he was surrounded.

Harpers Ferry, Virginia

News reaches us that a flag of truce has been received from Imboden's Rebel forces, consisting of two regiments, proposing to surrender on the same terms granted Lee's army.

The Rebel General Rosser, on hearing of Lee's surrender, declared his determination to fight it out, but was deserted by his men, and he started to join Johnston in North Carolina.

Monday, April 17, 1865

Raleigh, North Carolina,
Union Account

On Monday, the 10th instant, we broke camp and marched by a circuitous route over a low swampy country to Pikesville, corduroying the roads for nearly half the distance. The Fourth Division of the Fifteenth Corps having been in rear of the command did not get into camp until near four o'clock the following morning, very much fatigued and soaked through with rain, but in the most admirable spirits. Pikesville is a station on the Weldon Railroad, and has a small settlement of some half-dozen houses which are inhabited by what are commonly known in the South as "the poor white trash."

From Pikesville the command marched on Tuesday morning to Lowell Factory, the rear of the column getting into camp at about ten o'clock that night. The Rebels tore up the planking of the bridge over Little River, expecting thereby to delay the march of our army. The damage, however, was easily repaired, and did not delay the command for over an hour; they would probably have done more damage to the bridge had they not been prevented by the timely arrival of the mounted infantry, who rapidly drove them away. The First Division of the Fifteenth Corps, under the command of General Hazen, was in the advance of the Corps, and deserves great credit for the speedy manner in which they repaired the bridge and removed all the obstructions on the road.

Lowell Factory, from which the place derives its name, is owned by a Quaker, and is a small settlement of about seventy-five inhabitants, consisting principally of women and children, who are all employed as operatives in the cotton factory.

While waiting at Lowell Factory for the repairing of the roads toward Smithfield, the glorious news of the surrender of Lee's Army was officially communicated to the Command, and produced the wildest excitement.

The Fourth Division of the Fifteenth Corps were summoned together by their gallant commander, Major General John M. Corse, and after the playing of several national and patriotic airs by the band, the whole command joined in singing "John Brown," and the "Star Spangled Banner," with a zest which has seldom been equaled, and never excelled.

After repeated calls for General Corse, their gallant and popular leader, he was induced to come forward and address them, which he did in a short, eloquent and inspiring speech, reminding his listeners *"That there was yet a man named Johnston in the field, commanding a ragged mob commonly known as the Confederate Army of the West, and that by patient perseverance and a few more miles of corduroying, he would be brought to bay and forced also to surrender his command."* General Corse's remarks were loudly applauded, and he was in turn followed by General Rice, commanding a Brigade of the Fourth Division.

After this grand jubilee was over, the bugle sounded the assembly, and the men fell into the ranks and marched forward with the utmost spirit and enthusiasm. On Wednesday night the Fifteenth Corps encamped at Pineville, and the Seventh Corps, after crossing the Neuse River at Watson's Bridge, encamped for the night, and the next day moved forward to within a short distance of Raleigh. The Fifteenth Corps, in the meantime, advanced on the east side of the Neuse River by Eagle Rock, crossing at Hinton's Bridge and marching to within five miles of Raleigh, into which place they made their triumphal entry today at about ten o'clock, and were reviewed, together with the Seventeenth Corps, by Major General Sherman and Major General Howard, and their respective staffs, in front of the State House or Capitol Buildings.

Generals Sherman and Howard took their position on the south side of the capitol building and immediately in front of the bronze statue of Washington.

The different divisions composing the Army of the Tennessee marched "by column of companies right in front," bands playing, drums beating and colors flying, and presented a most imposing spectacle, with their tattered and ragged battle flags which they had heroically carried on battle-fields far too numerous to mention.

What a grand and glorious spectacle to witness! In eight hours and a half one continuous, almost never ceasing flow of men, and such men as are seldom seen in any army in the world. Strong, stout, athletic veterans, who have stood the shock of battle, and come out proud victors on innumerable battle-fields, from Fort Donelson, Tennessee, to Raleigh, North Carolina, their dead but never-to-be-forgotten heroes who sleep in the soldier's grave, on many well-fought battle-fields, strew the line of march, and bear undying testimony to their valor and devotion to the cause in which they all embarked. God bless them! May their memories ever be green in the hearts of their countrymen!

Some forty-six railroad cars and several engines were captured by Kilpatrick's cavalry, together with several thousand prisoners, some of whom have voluntarily come inside of our lines and given themselves up after becoming convinced of the utter hopelessness of their cause.

Johnston's Army, which retreated the day before our advance arrived here, is known to number from twenty to twenty-five thousand men. Some of his command retreated through Hillsborough to Greensborough, but the main portion of his army is known to be encamped this side of Greensborough, which is the junction of the Raleigh and Richmond railroad, at which place Jeff. Davis is known to be.

Governor Vance left this town a few hours before the arrival of our advance. It is stated by good authority that he is desirous of returning inside the lines and surrendering the State to General Sherman. If this be so General Sherman will give him every protection, and is really anxious that he should return and convene the Legislature, a majority of which are known to be loyal men.

It is expected that Sheridan's, Stoneman's and Kilpatrick's Cavalries will form a junction sometime within the next five days, and hold Johnston in check until this army can come up with him and deliver the final blow to the Rebellion which has for nearly four years cursed this fair laud. The citizens here all express a desire, now that Lee has surrendered his army that Johnston will do the same thing and put an end to this desolating war. It is questionable whether or not he has heart and sense sufficient to take this view of the subject.

It is stated on good authority that the cavalry belonging to Lee's army have nearly all succeeded in making a junction with Wheeler and Wade Hampton, and that the united cavalry force of the enemy now in our front numbers at least ten thousand men. It is also rumored, but not generally credited, that a number of stragglers from the Rebel Army of Northern Virginia have made their appearance inside of Johnston's lines and have been pressed into the ranks of his army.

Louisville, Kentucky

The guerrilla chief Major Walker Taylor, Captain Taylor, and five of his men, who surrendered themselves to Dr. Owens, a member of the Kentucky Legislature, under the late order of General Palmer, arrived here today.

Washington, D.C.

A large body of guerrillas has been hovering along the opposite bank of the Potomac the past few days. Our forces have had one spirited skirmish with them, in which we drove them after an obstinate resistance. It is supposed they came there to cover the retreat of the Washington assassins.

Secretary Seward's symptoms are much improved from this forenoon. He sat up in bed and had the papers read to him. Frederick Seward recovered his consciousness this afternoon so far as to recognize his wife.

Numerous arrests of indiscrete or suspected parties have taken place today. They cause much excitement. Reports prevail that Surratt is among the number, but this is not true.

David Herold   Mary Surratt   George Atzerodt

Information has been received by the Government from General Sherman that he was in communication with General Johnston with a view to the surrender of the latter.

General Sherman would offer the same terms that General Grant did to General Lee, and it was supposed they would be accepted.

Army of the Potomac, Burkesville Junction, Virginia

Quite an interesting event took place at headquarters this morning. The Sixth Corps having taken eighteen flags during the recent short campaign, it was arranged that the men who captured them, accompanied by their commands, should march to the vicinity of General Meade's quarters, and there turn in the colors taken from the Rebels. General Meade addressed these heroes in an appropriate speech, in which he thanked them individually for their gallantry, and the entire corps for the important part they had performed in being the first to break through the enemy's line at Petersburg, as well as for their conduct in pursuing and aiding in the utter defeat and capture of the principal army of the Confederacy. In conclusion, General Meade announced that every man who had taken a flag should have a furlough for thirty days, and that each one should carry his own and present it to the War Department at

Washington. The scene was brilliant, and much enjoyed by all who witnessed it.

The announcement of the assassination of Mr. Lincoln and Mr. Seward and his son was received throughout this army with the utmost sorrow. Every man seemed to think it the greatest calamity that could have possibly happened just at this time. Should the assassins be found and turned over to the army to be dealt with their punishment would be swift and sure, and such as to strike into the heart of every sympathizer with treason in the United States. The citizens living in the country here express their deep regret at the occurrence, and think it the worst thing that could possibly have happened for the Southern people just at this juncture.

The larger part of this army is now concentrated at Burkesville Junction, and is taking a short rest after their recent hard work. But it is thought that a movement of the main body of troops will soon be made toward Petersburg and Richmond. The cavalry and the colored divisions of the Twenty-fifth Corps have already gone in that direction. In fact such a change will have to be made in a few days, as the capacity of the Southside Railroad in its present condition is wholly inadequate to supply so many troops with rations and animals with forage. The latter have suffered much the past week, and large numbers have been abandoned for want of feed. The train which arrived this evening was thirty-two hours on the road from City Point to the junction, three or four engines having run off the track at different points.

Winchester, Virginia

Mosby surrendered his force to General Chapman at Berryville today. The terms of surrender were the same as those accorded General Lee and his army.

Raleigh, North Carolina,
Union Account

General Sherman and staff left the Central Depot at 8 o'clock this morning, with an engine and two cars, for Durham's Station, to meet General Johnston. None but his staff accompanied him.

The train which bore General Sherman to the front to receive the surrender of Johnston's army had been gone less than an hour, when the telegraph flashed to General Howard's headquarters the horrible and astounding news of the assassination of the President of the United States, and the fatal wounding of Mr. Seward and his son. For the greater part of the forenoon, the dreadful tidings were suppressed, and only known to a few persons immediately about headquarters; but by degrees it began to circulate about in whispers through the town, and though generally disbelieved, created a profound feeling of horror and alarm. A courier was immediately dispatched with the news to General Sherman, who had already arrived at Durham's Station, and was in conference with Johnston when the messenger arrived. Officers hurried into town from the camps to learn the facts, or to verify the report. It was too dreadful to be believed. Crowds of officers and soldiers met and discussed in suppressed breath the probabilities of its truth, and it was not until noon that the report could be traced to a trustworthy source—the telegraph operator and officers at General Howard's headquarters, fearing the effect of the news upon the soldiers, kept it quiet. A feeling of awful suspense, of horrible foreboding, spread over city and camps. Officers met and passed in silence, scarcely daring to break the dreadful secret to each other. Universal gloom settled like a pall over the place. Sad faces were everywhere, all hearts were heavy, all minds appalled by the dreadful news of this triple murder. At General Schofield's headquarters and other places I have seen officers and men in tears, as if mourning for the loss of a father or beloved friend. A sorrow like that which fell upon Egypt when the angel of death smote the first born, broods over all minds. Others with clinched fists and firm-set teeth were calling for vengeance upon the *whole race of traitors, from Jeff Davis down.* A people who could conceive of such transcendent wickedness and everyone who can apologize for or excuse it, say they ought to be *blotted from the face of the earth.*

The whole current of feeling in the army has been changed by this crowning act of villainy—this final fiendish stab at the Nation's life. Brave and noble men who but yesterday were reading the God-like plea of Mr. Beecher for pardon and conciliation for the Rebels, and were half consenting to a general amnesty to the bad men who have bathed the land in blood, and brought so much woe upon us, today cry with trumpet tongues for justice. General Johnston on hearing the news declared it was the heaviest blow which has ever fallen upon the Confederacy. He appeared very much troubled by the intelligence.

Among intelligent officers this is regarded as only the beginning of a reign of terror which has been long maturing—the opening of a bloody drama to be enacted by hired assassins, in obedience to a deeply laid conspiracy. That now, beaten in the open field, honorably defeated in war, they intend to adopt the assassin's last resort; and that our chief public men, and even our generals, are marked as victims of the bullet or the knife. This is the natural fruit of rebellion—the appendix to the May mob and the firing of New York hotels.

The officers and soldiers everywhere speak in terms of the highest admiration of the great and good man who has fallen. He seems to have been spared by a kind Providence to witness the fruit of his long and wearisome labors for the salvation of his country, and then, has mingled his blood with the thousands who have fallen in the struggle, in a manner to show to the world as no other event could teach, the fiendish spirit which has animated these enemies of liberty, of the country, and of mankind. I hear nothing but words of the most affectionate eulogy of the departed President, and earnest prayers ascend from many thousand hearts that God would disappoint the assassins, and yet spare the precious lives of Mr. Seward and his son.

Augusta, Georgia, Confederate Account

The Yankees assaulted Columbus on Sunday, the 16th, at noon, and skirmished with our forces through the streets until sunset, when they occupied the city.

The command of the enemy, supposed to number four thousand, advanced from Montgomery and destroyed the Montgomery and West Point Railroads.

Private property at Montgomery was respected. All the cotton, Government stores, manufacturing establishments, railroads and boats, were destroyed.

Salisbury, North Carolina, was re-occupied by our troops on the 14th. The Yankees did not do much damage in the place.

Telegraphic lines are open today, but nothing has been received north of that place.

The Yankee raid destroyed the depot and some rolling stock at Sumterville, South Carolina. No private property molested.

The enemy then moved on Camden, where a large amount of stock of the South Carolina Railroad had been accumulated.

General Lewis, with his Kentucky brigade, overtook the enemy about Camden, and after a short but spirited battle the Yankees were forced to retreat rapidly, being driven in confusion toward Georgetown. The Kentuckians pursued with alacrity.

From Columbus papers we cull the annexed news in regard to the situation in Alabama:

A large number of refugees have arrived in Columbus from Montgomery.

General Forrest, when last heard from, was twelve miles from Selma. It was thought he would cross the river and pursue the Yankees.

The Yankee force is composed entirely of cavalry and mounted infantry, with some artillery.

Among the refugees who arrived in Columbus are Governor Watts and other officers of the State Government of Alabama. They are deeply chagrined at the capture of their capital by six thousand Yankees, but feel conscious that they did all in their power to prevent it. The Governor has proceeded to Eufaula.

A dispatch from Talladega, dated April 7, states that a division of Yankees from Elyton are at Montevallo; a portion of them are also at Shelby Springs. Scouts report a body of the enemy at Ashville, taking stock, &c.

It is stated that there were about eighty thousand bales of cotton in Montgomery, in the warehouses. This was burned on Tuesday evening. There was a large quantity of cotton scattered through the streets; whether this was burned also is not known. If it was, a large part of the city must also have suffered a similar fate from its close proximity to the combustible material. That portion of the city in the neighborhood of the different warehouses must have suffered, and it is hardly possible that the buildings adjacent could pass unscathed.

The latest telegraphic dispatch from Montgomery was sent from that place at half past five o'clock on Tuesday evening.

Montgomery was evacuated in great confusion. Liquor was used freely. All commissary stores were distributed to the people. It is feared that much private property has been destroyed.

The Columbus Times speaks of the situation as follows:

"Thus is the great State of Alabama abandoned to the mercy of six thousand or eight thousand Yankees, who have in their power to desolate the whole of the territory unopposed. It is certainly the most disgraceful incident of the war. Alabama will now reap the fruits of the policy of her Legislature in refusing the Governor the power which he asked, of organizing her able bodied population at home and compelling them to fight in defense of the State."

Tuesday, April 18, 1865

Raleigh, North Carolina

After a two days' conference between Major General Sherman and Major General Joseph E. Johnston, commanding the Rebel forces east of the Mississippi River, with the concurrence of Jefferson Davis, and in the presence and with the advice of General John C. Breckenridge, the whole remaining Rebel army from the Potomac to the Rio Grande has been surrendered to the forces of the United States.

The conference was sought by General Johnston on the day following the occupation of Raleigh by the Union Army—the 14th—a flag of truce being sent in, with a request for an armistice, and a statement of the best terms on which General Johnston would be permitted to surrender the army under his command. General Sherman sent out Colonel McCoy with his ultimatum, and after some two days' delay, during which General Johnston's efforts were somewhat embarrassed by the refractory and mutinous position of Wade Hampton, of South Carolina, a personal interview took place between the two chiefs of the opposing armies, at Bennett's house, five miles beyond Durham's Station, on the North Carolina railroad, midway between the lines.

The conference was strictly private, only Wade Hampton being present with General Johnston on the first day, Monday, and John C. Breckenridge taking Hampton's place on the second day, Tuesday. The only members of the Rebel staff present were Captains Johnston and Hampton, the latter a son of the Rebel South Carolinian, a chip of the old block. The generals were treated with in their characters as simply commanders of the insurrectionary forces. The Southern Confederacy was not recognized, although Jefferson Davis was understood to be a party consenting to the surrender. Wade Hampton is understood to have withdrawn from the conference, and signified his intention, like the Irishman, to continue the fight on his own hook, which, it is devoutly hoped, he will do. If he and South Carolina have not enough of the war, they can readily be treated to another dose.

The terms settled for the surrender are understood to be substantially those accorded to General Lee by General Grant, with this exception, that the troops of each State are required to march to their respective capitals and then turn over their arms and all the public property in their possession, and be paroled under the supervision of officers to be designated for that purpose. Thus, the army is to be disbanded, and each soldier is required to return home, and not again to take up arms against the Government. The officers, like those of General Lee's army, are permitted to carry with them their side-arms and private effects. These terms are subject to the approval of the Washington Government, and only go into effect upon such ratification. Meantime the two armies maintain their respective positions, and all hostilities cease—until the return of the messenger of General Sherman, who has already proceeded to Washington with the stipulations, of which the foregoing is a brief outline.

This sweeps from existence as an armed force against the Government all the Rebel troops known to the Confederacy, and makes outlaws and guerrillas of all parties who remain in arms against the constituted authorities: The forces of Kirby Smith west of the Mississippi; all the irregular cavalry and roving bands in Texas, Missouri and elsewhere; the garrison at Mobile and at other points in Alabama and Southern Tennessee—all troops of whatever name and nation who have been ranged on the side of the Rebellion, whether as belonging to any recognized commander, or playing the guerrilla upon their own hook for private plunder.

General Johnston expresses deep and apparently sincere sorrow and much concern at the assassination of President Lincoln, in which he was joined by each Confederate officer present. General Johnston regards it as the most terrible blow yet inflicted upon the Confederate cause, and the Southern people, and seems deeply to deplore the event, coming as it does upon the close of this great struggle.

The Progress, of this city, contains the following order from General Sherman, following the announcement from Secretary Stanton:

Washington, D. C, April 15—p. m.

Major General Sherman:

President Lincoln was murdered about ten o'clock last night in his private box at Ford's Theater, in this city, by an assassin who shot him in the head with a pistol ball. About the same hour Mr. Seward's house was entered by another assassin, who stabbed the Secretary in several places, but it is thought he may possibly recover, but his son, Fred, may possibly die of wounds received from the assassin. The assassin of the President leaped from the box brandishing a dagger, exclaiming, *Sic semper tyrannis,* and that

Virginia was revenged. Mr. Lincoln fell senseless from his seat, and continued in that state until 7:22 this morning, at which time he breathed his last. Vice President Johnson now becomes President and will take the oath of office and assume the duties today.

E. M. Stanton,
Secretary of War

Headquarters Military Division of the Mississippi In the Field, Special Field Order No. 50

The General commanding announces, with pain and sorrow, that on the 11th inst., at the theater in Washington City, his Excellency the President of the United States, Mr. Lincoln, was assassinated by one who uttered the State motto of Virginia. At the same time the Secretary of State, Mr. Seward, whilst suffering from a broken arm, was also stabbed by another murderer in his own house, but still survives, and his son was wounded, supposed fatally.

It is believed by persons capable of judging that other high officers were designed to share the same fate. Thus it seems that our enemy, despairing of meeting us in manly warfare, begins to resort to the assassin's tools. Your General does not wish you to infer that this is universal, for he knows that the great mass of the Confederate army would scorn to sanction such acts, but he believes it the legitimate consequence of rebellion against rightful authority.

We have met every phase which this war has assumed, and must now be prepared for it in its last and worst shape, that of assassins and guerrillas; but woe unto the people who seek to expend their wild passions in such a manner for there is but one dread result.

By order of
W. T. Sherman,
Major General
L. M. Dayton,

Major and Assistant Adjutant General

There is much evident anxiety among the citizens on account of the changed feeling in the army, and the crisis is now a most painful one, which is greatly aggravated by the delay in the surrender of Johnston's army. Should anything go wrong now, and negotiations fail, woe to North Carolina when this army resumes its march—woe to Rebels everywhere.

General Sherman went back to Durham's Station at eight o'clock this morning to resume negotiations. There is no difficulty about the surrender of the Rebel army, but there are other and collateral questions on a settlement of which Johnston insists, and which General Sherman hesitates to approve. It is supposed to cover some guarantee for the lives or pardon of Jeff Davis and the chief traitors, which it is doubtful if he obtains. I give this only as rumor—not as official. Pending negotiations there is, properly, much reticence at headquarters. I have arrangements for giving you the fullest and quickest news of the result.

The great and overshadowing calamity, however, will chill all enthusiasm over the event, and I doubt if we hear a single cheer upon the occasion from the troops.

Washington, D.C.

Our capture of Rebel artillery, since the 1st of December last, may be briefly summed up as follows:

Captured by General Thomas, from the Rebel General Hood in his Nashville campaign – 72.

By General Sherman at Savannah - 160.

By General Terry, Admiral Porter and General Schofield from Fort Fisher to Wilmington, inclusive – 180.

By General Gilmore at Charleston, from Sherman's flank movement – 450.

By General Sherman, enroute through South and North Carolinas – 85.

By General Sheridan in the Charlottesville raid – 17.

By General Grant's forces around Petersburg – 75.

Around and in Richmond – 500.

By Canby at Mobile – 75.

By Stoneman at Salisbury -19.

By Wilson at Selma – 22.

Grand total - 1,655.

Wednesday, April 19, 1865

Raleigh, North Carolina
Special Field Orders No. 58

General Sherman publishes the following order to the army:

The General Commanding announces to the army a suspension of hostilities, and an agreement with General Johnston and other high officials, which, when formally ratified, will make peace from the Potomac to the Rio Grande.

Until the absolute peace is arranged, a line passing through Terrell's Mount, Chapel Hill, Mount University, Durham's Station and West Point, on the Neuse, will separate the two armies.

Each Army Commander will group his camps entirely with a view to comfort, health and good police. All the details of military discipline must still be maintained, and the General believes that in a few days it will be his good fortune to conduct you to your homes.

The fame of this army for courage, industry and discipline is admitted all over the world. Then let each officer and man see that it is not stained by any act of vulgarity, rowdyism or petty crime.

The cavalry will patrol the front line. General Howard will take charge of the district from Raleigh, up to the cavalry; General Slocum to the left of Raleigh, and General Schofield in Raleigh, its right and rear.

Quartermasters and Commissaries will keep their supplies up to a light load for their wagons, and the Railroad Superintendent will arrange a depot for the convenience of each separate army. By order of

> W. T. Sherman,
> Major General
> L. M. Dayton,
> Assistant Adjutant General

The order on being read to the different commands at evening parade caused the greatest enthusiasm among the troops.

General Schofield has issued his order for a review by the General in Chief of the Army of the Ohio. The Tenth Army Corps, Major General Terry, commanding, will pass in review tomorrow, and the Twenty-third Army Corps on the day following.

He makes a disposition of the troops for garrison duty, and appoints their different camps around the city. A brigade of General

Ames's Division of the Tenth Army Corps will relieve the Twenty-third Army Corps on duty in the city, and, until further orders, constitute the garrison of the town. He closes the order as follows:

"The attention of all officers and soldiers is called to special orders No. 58, Headquarters Middle Division of the Mississippi, announcing a suspension of hostilities, preliminary to peace throughout the land. It is the duty of every officer and soldier to aid in sustaining the honor of the army in this new relation, as they have so nobly done in many a bloody field. Let everyone determine that a few individuals shall not tarnish the fair fame of all."

Raleigh, North Carolina

The negotiations between Generals Sherman and Johnston end today. A meeting between Generals Johnston and Sherman was effected on the 17th, a few miles beyond Morrisville. General Sherman left Raleigh on a special train, accompanied by his staff. No accidental "Bohemians" being on the spot to chronicle the performances we write from hearsay. I should not forget to say that a pencil-bearer for one of our illustrated journals was discovered by the General after the train had left Raleigh, six miles distant, and he was dropped and it is said made way on foot to the village.

The General and party reached General Kilpatrick's headquarters, some twenty miles distant, where the iron horse was changed for those of flesh, and the party, preceded by Captain Hayes of Kilpatrick's staff, with a small squad and a truce-flag, started, after a ride of nearly four miles. The truce-flag of General Johnston's party was met advancing to meet ours. General Johnston suggested that the party should ride on to the house of Mr. James Bennett. Generals Sherman and Johnston went into the house, leaving their staffs to entertain each other, which it is said they did. Kilpatrick discovered that the small man with the big sword was General Wade Hampton, and as is his wont "went for him"—more courteously than usual, however. Hampton is described as being loud in dress and language. General Johnston is said to be very quiet, and bears the stamp of a true gentleman in his every movement. The officers of his staff, too, are well spoken of by those who met them.

The death of the President, at this time is more than a misfortune. The invariable remark of the soldier is, "they have murdered their best friend." Some of the Generals have taken their guards off the houses that they have been protecting.

The guards in the town have been strengthened, and all Fifteenth Corps men are scrutinized with a careful eye. The pickets in the extreme front are doubled, to prevent the soldiers of the advanced divisions from attacking the Rebel truce parties. If this army moves again, I think it is safe to say that the track of the army through South Carolina will not compare with the one that will be left by some of the corps.

The march from Goldsboro to this place is said, by those that have been to the rear, to have been very easy on the country passed through. One person, who came through on the road taken by the Twentieth Corps, went so far as to say that the corps was becoming demoralized and inefficient. He knew because there were chickens, pigs and cattle left at the houses by the road, and only one house burnt, and that is said to have been done by the Twenty-third Corps, for the reason that one of their men was found pendant to a tree nearby.

The picturesque town of Raleigh is certainly very little harmed. The devastation that has been done was done by "Wheeler's cavalry."

Poor Wheeler, what an amount of scoundrelism his diminutive shoulders have laid upon them—any respectable "Confed." disclaims entirely that he is even acquainted with anyone connected with Wheeler's cavalry.

That the war is over is now generally conceded, and the soldiers are many of them casting a longing eye toward home. That they will not make peaceful citizens is, I am sure, a mistake. This war has educated many of them.

Raleigh, North Carolina

It is now settled that as soon as the ratification of the terms of surrender or capitulation of the Rebel armies is made known from Washington, General Sherman will march his army northward to Harrisburg, Pennsylvania, where it will be mustered out of service.

General Schofield, commanding the Department of North Carolina, will probably remain with the Army of the Ohio, to maintain order until affairs become settled in the State. An earnest wish prevails among the citizens that our forces will continue to extend protection over them until the civil authorities are fully established, and there is a chance for a free expression of the choice of the people, for their future rulers, at the ballot-box. If the signs of the times indicate anything, they point to a complete overthrow of the unprincipled demagogues who have ruled the State.

The prospects of peace and of an early march home produce much rejoicing among the old soldiers of the army. They will go in light marching order, the heavy army material such as ordnance stores, and all superfluous impediments being sent by sea from

Beaufort. But this is anticipating. No orders, of course, have yet been issued on the subject. The return of Colonel Hitchcock, the bearer of the dispatches to Washington, will be looked for with intense interest. Already officers and men are casting about them for the future in view of their early release from service in the army.

The weather is delightful, and all nature seems to sympathize in the general joy which pervades the army over the return of peace.

President Lincoln's Funeral,
Washington, D.C.

The great and solemn pageant of removing the remains of the Nation's revered and beloved Chief from the White House to the Capitol is closed. Never was such a scene witnessed where each and every one of the vast throng moved in silent sadness, as if bearing the burden of a personal bereavement. It has been the writer's fortune to witness the funerals here of John C. Calhoun, Henry Clay, and President Taylor. These were solemn and imposing, yet the event of today was as the loss of an ardently loved parent to the death of a stranger.

At the White House the body lay uncoffined in the center of the East Room, as heretofore described, the head resting to the north. From the entrance door at the northwest end of the room were placed the pallbearers, next the representatives of the army, then the judiciary. At the corner, the Assistant Secretaries of the Departments. First on the eastern line the Senators of the States; next the Diplomatic Corps, who were out in very large numbers and in full court suits. Then the ladies of the Cabinet Ministers; next the Judges of the Supreme Court. Next in the center and in front of the catafalque, stood the new President and behind him the Cabinet Ministers. The members of the Senate joined their left, the House came next; at the corner turning southward stood the Kentucky delegation divided on the left by the delegation from Illinois; on the south end were first the clergy, then the municipal delegations, the Smithsonian Institute, New York Chamber of Commerce, Common Councils of New York and Philadelphia, Union League delegations, and around beside the southwest door of the Green Room were stationed the citizens' delegations from various quarters. The space surrounding the body to within about ten feet was filled by a raised platform, upon which the several bodies described above stood.

Throughout the ceremonies, within the reserved space on the north corner were seated the officiating clergy, on the south corner the mourners, consisting of the late President's two sons, his two private secretaries, and members of his personal household. Mrs.

Lincoln was so severely indisposed as to be compelled to keep her room. The recess of the double center doors leading to the large vestibule was assigned to representatives of the press.

The services were peculiarly impressive, and the quotation concluding Dr. Gurley's sermon was most aptly appropriate and significant. The sermon over, the body was removed to the funeral car for transportation to the Capitol, the pall bearers, mourners, Diplomatic Corps and Supreme Court riding in carriages, all others walking.

The exercises had commenced at precisely half past twelve o'clock and it was two o'clock as the cortege from within began to move out at the northwestern gate.

Outside the great gateway leading from the White House grounds and extending far back upon all the radiating streets were the thousands of delegations from nearly every loyal State who marched into line at the proper moment and moved on with the immense mass following the hearse.

No more beautiful morning, no brighter sunnier day, with sky clear as crystal and the air all charged with the ethereal mildness of spring, ever dawned in glory, ascended to the meridian splendor and sat in peace, than this, the day of the obsequies of Abraham Lincoln.

In the early morning the whole city thronged upon the streets, not as on a gala day, not as when Richmond fell, not as when Lee surrendered; then there was rejoicing—today there was sorrow. The closed shutters and barred doors of all places of business, the black drapery of mourning that festooned every home, the profound solemnity that dwelt upon every face, and the tears of strong men in the streets, and the more than one instance where women fainted in the houses, these were the incidents and attendants of joy; but in the attestations of grief, ordinary words lose their significance in the presence of facts and feeling never known before. Pennsylvania avenue, down which the cortege was to move, was densely packed before ten o'clock, and yet the procession was not to move until two o'clock.

The privilege of viewing it from a window was sold for ten dollars. A newsboy gave twenty-five cents to another for his place in the top of a tree. Boys pressed through the mass selling crape, and found many purchasers. Everybody wore crape; everybody was silent, grave, solemn; everybody stood and patiently awaited for hours; there was no disorder, no disquiet—all were chief mourners. None betrayed any thought unbefitting the occasion, all seemed to feel that the great national family had lost its head, that this was the funeral of the foremost man in all this world.

Meanwhile there were ceremonies in the house, simple, solemn, fitting, and promptly at two o'clock the procession moves, and there are sobs and tears now.

The dead march wails in the people's ears, the cortege is hours passing a given point—first the troops of the cavalry, the measured tread of the infantry and the bands, and the long guns and the flags, and every man and every horse, and every saber and every gun, and every fife and drum, and every flag, black with the emblems of grief.

The stricken family; a hundred Illinoisans and chief mourners, the Lieutenant General as a pall-bearer, various Generals and their staffs, General Butler in citizen's dress on foot, with the other Bay State men, and then the great funeral, all slowly moving to the music of dirges, twenty thousand following him, the man of amplest influence, yet clearest of ambitious crime, to the tomb, and fifty thousand more of the mourners, looking on in sympathy and sorrow, and then we all went each his way.

We had all come to bury our more than dead Caesar and to praise him; yet there was no thought to stir up a mutiny as at that Roman funeral. The feeling was too holy for turbulence, yet not too abstract or sentimental for justice. Men said, let not the traitors who are guilty of this, let not the traitors who are guilty, let none of the prominent ones of this Rebellion ever again become American citizens. We do not cry for their blood, but we demand that they shall never vote at the same polls with us, never claim a part in the flag they would have dishonored.

Thursday, April 20, 1865

Selma, Alabama, From "The Daily Rebel", Confederate Account

If the news we published yesterday from Senatobia is true, William H. Seward, the cold-blooded and heartless political miscreant, who guided the infernal policy which plunged us into this bloody and desolating war, has been arrested by an angry God in the midst of his iniquities, and has paid the penalty of his crimes at the hand of an unknown assassin.

For many years Mr. Seward has been the moving spirit of Northern hostility to the South, and to his enmity and ambitious designs do we owe this war. It is doubtful whether Lincoln would have had the nerve to press the differences between the two sections to the point of actual collision, if Mr. Seward had not stood at his back, and with his devilish malice urged him on.

Doubtless, Seward had conceived in his own mind some mighty scheme of government, in which the Southern States should play but a subordinate part, to "the success of which it was necessary that the institution of slavery, which was a paramount interest, and gave strength and unity to the South, and enabled it to exercise an important, if not a controlling interest in the Government, should be destroyed. He declared years ago that there was an "irrepressible conflict" between the Northern and Southern systems of labor, and that the one must supersede the other.

He steadily and persistently pursued the warfare upon our institutions, until he had created a party sufficiently strong to elect a President, and then taking the Premiership under that President, he inaugurated the war with the view to the extinction of slavery, though it should involve the slaughter and ruin of the entire white population of these States.

His ambitious plans have been brought to a bloody, we do not say a fitting, conclusion. If it was light for Brutus to slay the despotic Caesar; who shall say that the man who slit the throat of this arch plotter against the lives and liberties of these people is not worthy of the laurel wreath?

And Abe Lincoln, too, the political mountebank and professional joker, whom nature intended for the ring of a circus, but whom a strange streak of popular delusion elevated to the Presidency—he also has fallen. His career was as short as it was bloody and infamous. He has gone to answer before the bar of God, for the innocent blood which he has permitted to be shed, and his efforts to enslave a free people.

The dispatches are not sufficiently particular to enable us to judge in regard to the motives which prompted the assassins to their work. We presume that the South will be charged with inciting them to their bloody work, and that a high degree of exasperation against us will be the consequence. But while we do not know anything concerning the cause of these deeds, we do know that they have struck our people here with as much surprise as they have the people of the North. While they rejoice at the destruction of their enemies, they would neither have suggested nor will they sanction cold-blooded murder, however much the victims may deserve the fate they met.

Sherman's Army
Near Raleigh, North Carolina

Several important subjects connected with the war may be gathered from the gist of a conversation which General Sherman held with his Lieutenants after the review of the Tenth Corps today.

The most interesting theme among all upon which the conversation touched was the recent interview with General Johnston at Durham's Station. With this interview General Sherman expressed himself as highly pleased. Johnston was courteous and affable, and freely acknowledged that the cause of the Confederacy was hopeless and that humanity demanded an immediate cessation of hostilities.

To meet this end Sherman proposed that Johnston, as the ranking officer of the Confederacy, now that General Lee is a prisoner, should surrender the entire remaining armies of the insurgent States. To this proposition Johnston only objected that he doubted whether his authority would be recognized by the South and that he lacked the power to enforce such a capitulation as the one proposed. Sherman, however, rather humorously remarking that he would lend him all the power he needed, Johnston agreed to do "what in him lay" to pacify the nation, especially as the great Mogul of the Confederacy when its fortunes were prosperous, but its "small potato" when its fortunes are failing, could not be found.

The last that was heard by General Johnston of the chivalrous chief of the last ditchers, Jefferson D., was that he had started away for parts unknown in an ambulance and was supposed to be hidden somewhere in the mountains. May this be the end of him. There could be no more ludicrously insignificant termination to the career of this arch Rebel than in the flight which he has ignominiously chosen. There is nothing of the heroic in this. Had he bravely yielded himself a prisoner with chivalrous Lee, perhaps a bard or two in ages to come might have sung the life, fortunes, and tragic death of J. Davis, but now there will none be found so poor as to do him reverence.

Very little difficulty was experienced by the two chieftains in agreeing to the terms of the capitulation of the Southern armies. Sherman offered and Johnston accepted substantially the same terms which were offered by General Grant to General Lee. Johnston further agreed to issue a proclamation to the Rebel Legislatures, calling upon them to meet at their respective capitals and take the oath of allegiance to the Government of the United States.

John C. Breckinridge, who was present on the grounds before the interview, evidently thought that being a politician; he would be able to outwit Sherman in obtaining for him a recognition of his right to treat with him as a civil officer of the Confederate Government, who might be supposed to represent the views of its President. But General Sherman foiled all his attempts, and merely recognized him in his capacity as Lieutenant General of the Confederacy, and did not negotiate with him at all.

During the day, General Sherman communicated to General Johnston the intelligence of the assassination of President Lincoln, and it is only just to a sworn though honorable enemy, to say that General Johnston was grieved by the news, and seemed to be as much shocked by it as if he were a Northern man and a friend of the President's.

Something being said about State rights, Sherman made one of his characteristic remarks in reply. Said he: "The American citizen has some rights too. I have some rights, among them is the right to go where I please, and jump what fences I please." "That," said Johnston, "is because you have a large force to back you." Said Sherman, "That is the identical thing."

General Wade Hampton, Sherman describes as a foolish fire-eater, who vows that *he* never will surrender, but will cut his way through the lines somehow somewhere and sail away to an elysium of independence. Hampton says he will never speak to a Northern man after the war is over. Poor fool!

Lt. Gen. Wayne Hampton

Friday, April 21, 1865

Fauquier, Va., Mosby's Farewell Address, Confederate Account

"Soldiers: I have summoned you together for the last time. The vision we have cherished for a free and independent country has vanished, and that country is now the spoil of a conqueror. I disband your organization in preference to surrendering to our enemies. I am no longer your commander. After an association of more than two eventful years, I part from you with a just pride in the fame of your achievements, and grateful recollections of your generous kindness to myself; and now at this moment of bidding you a final adieu, accept the assurance of my unchanging confidence and regard. Farewell."

Washington, D.C.

General Ewell, in conversation with the editor of The National Intelligencer, yesterday, stated his last letter to General Lee, as follows:

General Lee:

For God's sake, and humanity's sake, surrender your army. You are outnumbered and beaten. To continue the contest longer is to court nothing but slaughter in vain.

Ewell

Brig. Gen. Richard Ewell

Sunday, April 23, 1865

Army of the Potomac

This glorious army is now being broken up. The Sixth Corps, which has earned the word Ubique* and might bear it on its flag, was put in march this morning for Danville, in order to hold that point, and it would seem, to guard the communication of the army under General Sherman.

*Ubique: Latin for 'Everywhere".

The Fifth Corps is now posted along the Southside railroad, guarding that line, and the Ninth, which did that duty till lately, is now on its way to the Capital, from which, report says, it will be transported to a certain distant point of the Rebel country.

The Twenty-fourth Corps is in march for Richmond, where the bulk of it now is, and lastly, the Second Corps is here waiting for orders.

Vicksburg, Tennessee

Eight thousand Andersonville prisoners are here getting ready to return to their homes.

Knoxville, Tennessee

Among the trophies of Stoneman's expedition are twelve battle flags and banners, one old United States flag found in the house of a loyal citizen of Salisbury. The poisonous pen, where many unfortunate Union prisoners pined their lives away, was burned to the ground. A few Union prisoners were found, skeletons of their former selves. Almost all of them died on the way to Knoxville. They preferred rather to die under the Stars and Stripes than to be left in the loathsome hospitals of Salisbury.

A drawing from 1862 showing Union prisoners playing baseball at Salisbury Prison.

Monday, April 24, 1865

Selma, Alabama, From "The Daily Rebel",
Confederate Account

The people of the North are now reaping the natural and inevitable harvest of crime growing out of the demoralization incident to a state of war. The last dispatches exhibit a most shocking and horrible state of society. The President and his Prime Minister killed by assassins and the new President and the Secretary of War murdered by a mob which has obtained and holds possession of the Capital of the Nation. Other cities sacked and a great popular revolution against the rulers impending. While their armies are devastating our land, their own down-trodden populace, infuriated by tyranny and driven to despair by want, bursts the bonds of law, and a reign of terror and of ruin is established.

That Nation, which prided itself upon its strength and prosperity, finds three different Presidents occupying its Executive Chair within a space of a single month, two of whom were murdered; discord and anarchy riding rampant and ruling the hour. Perhaps they may yet find it necessary to recall the armies they have sent to these States to ruin us to restore order and law among themselves. God grant it.

Chattanooga, Tennessee

The Atlanta papers know of the assassination of President Lincoln, but make no comment. They deny the surrender of Lee's Army, and say he was all right on the 16th inst.

Chattanooga, Tennesee 1865

Wednesday, April 26, 1865

Raleigh, North Carolina General
Grant's telegram of today:

Johnston surrendered the forces in his command, embracing all from here to the Chattahoochee, to General Sherman, on the basis agreed upon between Lee and myself for the Army of Northern Virginia.

The 26th of April, 1865, will remain celebrated in our annals as the day which witnessed the final surrender of the Rebel army under Joseph E. Johnston, and closed the Slaveholder's Rebellion.

The presence of Lieutenant General Grant at Raleigh with the ultimatum of the Government has been known to Rebel officers for four days, and, no doubt, had a salutary influence upon the negotiations which hitherto have hung fire. General Sherman, General Schofield and General Howard, with several members of their respective staffs, among others Colonel W. H. Wherry, of General Schofield's staff, left for the front at eight o'clock this morning by train.

Bennett's house, five miles beyond Durham's Station, and about thirty from Raleigh, was the place of conference, the same as that where the former interview took place. It is a small and unpretentious country dwelling, with only two rooms, and a small allowance of windows in each room. The house, however, was scrupulously neat, the floors scrubbed to a milky whiteness, the bed in one room very neatly made up, and the few articles of furniture in the room arranged with neatness and taste. The grounds were ornamented with a few flowers and a little shrubbery. Opposite the house is a fine oak casting a broad shadow; and other trees about the premises had been trimmed by the Rebel officers and soldiers to give them an inviting appearance.

The train, bearing the Union Generals, arrived at the station, or house, about two o'clock in the afternoon. General Johnston, with Captain Wade Hampton, Jr., and Major Preston of his staff, with several other officers arrived about half past two o'clock, and after a very civil but not over warm greeting between the officers, and the introductions of the officers, General Johnston and General Sherman held a short private interview in the room set apart for the conference, meanwhile the Rebel officers withdrew to some distance, and remained in conversation among themselves, the Union officers doing the same.

Generals Schofield and Howard then joined the Conference, which lasted about one hour. Wade Hampton, having been relieved of command, was not present, neither was Breckinridge. The basis of surrender was the same as that on which Lee handed over his shattered army to General Grant. Instead of marching to their respective capitals to deliver their arms, the whole force, estimated at twenty-five thousand men of all arms, with all the artillery and material of war, are to be delivered at Greensborough, North Carolina.

The terms include no recognition of the existing State Governments, the whole civil feature of the settlement being left to the people and the general Government. The surrender includes all the Rebels in arms in the four States of North Carolina, South Carolina, Georgia and Florida to the Chattahoochee river. The remainder of the Rebel armies—Kirby Smith's and others'—will undoubtedly follow suit.

General Johnston throughout has shown unmistakable anxiety to close the war without further bloodshed. He seemed considerably oppressed with care and responsibility, but maintained his affable and gentlemanly bearing throughout.

The officers finally mingled freely in conversation upon the war, and the men argued and disputed about the merits of various battles in which they had taken part. The conference closed cordially, the officers shook hands and parted with mutual expressions of good will. Thus closes the drama of a four years' bloody and most inexcusable war. The train returned to Raleigh at nine o'clock in the evening. An order will be published tomorrow announcing the surrender of the Rebel Army. General Grant goes north on a special train in the morning. The Twenty-third and Tenth Army Corps remain here.

Thursday, April 27, 1865

Washington, D.C.
Booth's Capture and Death

About eight o'clock last evening we received the intelligence of the capture of J. Wilkes Booth, the assassin of Abraham Lincoln, and one of his accomplices in the murder, David C. Herold. The following are such of the particulars as we were enabled to gather, which, with the exception of the precise locality where the occurrence took place, we give as being trustworthy and correct. Booth and his accomplice had crossed the Potomac River at or near Acquia Creek. Our cavalry scouts in that vicinity have been in consequence unusually active in their endeavors to get on their trail.

Early yesterday morning a squad of about twelve men belonging to the Sixteenth New York Cavalry, under command of a lieutenant whose name we did not learn, succeeded in discovering the fugitive in a barn on the road leading from Port Royal to Bowling Green, in Caroline County, Va. As soon as they were discovered the place was surrounded, and the assassins ordered to surrender. This they both refused to do, Booth declaring that he would not be taken alive, and offering to fight the whole squad if he would be permitted to place himself twenty yards distant from them. His proposition was not, however, acceded to, and as they persisted in their refusal to surrender, the lieutenant determined to burn them out, and accordingly set fire to the barn. Shortly afterward Herold came out and gave himself up. Booth remained in the burning building for some time and until driven out by the fire, when he rushed out and was immediately shot through the neck by the sergeant of the squad.

Since the above was put in type, we have had an interview with two of the cavalrymen engaged in the capture of the assassins.

From them we learn that the whole party consisted of twenty-eight, including two detectives. The first information respecting Booth's crossing the river and his probable whereabouts, was obtained from disbanded Rebel soldiers who were met with in all directions in that part of the country. From one and another of these the clue to Booth's movements was gathered and held until just at daybreak they came upon the barn where he and Herold were secreted.

A parley was had, and Booth manifesting the most desperate determination not to be taken alive, and to take as many of the lives of the party as possible, Lieutenant Edward P. Doherty, who commanded the scouting party, determined to make short work of him. When Herold saw the preparations for firing the barn, he declared his willingness to surrender, and said he would not fight if they would let him out. Booth, on the contrary, was impudently defiant, offering at first to fight the whole squad at one hundred yards, and subsequently at fifty yards. He was hobbling on crutches, apparently very lame. He swore he would die like a man, etc.

Herold having been secured, as soon as the burning hay lighted the interior of the barn sufficiently to render the scowling face of Booth, the assassin, visible, Sergeant Boston Corbett fired upon him, and he fell. The ball passed through his neck. He was pulled out of the barn, and one of his crutches and carbine and revolvers secured.

The wretch lived about two hours, whispering blasphemies against the Government and messages to his mother, desiring her to be informed that he died for his country.

The time Booth was shot he was leaning upon one crutch and preparing to shoot his captors. Only one shot was fired in the entire affair, that which killed the assassin.

Lieutenant Doherty is one of the bravest fellows in the cavalry service, having distinguished himself in a sharp affair at Culpepper Court House, and on other occasions. The Sixteenth New York Cavalry is commanded by Colonel Nelson Sweetzer, and has been doing duty in Fairfax County. This regiment formed part of the cavalry escort on the day of the President's obsequies in Washington. The body of Booth and the assassin's accomplice, Herold, were placed on board the Ida, and sent to Washington, arriving here about one o'clock this morning.

Sgt. Boston Corbett

Later.—Booth's body has been fully recognized and placed upon a gunboat in the stream. The knife he brandished, with the blood of Captain Rathbone dried thereon, is here; also his revolvers and Spencer rifle. He claimed to have been deserted by all his confederates, except Herold, and that he rode twenty miles with the bone of his leg protruding and chafing against his saddle.

Memphis, Tennessee,
Sultana Disaster

From the Memphis Argus Newspaper

April 28, 1865

Yesterday morning our city was startled with the news of one of the most appalling disasters which ever occurred on American waters. By this terrible catastrophe no less than twelve or fifteen hundred persons were hurried into eternity

The steamer Sultana, one of the People's and Merchants' line of packets, Capt. Cass Mason commanding, bound from New Orleans to St. Louis, arrived up on the evening of the 25th at 6:30 o'clock, having on board, it is understood, 1,966 men and thirty commissioned officers. Besides this there was a considerable passenger list, including forty ladies and the boat's crew.

Having discharged the freight for this city, the Sultana proceeded on her way up the river, leaving our wharf at about 2 o'clock yesterday morning. When about seven miles above the city she exploded her boilers; the entire middle portion of the boat, including the Texas and pilot house, was hurled high in the air and scattered over the water. Immediately after the explosion fire broke out; a vast volume of flame swept through the cabin from the front to the stern of the boat. Then ensured a scene which language cannot describe - the most terrible that can possibly be conceived.

The explosion occurred in a wide portion of the river, there being no land for a mile on either side. Many were scalded to death immediately; those who were not injured were jumping overboard. The river for a mile around was full of floating people; the light of the burning boat shone over a scene such as has never before been witnessed; such as language cannot paint or imagination conceive. The screams of women, the groans of those who were wounded and thrown from the boat by the force of the explosion, the cries for help when there were none to assist - all contributed to create a scene over which we are compelled to shudder with horror.

The steamer Bostona was on her way down and about a mile above the Sultana at the time the explosion occurred. Her officers, perceiving the light of the burning boat and hearing the cries and struggles of the drowning people, made all haste to the scene of the disaster. Her yawls were sent out, stage planks thrown overboard; everything that could float was thrown into the river for the sufferers. Every effort was made by the officers of the Bostona in this trying emergency to render aid to the drowning multitude.

A passenger from the Bostona, Mr. Deson, rendered noble service by his courage and daring. It is said that this gentleman took one of the foot planks from the Bostona and went out on it and succeeded in saving the lives of no less than eight persons. Such deeds should not go unnoted.

The flames burst in great fury in a very few minutes after the explosion on the Sultana. No time was allowed for the people to do anything. Ladies rushed forth from their berths in the night attire, and with a wild scream plunged into the angry flood and sank to rise no more. The pitiful cries of children as they, too, rushed to the side of the wreck and plunged into the water were mingled with the hoarser voices of manhood in the desperate struggle for life. More than 2,000 people were thus compelled to choose between a death by fire and a sleep beneath the wave. Hour after hour rolled away, and the struggle for the great multitude in the river continued. Manhood was powerless. Husbands threw their wives into the river and plunged into the water after them, only to see them sink in death. Some had secured doors and fragments of the wreck and were thus enabled to keep a longer time above the water. Those who were swimmers struck for the shore, where they could find trees and bushes to keep them above the water. Some were carried down by the current until opposite the city, where their cries attracted the attention of the people on the steamers lying at the wharf. Yawls, skiffs, and every available small boat was put into immediate requisition and sent out into the stream to pick up the survivors. A considerable number were thus rescued from a watery grave. One lady with an infant in her arms was forced by the current several miles, and was finally rescued by some of the small boats that were cruising around. She exhibited the most remarkable heroism--still clinging to her precious charge and supporting it above the water until rescued. The small boats from the United States gunboats did good service.

Messrs. John Fogleman, Thomas J. Lumbertson, George Malone and John Berry, citizens of Mound City, Arkansas are entitled to the eternal gratitude of every right-thinking mind. When they saw the burning, floating mass, and heard the cries of the struggling thousands, they made haste to construct rude rafts of logs and put into the stream. With these, they succeeded in saving the lives of nearly a hundred persons. They were unceasing and labored faithfully and courageously as long as there was any possibility of relieving a suffering fellow mortal. Mr. Fogleman's residence was converted into a temporary hospital for the sufferers, and every possible care and attention were bestowed on them by Mr. Fogleman and his family. The number who had been brought in-- rescued from the river--at 12 o'clock yesterday were 110 enlisted men, ten officers, four ladies and fifteen citizens.

The Sultana had been in service three years. She belonged to Capt. Cass Mason, Sam DeBow, W. J. Lewis and Mr. Thornberg, and was valued at $80,000. She was insured to a large amount.

The officers and crew of the ironclad Essex deserve unstinted credit and praise for the part they took in picking up passengers of the ill-fated steamer Sultana. Lieut. James Berry, ensign of the Essex, was awakened yesterday morning about 4 o'clock and informed that the steamer Sultana had blown up and was now burning; that the passengers were floating down the river and crying for help. The lieutenant jumped up immediately and was startled and horrified by the agonizing cries of the people in the river. He said that never in his life did he hear anything so dreadful, and hopes it may never be his lot to hear such screams again.

He immediately ordered the boats to be manned, which was done in very quick time. The morning was very dark; it was impossible to see twenty feet ahead; they had nothing whatever to guide them but the shrieks and groans of the wounded and scalded men.

The first man picked up was chilled through and through. Lieut. Berry, seeing the condition the man was in, very generously divested himself of his own coat and put it on this man. The second man they took up died a few minutes after being taken aboard. The men who had Capt. Parker's gig picked up a woman out of some drift. She was at that time just making her last struggle for life. About the time this woman was picked up a steamboat yawl came there and helped pick up some more who were clinging about the drift. Lieut. Berry said it was impossible for him to give any description of the scene; he said it beggared all description; that there were no words adequate to convey to the mind the horror of that night. He continually heard persons cry out, *"Oh, for God's sake, save us! We cannot hold out any longer!"*

The boats of the United States steamers Groesbeck and Tyler were on hand and displayed great vigilance and zeal in picking up drowning men. Lieut. Berry, with the help of the crew, picked up over sixty men... With commendable forethought Capt. Parker sent out ten boats to explore the shore from Memphis to the place of the disaster. Up to 3:30 yesterday afternoon only five of these boats had returned. They had found a few dead bodies, but could not find any survivors along the shore.

Had the disaster occurred an hour or two later Capt. Parker feels assured that the naval force could have saved several hundred lives instead of the sixty alluded to. Unfortunately the night was dark, and the boats were compelled to steer in the direction of the cries, being unable to see more than a few of those struggling in the water.

After the explosion of her boilers, and the rapid spread of the flames, the burning mass of what had been the fine steamer Sultana floated down with the current until within a few hundred yards of Mr. Fogleman's residence, where it grounded on the Arkansas shore. We visited the wreck about 10 o'clock. It was sunk in about twenty feet of water; the jackstaff was standing up before the black mass, as though mutely mourning over the terrible scene, a silent witness of which it had been. The boat was almost entirely consumed. The charred remains of several human bodies were found, crisped and blackened by the fiery element. The scene was sad to contemplate, and those who witnessed it can never forget it. The Rose Hambleton, Pocahontas, Jenny Lind and Bostona were cruising around the place, ever and anon picking up the breathless body of some unfortunate who slept the sleep of death; or some more fortunate who had escaped a watery grave, though exhausted by a fearful night of struggle for life.

The names and places of many of those who were hurried into eternity by this terrible catastrophe will never be known. Capt. Cass Mason, who was in command of the Sultana, was among the lost. Capt. Mason was well-known to many of our business men as the former commander of the Belle of Memphis. It is said that he did well his part. During the trying scenes ensuing the explosion he stood upon the deck of the fated vessel, throwing buoys into the water, or anything that would float, encouraging others by his example; and was last seen after everybody else had left the burning wreck. His body is probably beneath the mighty river's surging waves. The two clerks, W. J. Gamble and William Stratton, were among the lost. One of the engineers, lost. Harry Ingraham, one of the pilots, was lost. Mrs. Hardin of Chicago was among the lost. She was lately married, and was on a bridal tour.

DeWitt Clinton Spikes (whose father, mother, three sisters, two brothers and young lady cousin were all lost), a young Louisianian, with a noble courage that is beyond all praise, notwithstanding his exhausted condition, used every effort to assist his fellow sufferers and succeeded in saving no less than thirty lives. A soldier procured a log; several drowning men were seen; he directed his log toward them; they laid hold on the log, and were thus taken ashore. By this means he was instrumental in saving the lives of five men. Capt. Curtis, master of river transportation, sent out boats on the first intimation of disaster, and had the Jenny Lind fired up and dispatched her to the scene of distress. He and his assistants were very active, and performed many noble deeds.

Capt. George J. Clayton, pilot of the Sultana, was on duty at the time the explosion occurred. He says they were going on about as usual; that they had gotten about seven miles above the city, running at her usual rate of speed--if any difference, not as fast as usual. All of a sudden he saw a flash, and the next thing he knew he was falling into the water with a portion of the wreck of the pilothouse. He thinks that he must have been hurled at least forty feet into the air. When he reached the water he saw the flames bursting up from the furnace and soon enveloping the entire boat. The scene which ensued beggars all description. He says the river was full--a sea of heads for hundreds of yards around. Screams and cries arose, rendering the scene appalling. Mr. Clayton was slightly injured in his fall.

This photo was taken on April 26, 1865 in Arkansas. The ship is greatly over-crowded with over 2000 soldiers, most recently released from Andersonville and other Confederate prisons. They were still weak and suffering from mal-nutrition, disease and other maladies caused by their incarceration.

Friday, April 28, 1865

St. Louis, Missouri

A force of six to twelve thousand Rebels, comprising the remnants of Jeff. Thompson's and Joe Shelby's brigades are at Pocahontas, Arkansas, preparing to invade Missouri.

Three regiments have been sent down the river.

Gen. Joseph O. Shelby

Jefferson Barracks, St. Louis, Missouri

Saturday, April 29, 1865

Savannah, Georgia
Wilson's Raid,

The forces under Brevet Major General Wilson, after a march of over three hundred miles through a sterile and mountainous country, approached Selma, Alabama, surrounded by two lines of entrenchments, impassable swamps, covered by stockades and defended by seven thousand Rebel troops under the command of General Forrest. The Second Division swept over the defenses of the Summerfield road like an avalanche, while the Fourth Division carried those on the Plantersville road. The enemy, astonished and disheartened, broke from their works, and Selma was won. General Chalmers made a futile effort to drive in the pickets of the Second Division, and go to the Rebel garrison during the battle, and was compelled to retreat rapidly beyond Cahaba. The fruits of this victory were twenty-six field pieces and one thirty-pounder Parrott, captured on the field of battle, and over seventy pieces of heavy ordnance in the arsenal and foundry; two thousand prisoners, a number of battle-flags, the naval foundry and machine shops, the extensive arsenal filled with every variety of military munitions, and large quantities of commissary and quartermasters' stores in depot. This was on the 2d day of April. On Saturday evening, April 8, the troops commenced crossing the Alabama River on pontoon bridges, and by Monday, the 10th, all were across. From Selma to Montgomery is distant about fifty-six miles. On the 12th, Montgomery was surrendered to General McCook, commanding First Division. No resistance was met with, General Beauford having evacuated the place, after destroying a large quantity of cotton, commissary stores, &c.

Monday, 16th, left the camp early in the morning, marching thirty-eight miles, reaching Columbus between nine and ten o'clock. General Winstow's brigade of the Fourth Division forced its way through the lines, and about twenty-five Union soldiers rode across the covered bridge in company with a Rebel escort, without their knowledge, of course. After crossing the river these intrepid soldiers informed the Rebels who they were, and made an attack upon them with their sabers. The escort soon disappeared, and followed by the balance of the brigade, entered and took possession of the city. About two hundred pieces of artillery and a large number of small arms were captured in the arsenal, and about two thousand prisoners. General Howell Cobb was in command at Columbus, who skedaddled back to Macon as fast as he could on the appearance of the Union forces. From Columbus to Macon is ninety-six miles. General Wilson left the former city on the 18th, resuming his march for the latter place, passing by the double bridges. On the evening of the 20th, when about seventeen miles from Macon, he was met by a flag of truce sent out by General Cobb, with a copy of a dispatch from General Beauregard announcing the armistice between Generals Sherman and Johnston, and asking an interview at some point with a view to enforcing said armistice. Pending this, and before General Wilson had time to reply, the Seventeenth Indiana of the Second Division, commanded by General Long, dashed into the city about dusk, and took possession of it. A short time after General Wilson arrived in the city and took quarters at the Lanier House. General Cobb and staff, General Mercer and staff, and General A. W. Smith (commanding the militia) and staff, and some two thousand other officers and soldiers, were all taken prisoners. The stockade at Macon, where a large number of Union prisoners were formerly confined, was, soon after the arrival of our forces, totally demolished. The Lanier House was pillaged, supposed to have been done by the servants, and the jewelry store of E. J. Johnson, in which was the Confederate Depository, managed by W. B. Johnson. General Wilson's command consists of about sixteen thousand men, to whom much credit is due for the rapid marches they have made and important captures of the cities they have visited.

Sunday, April 30, 1865

Washington, D.C.

General Sherman's Army is enroute to Washington, overland. The Government today telegraphed to Baltimore, Philadelphia and New York for fifty bakers from each place, in order to be ready for the army. We have now here a very large body of troops, coming from the vicinity of Richmond and the Shenandoah Valley, and fifty thousand rations of soft bread are issued here daily.

Army of Georgia near the Neuse River

The day broke in the most delightful manner. The sun shone forth after the heavy rain of the previous night in all his splendor, and gave to the cool morning air his brightest and most cheery glances. So opened the day on which the left wing of the grand army commenced its joyful march toward home—sweet home. When at daylight their tents were struck, and the bugle gaily sounded the "forward," of all that host who proudly marched beneath the "bonnie blue which bears a single star," there was not one whose bosom did not swell with pride and exultation as he thought that he was marching north, crowned with victory.

Joy beamed from every eye when home was in the mind, and every eye looked joyful only to be dimmed as the melancholy tragedy at Washington was recalled by the over working brain. Yet as hope and joy are the ruling passions of the successful, the moments of grief, though poignant, were few. Joyfully then the Twentieth Corps, which led the advance of the Army of Georgia, marched from their camps on a march which cannot but be barren of the usual topics of interest which spring from the movements of an army, and yet will be fruitful in others more novel and as entertaining. How the troops are received on the route, what are the sentiments of the inhabitants upon the great social problem of re-union which now perplexes the profoundest minds, when the army will arrive at the principal towns on its way, when it will finally reach its destination at Alexandria, and a thousand other items which cannot be anticipated, will, fill the place in the public mind which has been during four years occupied by war and rumors of war.

Raleigh, North Carolina, from
"The Raleigh Progress"

We learn that Jefferson Davis, under a strong escort, and accompanied by a long train bearing away immense sums of gold filched from the people, and other plunder, has crossed the Yadkin river, near Salisbury, and is making his way to Texas, where he expects to re-establish *his Government.* Before leaving the rear of Johnston's army he harangued a portion of the troops, and asked them to follow him across the Mississippi, where he promised them to again rear the standard of Rebellion; and it is said a strong mounted force accompanied him, the train being over two miles long. After all that has happened recently we doubt his ability to reach the country beyond the Mississippi.

It is now evident that there is no peace for any part of this country, or for any State, but in a prompt return to the protection of the Union Government, and a ready, cheerful obedience to the laws; and if Jefferson Davis, and the desperate characters who have cast their lots with him should again attempt to defy the National authority, here or elsewhere, we trust that short work will be made of them. We had hoped that peace would so soften the hearts of rulers and people that the past would be a sealed book, and that punishment, even of leaders, if inflicted at all, would be very mild; but Jefferson Davis, and the leaders who helped him break up the Government and defy the National authority, are mainly responsible before men and high Heaven for the slaughter, sufferings and horrors that have accompanied this war, and the patriotic, loyal masses will no longer tolerate their infamous treason. Davis will, no doubt, betray and deceive this small band of misguided followers, as he has betrayed and deceived the great body of the people of the Southern States; and when they shall have given him safe conduct across the Mississippi, he will step into Mexico and desert them, as he has but so recently deserted the people east of the Mississippi. He is running for his life, and should he and Benjamin, the Jew, his prime minister, once clear the country, we shall never see them or their like again.

There are large bodies of Union troops in Georgia, Alabama, Mississippi, and Tennessee, with small forces in Arkansas and Missouri; and if the Rebel leader shall dare attempt to open shop in Texas, he and all his sympathizers will be swept away like broom-sedge before the devouring flame.

Farewell, Davis! You played the bold and successful tyrant over the deluded people of the South, for four long years, but if you will take your leading associates in infamy with you in your flight, we shall be disposed to forgive much.

You and your confederates in treason against a Government you had sworn to support will wear the mark of Cain wherever you may go, and in future times, when mothers shall recount your deeds of cruelty, oppression, and wrong, their children shall shudder and shrink back aghast at the horrid picture. Farewell, thou arch despoiler of one of the fairest lands that ever the sun shown upon! Go, and if you can make peace with your own conscience, we freely forgive you all the wrong you have done us.

A Black Confederate Soldier

Monday, May 1, 1865

Sherman's Troops,
Fairport, North Carolina

Another fine day for marching, starting at five in the morning, by three o clock in the afternoon the troops were in camp at Fairport, having marched twenty-two miles without experiencing more than usual fatigue, owing to the excellence of the roads.

Perfect order reigned along the lines of the Twentieth Corps. What occurred in the Fourteenth I am unable to say as it is marching upon a different road.

One of the halts of General Geary's Division was at the house of a quondam Rebel Quartermaster who had evidently been a thorough Secessionist. His thoroughbred terrier was named "Rebel," and his favorite game chicken was called "Bob Lee." A little daughter of this gentleman, three years old, was thoroughly imbued with rebellious spirit. Coax her, as all did, she would still defiantly say she "did not like Yankees." An officer failing to obtain the gift of one of her curls inquired why she refused him, and he was rather astonished when the little lips which had scarcely learned to frame an answer, said plainly—"she was going to sell the curl to help pay the National debt."

Artemus Ward at Richmond, Virginia

The old man finds himself once more in a sunny climb. I cum here a few days arter the city catterpillertulated.

My naburs seemed surprised & astonisht at this darin' bravery onto the part of a man at my time of my life, but our family was never know'd to quale in danger's stormy hour.

My father was a sutler in the Revolootion War. My father once had an intervoo with Gin'ral LaFayette.

He askcd LaFayette to lend him five dollars, promisin' to pay him in the fall; but Lafy said he couldn't see it in those lamps. Lafy was French, and his knowledge of our langwide was a little shaky.

Immejutly on my 'rival here I perceeded to the Spotswood House, and, callin' to my assistans a young man from our town who writes a good runnin' hand, I put my ortograph on the register, and handin' my umbrella to a bald-headed man behind the counter, who I s'posed was Mr. Spotswood, I said, "Spotsy, how does she run?"

He called a cullud purson, and said:

"Show the gem'mun to the cow yard, and giv' him cart number one."

"Isn't Grant here?" I said. "Perhaps Ulyssis wouldn't mind my turnin' in with him."

"Do you know the Gen'ral?" inquired Mr. Spootswood.

"Wall, no, not 'zackly; but he'll remember me. His brother-in-law's aunt brought her rye meal of my uncle Levi all one winter. My uncle Levi's rye meal was—"

"Pooh! pooh !" said Spotsy, "don't bother me," and he shuv'd my umbrella onto the floor. Obsarvin' to him not to be so keerless with that wepin, I accompanied the African to my lodgins.

"My brother," I sed, "sir are you aware that you've bin 'mancipated? Do you realise how glorus it is to be free? Tell me, my dear brother, does it not seem like some dreams, or do you realise the great fact in all its livin' and holy magnitood?"

He sed he would take some gin.

I was show'd to the cow yard and laid down under a one mule cart. The hotel was orful crowded, and I was sorry I hadn't gone to the Libby Prison. Tho' I should hav' slept com't'ble enuff if the bed cloths hadn't bin pulled off me durin' the night, by a scoundrul who cum and hitched a mule to the cart and druv it off. I thus lost my cuverin', and my throat feels a little husky this morning.

Gin'ral Halleck offers me the hospitality of the city, givin' me my choice of hospitals.

He has also very kindly placed at my disposal a smallpox amboolance.

There is raly a great deal of Union sentiment in this city. I see it on ev'ry hand.

I met a man today—I am not at liberty to tell his name, but he is an old and inflooentocial citizen of Richmond, and sez he, "Why! we've bin fightin' agin the old flag! Lor' bless me, how sing'lar!" He then borr'd five dollars of me and bust into a flood of tears.

Sed another (a man of standin' and formerly a bitter rebul) "let us at once stop this effushun of Blud! The Old Flag is good enuff for me. Sir," he added, "you air from the North! Have you a doughnut or a piece of custard pie about you?"

I told him no, but I knew a man from Vermont who had just organized a sort of restaurant, where he could go and make a very comfortable breakfast on New England rum and cheese. He borrowed fifty cents of me, and askin' me to send him Wm Lloyd Garrison's ambrotype as soon as I got home, he walked off.

Said another, "There's bin a tremendous Union feelin' here from the fust. But we was kept down by a rain of terror. Have you a degerretype of Wendell Phillips about your person? and will you lend me four dollars for a few days till we air once more a happy and united people?"

Jeff Davis is not pop'lar here. She is regarded as a Southern sympathizer, & yit I'm told he was kind to his parents. She ran away from them many years ago, and has never bin back. This is showing them a good deal of consideration, when we refleck what his conduct has been. Her captur in female apparel confooses me in regard to his sex, and you see I speak of him as a her as frequent as otherwise, and I guess he feels so herself.

Robert Lee is regarded as a noble feller.

He was opposed to the war at fust, and draw'd his sword very reluctant. In fact, he wouldn't hav' draw'd his sword at all, only he had a large stock of military clothes on hand, which he did not want to waste. He sez the colored man is right, and he will at once go to New York and open a Sabbath school for Negro minstrels.

The surrender of R. Lee, J. Johnston, and others leaves the Confedrit Army in a rather shattered state. That army now consists of Kirby Smith, four mules, and a Bass drum, and is movin' rapidly to'ds Texas.

Feelin' a little peckish, I went into a eatin' house today, and encountered a young man with long black hair and slender frame. He didn't wear much clothes, and them as he did wear looked onhealthy. He frowned on me, and sed, kinder scornful, " So, sir—you cum here to taunt us in our hour of trouble, do you?"

"No," said I, "I cum here for hash!"

"Pish-haw!" he said sneeringly, "I mean you are in the city for the purpose of gloatin' over a fallen people. Others may basely succumb, but as for me, I will never yield—Never, Never!"

"Hav' suthin' to eat!" I pleasantly suggested.

"Tripe and onions," he said furely; then he added, "I eat with you, but I hate you. Your a low-lived Yankee!"

To which I pleasantly replied, "How'll you have your tripe?"

"Fried, mudsill, with plenty of ham fat!" He et very ravenus. Poor feller! He had lived on odds and ends for several days, eatin' crackers that had been turned over by revellers in the bread tray at the bar.

He got full at last, and his hart softened a little tu'ards me. "After all," he said, "you hav sum people at the North who air not wholly loathsum beasts!"

"Well, yes," I sed, "we hav now and then a man among us who isn't a cold bluded scoundril. Young man," I mildly but gravely said, "this crooil war is over, and you're likt! Its rather necessary for somebody to lick in a good square, lively fite, and in this 'ere case it happens to be the United States of America. You fit splendid, but we was too many for you. Then make the best of it, & let us all give in and put the Republic on a firmer basis nor iver.

"I don't gloat over your misfortins, my young fren'. Fur from it. I'm a old man now, & my hart is softer nor it once was. You see my spectacles is misten'd with suthin' very much like tears—I'm thinkin' of the sea of good rich blood which has been spilt on both sides in this dredful war. I'm thinkin' of our widders and orfuns North, and of your'n in the South. I kin place my old hands tenderly on the fair yung hed of the Virginny maid whose lover was laid low in the battle dust by a fed'ral bullet, and say as fervently and piously as a vener'ble sinner like me kin say anything, God be good to you, my poor dear, my poor dear."

I riz up to go, & takin' my young Southern fren' kindly by the hand, I sed, "Yung man, adoo! You Southern fellers is probly my brothers, tho' you've occasionally had a cussed queer way of showin' it! It's over now. Let us all jine in and make a country on this continent that shall giv' all Europe the cramp in the stummuck ev'ry time they look at us! Adoo! adoo!"

And as I am through, I'll likewise say adoo to you, jentle reader, merely remarkin' that the Star Spangled Banner is waving round loose again, and that there don't seem to be anything the matter with the Goddess of Liberty beyond a slite cold.

Artemus Ward

Tuesday, May 2, 1865

Twentieth Army Corps near Williamston

It is painful to be obliged to record the lawless conduct of our soldiers at any time, particularly is it so when that conduct is utterly without extenuation. Despite the stringent orders issued in regard to the peaceable behavior of our troops upon their inarch to Richmond, some of the soldiers both of the Army of Georgia and the Army of Tennessee have been permitted to straggle from their commands, and have committed depredations upon the inhabitants much to be deplored. It would seem that the roving spirits fostered by army life cannot at once be chastened into a domestic one by the white-winged angel of peace.

Most of the depredations which have come under my notice, and I am cognizant of many, have been committed by men of the Fourteenth Corps, which seems to conduct itself as it used to when living upon the enemy's country. Houses have been entered and robbed of eatables, stables have been opened and plundered of horses and cattle, and numerous smaller offenses have been committed. It is of no use for corps commanders to make rules if they do not take the trouble to enforce them.

The Twentieth Corps has not been entirely guiltless of such conduct; but in every instance where the perpetrators of an offense could be discovered they have been severely punished.

Robertson County, Texas,
Confederate Account

Brigadier General William P. Hardeman's Brigade assembled in mass this evening, and, with General Hardeman in the chair, resolved, among other things, that in spite of the reverses to the cis-Mississippi armies, they would not abandon the struggle until the right of self-government is fully established. It was also

Resolved, That we denounce as cravens those men who, having evaded service in the army, use unceasing endeavors to instill a want of confidence in the public mind as regards the final issue, and hold them as more dangerous (being more insidious) than our Yankee foe, who avows his object to be our subjugation.

Resolved, That we will prosecute this war until our independence is achieved, holding in equal esteem the vandal foe who seeks to enslave us and the scarcely concealed traitor at home, who, by act or word, attempts to paralyze our efforts to obtain our just rights—self-government.

Resolved, That to our brethren in arms in the cis-Mississippi Department we say, "Be of good cheer;" anxiously awaiting for orders, we are ready to march to your immediate aid; but if driven from your homes and firesides, with high resolves and actuated by stern ambition, tread your way to the soil of Texas, where our army, determined to be free, awaits your coming; together here, we can yet toil, and struggle, and conquer.

Resolved, That we will never forget the true patriots of our land, the fair women of the South; they have always been found ministering angels around the couch of the sick and dying soldier; with their own hands they wrought the comfortable fabrics that have clothed and warmed us amid the frozen blasts of winter. Others may have despaired; women never; and in the future as in the past, we confidently hope to receive from her the same bright smile of approval and gentle words of encouragement.

Greensborough, North Carolina
Confederate Account

General Orders, No. 22. — Comrades: In terminating our official relations, I earnestly exhort you to observe faithfully the terms of pacification agreed upon, and to discharge the obligations of good and peaceful citizens at your homes, as well as you have performed the duties of thorough soldiers in the field. By such a course you will best secure the comfort of your families and kindred, and restore tranquility to the country.

You will return to your homes with the admiration of our people, won by the courage and noble devotion you have displayed in this long war. I shall always remember with pride the loyal support and generous confidence you have given me.

I now part with you with deep regret, and bid you farewell with feelings of cordial friendship, and with earnest wishes that you may have hereafter all the prosperity and happiness to be found in the world. [Official.]

> J. E.Johnston, General,
> Archer Anderson, Assistant Adjutant General,
> Lieutenant Colonel Kennard, Chief of Ordnance.

Wednesday, May 3, 1865

Twentieth Army Corps near the state line, Virginia

On the 3d of May, 1863, the troops now composing the Twentieth Corps (then the Eleventh and Twelfth Corps), fought the last day's fight at Chancellorsville.

On the 3d of May, 1864, the same troops crossed a State line passing from Bridgeport, Alabama; to Shell Mound, Tennessee. This was the opening of the Atlanta campaign.

On the 3d of May, 1865, the same troops cross another State line, passing from North Carolina into Virginia.

Thus it will be seen that this day has been an eventful one with the Twentieth Corps.

All along the road on which the army marches, little knots of Negroes congregate, many of them from mere idle curiosity, others from higher motives touching upon their ideas of freedom. These persons are a source of unfailing merriment to the soldiers who treat them very kindly. They will cheer for whatever they are told, and in order to be sure of being on the right side, they will hurrah for the *Nunion,* as they call the Union, and Jeff. Davis in one and the same breath. Some of them, through neglect of their masters, are more ignorant than I had imagined it was possible for a human creature to be. Some of the bands amuse themselves by discoursing music to these colored auditors, and today a very funny incident happened upon one of these outbursts of music.

A brigade band, seeing a large gathering of Africans by the side of the road in advance, reserved its music until exactly opposite them and then commenced a tune with a tremendous blast of its trumpets and a thundering thump of its bass drum. The effect was amazing. Like the dried leaves of autumn before a hurricane, they fled as from a hideous and many tongued monster. Once arrived at a safe distance from the beast they hid behind trees and viewed, with cautious eyes, the cause of their dismay.

The Fourteenth Corps encamped for the night near Oxford, and the Twentieth around Williamsborough

Fifth Army Corps, Richmond, Virginia

The old pine woods south of Manchester are luminous tonight with the camp fires of the returning veterans of the Fifth Army Corps. Tomorrow they will be gratified with their first view of the city for which they so long and so nobly battled. Their first view, did I say? No, for in the long column are scores to whom the town will only serve to bring back to memory the long days and longer nights of privation and suffering endured in the former prison dens of the enemy. Following the Fifth will march the Second Corps, both on their way to Alexandria, where they will enjoy for a season the rest and relaxation to which they are so eminently entitled by their arduous service in the field. The battle fields of Cold Harbor, North Anna, Spotsylvania and Fredericksburg will probably be passed on their way to their point of destination.

Thursday, May 4, 1865

Citronville, Alabama

"Lieutenant General Taylor has this day surrendered to me with the forces under his command, on substantially the same terms as those accepted by General Lee.

E. R. S. Canby."

Twentieth Corps near the Meherrin River, Virginia

This morning both corps reached the Roanoke river, at Taylor's Ford, joined their pontoon trains, forming a bridge three hundred and eighty-five yards long, and crossed, the Fourteenth Corps thence taking the road to Nottoway Cross Roads via Boydtown and Lewistown, and the Twentieth making for Black's and White's.

The day passed without much incident, both commands making good marches.

Mobile, Alabama,
Union Account

Lieutenant General Taylor has this day surrendered the forces under his command on substantially the same terms as those accepted by General Lee.

The interview took place at Magee's plantation, fourteen miles from Mobile, on the Baltimore and Ohio Railroad. General Canby was accompanied by his Chief of Staff, General Osterhaus, and Captain C. T. Barrett, Aid-de-Camp, Generals Granger and West, and Commodore Palmer, with members of their staffs, also went out with the party. General Taylor was accompanied by Colonel Levi, Major Cornell and Captain Bullard.

The interview lasted five hours, three of which were private between Canby and Taylor, and what transpired during that time is not yet made public; but there is little doubt, from Canby's well-known sentiments, that the terms he offered to the Rebel commander were the same as granted by Grant to Lee. General Taylor was desirous to obtain similar terms as those at first granted by Sherman, but failed. What the exact understanding arrived at was, we cannot say; but at the termination of the interview, which was very pleasant throughout, General Taylor started for Meridian, Mississippi, and General Canby returned to Mobile.

Friday, May 5, 1865

Twentieth Army Corps near the
Big Nottoway River, Virginia

As the army nears Richmond it begins to grow impatient. Home becomes near and more vivid in the mind's eye, and hearts beat more longingly for the loved ones at home. The soldiers eagerly discuss the prospects of their early muster out of the service, and universally hope that they will not be detained any longer than is absolutely necessary.

Since leaving Raleigh the Twentieth Corps has marched one hundred and eleven miles in six days, going into camp nearly always at three o'clock in the afternoon, and the Fourteenth Corps has done- equally well. There is no trouble in marching troops toward home. By Tuesday noon the Army of Georgia will be encamped around Richmond.

Sixteenth Army Corps, Montgomery, Alabama

We arrived here from Blakely, on the 25th of April, marching by way of Greenville. The distance is one hundred and eighty miles; time of marching, thirteen days, including one day of rest at Greenville. Major General Grierson, with a cavalry command, passed us at Greenville, striking out to Americus, Georgia. He has been heard from at Eufaula, Alabama, where Governor Watts had taken up his abode and located the fugitive seat of Government of Alabama.

The first half of the march from Blakely was through pine woods—*barrens* the country is called, the soil being light, but by no means barren—with very few clearings or settlers. A few families of Creek half-breeds, and of the "poor white trash," were the only inhabitants of the country.

For two days before we reached Greenville, and from Greenville to Montgomery, the country is well settled and cultivated.

No Union army had passed through the country before us, and the people were greatly excited and terrified. The wealthy planters tried to hide their stock and supplies, but in vain. The mules and loads of bacon were dragged out of the swamps and hiding places, to replenish our scant commissary supplies, and to replace worn-out animals in the train.

The Negroes hailed us as deliverers. They thronged the highways, almost impeding our march. I have heard the number that came into Montgomery with the corps estimated as high as five thousand.

In many cases we advised them to stay with their old masters, but they said "No da was going to be free," and that their old masters had treated them too cruelly.

One old man seventy-eight years old, born in the North and a free man, had been kidnapped at the age of fifteen and had been held in slavery *sixty-three* years. He said this was the first chance he had had in all these long years of slavery to regain his liberty, and he was bound to avail himself of it; he wouldn't risk staying with his old master and take the chance of being made free by the laws.

It was truly surprising to see the correct knowledge these Negroes had of the war. They knew the "Yanks" were their friends; they knew that the approach of the Federal army meant deliverance.

Saturday, May 6, 1865

Richmond, Virginia

The author of the Southern History of the War, E. A. Pollard, and his brother, H. E. Pollard, were arrested last night and committed to Castle Thunder. They were connected with The Examiner, and have been and are now exceedingly bitter against the United States Government. Mr. E. A. Pollard, as will be remembered, was for a while prisoner in Fort Warren, was paroled and allowed to come to Richmond to be exchanged for Mr. A. D. Richardson, but before his arrival here Mr. Richardson made his escape from Salisbury. General Butler says that he was to be exchanged for Mr. Richardson and no one else. He has been at large through the week and has not bridled his tongue.

He was arrested by Colonel Coughlin, of the Tenth New Hampshire, who is Provost Marshal of the District of Virginia, an able and efficient officer. When brought before Colonel Coughlin, he said: "Do you take away my parole?"'

"O no, you may keep your parole, I do not arrest you because you have been connected with The Examiner, or for what you have published, but for what you have said since the occupation of the city."

When informed that he was to be sent to Castle Thunder, his countenance fell. He asked permission to take his clothes, which was granted, and at sunset Saturday night he and his brother entered the door where many better men than they have suffered long imprisonment—eaten by vermin, suffocated by intolerable stench, and starved till they were walking skeletons. So the wheel turns, grinding the grinders."

E. A. Pollard

Castle Thunder Prison, Richmond, Virginia

Vicksburg, Mississippi

"The Vicksburg Herald" extra of this date gives additional official information confirmatory of the surrender of General Dick Taylor and command to General Canby on the 4th. This makes almost a clean sweep of the Rebel troops in arms east of the Mississippi river, there being no other important commands in that section to oppose the progress of Union troops. It is also stated in the dispatch which was received through the Rebel lines, that points in the interior will be immediately occupied as garrisons by our troops, in order to suppress jayhawkers and guerrillas, preserve order and protect the people. The extra says that General Dana will probably make his headquarters at Jackson, Mississippi, at a very early period. Up to today about four thousand Rebel prisoners of war have been received at this city (Vicksburg) for delivery to the Rebel Bureau of Exchange. Colonel N. G. Watts, of the Confederate Exchange Bureau, made the following speech to the Confederate prisoners on board:

Fellow Soldiers: I have received this morning official information of the surrender of Lieutenant General Dick Taylor. I *am afraid the Confederacy is no more.* Jackson is no longer ours. I am now the only man that has authority to parole you. Those belonging to the Trans-Mississippi Department wishing to go there will be sent. Those of this Department can go to their homes, there to remain law-abiding citizens to those laws under which you have fallen. You will remain at your homes until further orders.

Lt. Gen. Richard Taylor

Monday, May 8, 1865

Army of the Tennessee, Petersburg, Virginia

At eight o'clock this morning, Major General Howard and staff, commanding the Army of the Tennessee, took position in front of Jarrett's Hotel for the purpose of reviewing the Seventeenth Corps, Major General Frank Blair commanding, as they marched through Petersburg on their way to Richmond and Alexandria.

According to orders previously received from Headquarters Department of the Tennessee, the Corps marched in "column of fours by the flank," which, strictly speaking, was not in " order of review."

As the different Brigades and Divisions of the Corps passed through the city, their excellent marching, elasticity of step and fine soldierly appearance was the subject of remark of every one who witnessed them, every man was in his proper place, and the different regiments were well closed up; the men looked just as fresh as when they started from Raleigh, and were in excellent spirits at the prospects of an early return to their homes.

More than two-thirds of the men comprising the Army of the Tennessee are veteran troops, who have marched through the greater portion of the so-called Southern Confederacy, and there are but few regiments in the command who have not marched upward of six thousand miles, incredible as it may appear, since their first enlistment and muster into service. They are consequently trained to marching, and it is doubtful if there is any other army in the world capable of making the extraordinary marches which Sherman's Army can now make with comparative ease.

The flags which the different regiments and brigades carried, by their tattered and ragged appearance, told unmistakably of the many hard-fought battles which now form a portion of the history of the country, and were frequently applauded and saluted as they passed through, by the crowds of soldiers from the garrison of this city, who lined the streets and sidewalks along the line of march.

The transportation was in excellent condition, and reflected the greatest credit of the General commanding and his subordinate officers. They followed in rear of the infantry column, and were the subject of remark by the officers of the Potomac Army present.

The Seventeenth Corps will march to Swift Creek, a point about six miles distant from Petersburg, and there go into camp for night. Tomorrow morning they will resume their march and proceed as far as Manchester, halting on this side of the river, where preparation has been made to provide the army with full rations for the remainder of the march to Alexandria.

The Fifteenth Army Corps, Major General John A. Logan, will be reviewed tomorrow at about eight o'clock in the morning, as they pass through this city to Alexandria, via Richmond.

Dick Turner, the noted turnkey of Libby Prison, is securely locked up in the most dismal, subterranean dungeon of that place of torture. There is no pity felt for him in Richmond. He is as pale as leprosy, his beard whitening, his deficient teeth ajar and his eyes full of terror. He is now as mean and cringing in his behavior as, in power, he was insolent and cruel. When turnkey, he shot men dead with a revolver, who came to the windows for air and light, kicked and knocked down others, and took delight in augmenting the untold miseries of the poor prisoners under his charge. He has heard, in his loathsome cell, that the soldiers have decreed his death so soon as they are fully assured of his identity, and his pleadings for mercy are presented to all who come near him; but he pleads to hearts of stone.

Tuesday, May 9, 1865

Petersburg, Virginia

The Seventeenth and Fifteenth Corps of Sherman's Army—dusty and tired infantry columns, mounted officers, cavalry battalions, martial bands in full blast, fluttering banners, rattling artillery trains, and rumbling army wagons—have been passing through Petersburg all day, bound for Manchester, opposite Richmond, and thence for Alexandria, by way of the battlefields of last spring.

The entire army (that is, all that is coming north, at present), struck the Southside Railroad at White's and Black's Station, the Twentieth and Fourteenth Corps marching direct for Manchester by way of Beverly's bridge across the Appomattox, and the other two corps coming this way, for the sake of more marching room.

The dusty veterans of the South were received by our troops here, and the loyal citizens, with every demonstration of respect and admiration. Many were the huzzas that greeted them from our own strong-lunged boys and many a waving banner and white handkerchief welcomed them, from the windows and balconies of Union appreciating citizens.

I was proud to recognize the native western element so strongly marked in this distinguished army.

Sheridan's Cavalry start from here, overland for Alexandria, tomorrow morning.

The Second Brigade of the Second Division, under Colonel Young, has gone in the direction of Lynchburg, for the present, to attend to any police duty that may be required of them.

A considerable amount of travel is now beginning to take place on the railroads in this vicinity, and on the James River, in the way of Northern people coming South, and Southern people going North. They mingle as harmoniously together, or more so, than the people of the two sections did before the war.

Paroling Johnston's Army, Raleigh, North Carolina

In the unfinished condition of the rolls at the close of my previous letter, the numbers actually paroled of J. D. Johnston's army could only be approximated. General Hartsuff has since completed the entire lists, from which I have been permitted to make up a resume, and I send it herewith.

The whole number of officers and men paroled proves to have been twenty-nine thousand nine hundred and twenty-four. The officers mentioned personally signed their own parole, and also the muster-rolls of their respective commands. Before doing this, however, they were careful to have an inspection of the men actually present, refusing to be held for a large number who were borne on the rolls, but who had absented themselves. The number of Johnston's army at the time hostilities were terminated, on the 17th and 18th of April, is estimated by General Hartsuff at fifty thousand men of all arms. The delay in concluding negotiations produced the belief that the war would be renewed, and a large number availed themselves of the peaceful interlude to make good their escape. It will be seen that this makes a clean sweep of the Rebel army east of the Mississippi, officers and men, with the exception of Hampton, Wheeler, Vaughn, Basil Duke, and one or two others, who have followed the fortunes of Davis toward the Trans-Mississippi.

A dispatch from General Wilson, commanding the cavalry in Georgia, brings the cheering intelligence that he had headed off Davis and his party, and had pressed them so hard that all his escort except a small number had deserted him (report says about forty), and these he was pursuing hard after. The news comes from Macon, Georgia.

Upon opening the paroling office at Greensborough, General Hartsuff observed a Confederate officer who had been standing near the door from a very early hour. He pressed in eagerly and first signed the following to a parole already written out in his own hand: "Rear Admiral and Brigadier General, C. S. N. and C. S. A., R. Semmes."

The following is a complete list of Johnston's army:

General Joseph E. Johnston, commanding Army of the Tennessee, personal and general staff and executive bureaus, total - 333
General G. T. Beauregard, "second in command," and staff - 24
Provost Marshal General, Army of Tennessee, and absentees reporting to him - 241
Unassigned officers and men - 106
Unattached officers and men, Army of Northern Virginia - 15
Major General L, L. Lomax and staff – 12
Lieutenant General Stewart, staff and headquarters attaches - 108
Major General E. C. Walthall - 74
Major General Loring - 15
Major General P. Anderson - 41

Officers and men of the corps - 8,586
Total 9,555

Beauregard evidently had regard to his family connections. There are two "Beauregards" and two "Toutants" on his personal staff. He had nine aids-decamp. His signature is one of the boldest and clearest of the whole list.

Lieutenant General S. D. Lee, staff and headquarters' attaches - 116
Major General Hill, staff and headquarters' attaches - 22
Major General Stevenson, staff and headquarters' attaches - 53
Officers and men of the corps - 4,765
Total - 4,956

Lieutenant General W. J. Hardee, staff and headquarters, &c - 201
Major General Brown - 82
Major General R. F. Hoke - 62
Major General Cheatham - 153
Officers and men 9,060
Major General Butler (cavalry), staff, &c. - 150
Cavalry Division - 2,346
Total – 12,054

NAVAL BRIGADE

Rear Admiral R. Semmes - 203
Other naval officers and men, under flag of Forrest - 103
Medical officers, stewards and attendants, and officers and men, patients in hospital - 1,002
Unattached, reserve artillery - 1252
Detachments reporting to the Commandant Post at Greensborough - - 717
Total – 3277

Grand total, present and paroled, officers and men - 29,924
The wasting effects of war were never more apparent than in this Southern army, as may be seen by an inspection of these muster-rolls. The following are a few sample cases:
The Forty-sixth North Carolina Volunteers had three officers, three non-commissioned officers and eight men —total, fourteen.

The Forty-seventh North Carolina Volunteers had two officers, two non-commissioned officers and three men—total, seven.

The Forty-eighth North Carolina Volunteers had three officers, three non-commissioned officers and fourteen men—total, twenty.

It required nine regiments of North Carolina troops to make a battalion of sixty-one officers and men.

The original number of these regiments was, maximum, one thousand men each.

The muster-roll of the Second North Carolina Reserves had indorsed upon it "18 men." This was scratched out, and the word "boys" substituted for men. They were all squirrel-hunting boys.

Five regiments of North Carolina troops had only, footed up, one hundred and fifty-seven men, including Brigade Headquarters.

The First, Fourth, Fifth and Sixth South Carolina Cavalry mustered, all told, two hundred and sixty men.

Wednesday, May 10, 1865

Capture of Jefferson Davis, Irwinsville, Georgia

Colonel Prichard learned yesterday where Jeff's party was encamped, and just before daylight this morning we surrounded the camp. It was supposed that Davis had a considerable force as guard and a severe fight was expected. By an unfortunate and so far unaccountable accident one part of the force fired upon another, and before the mistake was discovered two men were killed and six others slightly wounded. Captain Hudson had placed a strong guard around the tent where Davis was supposed to be, and when the firing commenced, thinking his duty called him to the fight, he left the tent in charge of a Corporal with orders to let no one pass out. The Corporal went to the door where he was met by a lady, who proved to be Mrs. Davis, and who said that tent was occupied by ladies and she hoped they would be permitted to dress before being disturbed. Very soon, she again and voluntarily appeared at the door, with another person in petticoats, morning dress and woolen cloak, with a hood closely drawn over the head and a pail on her arm. Corporal ordered halt! which was of course obeyed, but Mrs. Davis feelingly appealed to the Corporal to allow her *mother* to go to the spring for a pail of water—It was hard, even if they were prisoners, not to be allowed to get a little water for their morning ablutions. Mr. Corporal just then observed that the morning dress was not quite long enough to conceal a pair of boots looking rather too heavy for *"mother"* to wear, and, with his Spencer carbine presented to the aged lady's head, ordered her to remove that cloak. The argument was persuasive, even to the chivalry. The disguise was removed and Jeff. Davis appeared in full view. Davis said he should have defended himself if he had been armed—even if he had had a revolver he would have fought with it as long as he could. The Corporal replied to him, that he didn't appear to be in a very good fighting condition just at that time.

After a hurried breakfast the party was put in marching order. The prisoners, in ambulances, preceded by the band of the Fourth Michigan Cavalry, playing first "Yankee Doodle," which had evidently a depressing influence on the feelings of Mr. Davis; but when in a few minutes, the band struck into the somewhat familiar air of "John Brown's Body's Marching On," it was too much for endurance, and he actually fell prostrate in the ambulance, and was kept from view by his friends for a considerable time.

It was noticed in all his conversations, that his eyes were constantly toward the floor, as though the eye of a Yankee was not pleasant and agreeable to meet. He is dressed in a fine grey suit, and wears a drab soft hat. The last four years have added apparently more than ten to his age. With Mr. Stephens it is different. He is, for him, in tolerable health, and his eyes are keen and pleasant to look upon. He is very agreeable in conversation, and earnestly desires a permanent restoration of the Union. He says the advice and warning which he gave to the people of Georgia before she seceded were such as a wise man ought to give, but the majority overruled him. He concedes that slavery is at an end in this country.

Tallahassee, Florida

"The Rebel troops in Florida, with all the public property, surrendered to McCook today. The number of troops paroled and already reported is 7,200, and will, doubtless, reach 8,000 when the returns are complete.

The amount of property received from the Rebel authorities was: Ordnance stores—40 pieces artillery, 25,000 small arms, 450 sabers, 1,618 bayonets, 1,200 cartridge boxes, 710 waist belts, 63,000 pounds lead, 2,000 pounds niter, 200 sets accoutrements, 10,000 rounds artillery ammunition, fixed, 121,900 rounds small ammunition, 700 pounds musket balls, 325 pikes and lances, beside large amounts of various other ordnance stores. Quartermaster's stores—70 horses, 80 mules, 40 wagons, 4 ambulances, also tools of various kinds, with much stationery, clothing, and camp and garrison equipage. Commissary stores—170,000 pounds bacon, 300 barrels salt, 150 barrels sugar, 100 barrels syrup, 7,000 bushels corn, and 1,200 head of cattle, also quantities of flour, ground peas, &c. A large amount of hospital stores were also turned in to the medical officer, Dr. Chapman.

Totally unserviceable horses and mules were either exchanged for corn or forage, or loaned to the citizens, subject to the order of the Federal authorities."

Thursday, May 11, 1865

Fourteenth Army Corps, Richmond, Virginia

The great event of today was the passage through the city of a portion of Sherman's noble veterans, now homeward bound. The Fourteenth Corps, Brevet Major General Jefferson C. Davis commanding, and the Twentieth Corps, Major General John A. Logan, took tip the line of march from Manchester about seven o'clock this morning, crossing the pontoon bridge at Seventeenth Street, and marched through the town to Brook Avenue, the pike leading to Hanner Court House—the same route as that taken by the Army of the Potomac.

The appearance of the troops excited the admiration of all who had the pleasure of witnessing them on the march. The Fifteenth and Seventeenth Corps will pass through the city tomorrow.

Havana, Cuba

The Rebel Ram Stonewall, Page commanding, arrived this morning reporting from Teneriffe. She left that port April 1st, but it seems hardly probable that she has been forty-one days making the passage, and the report is that she has come from Nassau.

Some of the destruction Sherman poured upon Atlanta

Monday, May 15, 1865

Nashville, Tennessee, Union Account

Joe Brown, late Rebel Governor of Georgia, was brought to this city last night as a prisoner, and left for Louisville this evening. He has been a violent Rebel, but, on account of his opposition to Jeff. Davis, he has found some favor with the Union people of his State.

Jeff. Davis is under a strong guard, and will arrive in this city on Thursday evening.

Every Rebel body of regular soldiers, and every guerrilla organization in this State, and in northern Alabama, has given up to come under General Thomas's late order.

Thousands of Rebel soldiers have arrived here and taken oath, and are conducting themselves honorably.

Joseph E. Brown

Tuesday, May 16, 1865

General Sheridan's Account of the Battle of Five Forks

General Sheridan has made his report of the operations of the cavalry and such other forces as were under his command in the closing campaign in Virginia. It bears the date May 16, would make about three and a half columns of this paper, and is written in his usual clear pointed and spirited style. He says the effective cavalry force was nine thousand men.

He says his first orders were to make a raid on the Southside railroad, and thence to join General Sherman, or return to Petersburg as the circumstances might dictate. But after he had started, and during the night of March 29, General Grant sent him instructions to abandon the contemplated raid and act with the infantry under his immediate command, and if possible turn the right flank of Lee's Army. General Sheridan then details the operations of March 30, which resulted in the forcing back and partial discomfiture of our forces. He then continues:

"During the night of the 31st of March my headquarters were at Dinwiddie Court House, and the Lieutenant General notified me that the Fifth Corps would report to me and should reach me by midnight. This corps had been offered to me on the 30th, but very much desiring the Sixth Corps, which had been with me in the Shenandoah Valley, I asked for it; but on account of the delay which would occur in moving that corps from its position in the line in the front of Petersburg, it could not be sent to me."

At three o'clock on the morning of April 1st, General Sheridan issued his orders to General Warren. They were to attack vigorously at daylight, and he adds that had General Warren moved according to the expectations of the Lieutenant General, there would appear to have been but little chance for the escape of the enemy's infantry in front of Dinwiddie Court House. General Sheridan's report of this day's operations, known as the Battle of Five Forks, is written in his best style and is a most graphic picture. His plan is best told in his own words, viz.:

"I determined that I would drive the enemy with the cavalry to the Five Forks, press them inside of their works, and make a feint to turn their right flank, and, meanwhile, quietly move up the Fifth Corps with a view to attacking their left flank, crush the whole force if possible, and drive westward those who might escape, thus isolating them from their army at Petersburg."

~ 293 ~

Happily this conception was successfully executed.
After speaking of the operations of the cavalry, he continues:

"I then rode over to where the Fifth Corps was going into position and found them coming up very slowly. I was exceedingly anxious to attack at once, for the sun was getting low, and we had to fight or go back. It was no place to entrench, and it would have been shameful to have gone back with no results to compensate for the loss of the brave men who had fallen during the day. In this connection I will say that General Warren did not exert himself to get up his corps as rapidly as he might have done, and his manner gave me the impression that he wished the sun to go down before dispositions for the attack could be completed. As soon as the corps were in position I ordered an advance. The Fifth Corps, on reaching the White Oak road, made a left wheel and burst on the enemy's left flank and rear like a tornado and pushed rapidly on, orders having been given that if the enemy was routed there should be no halt to re-form the broken lines. As stated before, the firing of the Fifth Corps was the signal to General Merritt to assault, which was promptly responded to, and the works of the enemy were soon carried at several points by our brave cavalrymen. The enemy were driven from their strong line of works and completely routed. The Fifth Corps doubling up their left flank in confusion, and the cavalry of General Merritt dashing on the White Oak road, capturing their artillery and turning it upon them and riding into their broken ranks, so demoralized them that they made no serious stand after their line was carried, but took to flight in disorder. Between five thousand and six thousand prisoners fell into our hands, and the fugitives were driven westward, and were pursued until long after dark by Merritt's and McKenzie's cavalry for a distance of six miles. During this attack I again became dissatisfied with General Warren during the engagement. Portions of his line gave way when not exposed to a heavy fire, and simply from want of confidence on the part of the troops, which General Warren did not exert himself to inspire. I therefore relieved him from the command of the Fifth Corps, authority for this action having been sent to me before the battle, unsolicited."

In those extracts General Warren will find the answer to his late letter in the newspaper, in which he professes ignorance of the cause of his supercedure. General Sheridan speaks in the warmest terms of the Fifth Corps, as well as of his own cavalry force, saying they all seemed to realize that the success of the campaign and the fate of

Lee's army depended on the result of that day's fighting. The report then details, at considerable length, the pursuit of Lee's army. The opening paragraph of his account of the operations of April 3d is as follows:

"On arriving at Jettersville I learned without doubt that Lee and his whole army were at Amelia Court House. The Fifth Corps were at once ordered to entrench, with a view of holding Jettersville until the main army could come up. It seems to me that this was the only chance the Army of Northern Virginia had to save itself, which might have been done had General Lee promptly attacked and driven back the comparatively small force opposed to him, and pursued his march to Burkesville Junction."

In continuing the report, General Sheridan expresses regret at having, on the 3d, given up the command of Miles's Division of the Second Corps, on the 6th of the Fifth Corps, and expresses the belief that he could have accomplished more decisive results had he been allowed to retain control of these troops. He takes occasion to speak in the highest terms of the Sixth Corps, which was ordered to report to him on the night of the 5th. And he adds, "On the arrival of Major General Wright he reported his corps to me, and from that time until after the battle received my orders and obeyed them; but after the engagement was over and General Meade had communicated with General Wright, the latter declined to make his report to me until ordered to do so by the Lieutenant General."

Friday, May 19, 1865

Memphis, Tennessee

The influx of paroled Rebel troops into Memphis caused a great excitement among the Negro troops.

They got up a plot to assassinate every Rebel soldier in Memphis in revenge for the Fort Pillow massacre.

This plot was discovered last night, and the white troops were put on guard to watch the movements of the Negroes.

At a given hour the Negroes attempted to come out of the fort to carry out their purpose, when they were ordered back again by the white troops.

The Negroes refused to obey the order, and a fight forthwith ensued.

After a short conflict twenty of the Negroes were killed and wounded and driven back in confusion into the fort.

A strong guard is now kept over them.

Saturday, May 20, 1865

Washington, D.C.

It has been ascertained that while the Rebel General Imboden was in charge of Rebel prisons South, he issued an order to the effect that if any prisoner or prisoners of war confined in any of the military prisons in the States of Georgia, Alabama, or Mississippi shall engage in any meeting, or attempt by force to escape, the guard shall instantly fire upon the mutineers, and, if necessary, upon the whole body of prisoners, until perfect order is restored, and every prisoner found with arms in his hands at the time of any meeting or possible attempt to escape shall be instantly shot to death, and this penalty will in no case be remitted where such armed prisoners are overpowered by surrendering to the guard on the suppression of a meeting. He also directed that all prisoners of war who conducted themselves in an orderly manner should be treated with that humanity becoming the Christian people of the Confederate States.

Monday, May 22, 1865

Fortress Monroe, Virginia

At one o'clock this afternoon the steamer Silas B. Pierce left Baltimore Wharf at this place with Brevet Major General Miles, accompanied by other officers of prominence, and proceeded immediately to the steamer William P. Clyde, at anchor in the stream, with Jeff. Davis and remainder of the Rebel party on board. An hour, perhaps sufficient to give departing Rebels time to take a long farewell of friends and dear ones, was awarded them. The harbor, which usually is crowded with all kinds and classes of vessels, today looked almost deserted. Scarcely a dozen sail vessels could be counted, and even they seemed dull and listless. Colonel Roberts, Commander of Fortress Monroe, perceiving the absolute necessity of maintaining strict discipline in conformity with the wishes of the Government, that the transfer of the Rebel party to Fortress Monroe should be conducted in as quiet a manner as possible, very early in the morning stationed guards in the immediate vicinity of the casemates, wherein are cells intended for the incarceration of the prisoners, and also along the ravines, paths and routes they would be obliged to traverse while en route to the Fortress. In a short time after the Pierce reached the wharf the prisoners began to land. Such were the arrangements strictly enforced by the military authorities that no person was allowed to approach the wharf where the prisoners landed except at a distance of over five hundred yards. As the prisoners marched up the wharf, preceded by a guard of their captors of the Fourth Michigan cavalry, the tall, spare form of Jeff Davis, dressed in grey clothes and wearing a light felt hat, could be easily discerned. As soon as the prisoners were all ashore, they were marched up along the beach to the sallyport of the water-battery in the rear of the Fortress, and thence to their cells in the second tier of casemates. Clement C. Clay accompanied Jeff. Davis inside the Fortress, and also, it is supposed, the largest portion of his personal staff. Mrs. Davis and her four children, her brother and sister and the wife of Clement C. Clay remain on board the steamer Clyde; and, it is thought, will be sent south this evening, as orders have been received from the War Department prohibiting them from going north. The parting between Jeff Davis and his family is described to have been of an extremely affecting nature, during which the feelings of the once ambitious and desperate Rebel leader were completely overcome. Major General Halleck has been here during the past three days superintending the arrangements made for the confinement of the Rebel prisoners. Stringent orders in relation to visiting the Fortress have been issued, and all civilians are prohibited from entering it, unless duly provided with a pass from Major General Halleck.

Richmond, Virginia

The arrival of the Sixth Corps, now encamped without the fortifications of Richmond, has broken in upon the dull monotony of this city, and its crowded streets testify that these sturdy veterans enjoy with intense satisfaction the privileges of an ended campaign. They left Danville last Tuesday, reaching Manchester Saturday afternoon. Thursday this corps will pass through Richmond on its way to Alexandria, whether there to be mustered out, or to be detailed for a short and important service, cannot at present be known. Furloughs are granted twenty a day to each regiment, which will give the boys an opportunity to visit the points of interest, and see what a dilapidated condition even this center of Rebellion had fallen into.

Tuesday, May 23, 1865

Kirby Smith Ready to Surrender
Baton Rouge, Louisiana

Brigadier General Brent, and Colonels Deblau, C. Burke and Seip arrived here today as commissioners from Kirby Smith. General Herron and Lieutenant Commander Foster came down from Red River with them. General Herron has gone to General Canby, and it is believed here that terms are arranged for the surrender of Kirby Smith's whole army.

THE GRAND REVIEW IN WASHINGTON
AT THE CLOSE OF THE WAR
150,000 UNION TROOPS IN LINE

This morning, according to general orders, the Army of the Potomac entered Washington, and were reviewed by President Johnson. The weather was everything that could be desired. The atmosphere was pleasant, the sun shone with unclouded splendor, and the recent rains have laid the dust, thus rendering the streets in good marching condition. Thousands of persons, including many from other cities who had specially come to see the pageant, lined the sidewalks from the Capitol to the Executive Mansion, a distance of a mile and a half, while windows, and balconies and all eligible positions, including housetops, were occupied by deeply interested spectators. All public business was suspended, and there was a general holiday. The Capitol bore the motto in large letters, "The only national debt we never can pay is the debt we owe to the victorious Union soldiers." The national flag flew from all the public buildings, while from the windows on the line of procession the Stars and Stripes were profusely displayed.

At 9 o'clock the seemingly interminable lines of bristling bayonets and flashing sabers, borne by the boys in Federal blue commenced to unfold themselves around the National Capitol where, as was meet, the children of the city to the number of many thousands had come to greet the battle-worn and scarred heroes of the Republic with banners, mottoes, songs of cheer, garlands of flowers and approving smiles. The immense column moved in the following order:

ARMY OF THE POTOMAC

General George G. Meade, Commander and Staff

Squadron of the 1st Massachusetts Cavalry
as Headquarters Escort

CAVALRY CORPS
Major General MERRITT, Commanding
Headquarters Escort, 5th U. S. Cavalry

THIRD CAVALRY DIVISION
General George A. Custer, Commanding
1st Brigade, Colonel Wells, Commanding
15th N. Y. Cavalry
8th N. Y. Cavalry
1st Vt. Cavalry
2d Brigade, Colonel Capehart, Commanding
2d W. Va. Cavalry
3d W. Va. Cavalry
1st W. Va. Cavalry
1st N. Y. Light Cavalry
3d Brigade, Colonel Pennington, Commanding
2d N. Y. Cavalry
24th N. Y. Cavalry
1st N. J. Cavalry
1st Penna. Cavalry

This is Custer's Division, one which has accomplished more in a short space of time than any other division in the army. It is probably the finest division of troopers in the world. The following address of General Custer to his troops will give some idea of the tremendous blows struck at the Rebellion by this division:

Headquarters Third Cavalry Division
Appomattox Court House, Va., April 9, 1865

Soldiers Of The Third Cavalry Division: With profound gratitude toward the God of battles, by whose blessings our enemies have been humbled and our arms rendered triumphant, your Commanding General avails himself of this, his first opportunity, to express to you his admiration of the heroic manner in which you have passed through the series of battles which today resulted in the surrender of the enemy's entire army.

The record established by your indomitable courage is unparalleled in the annals of war. Your prowess has won for you even the respect and admiration of your enemies. During the past six months, although in most instances confronted by superior numbers, you have captured from the enemy, in open battle, one hundred and eleven pieces of field artillery, sixty-five battle-flags, and upwards of ten thousand prisoners of war, including seven general officers. Within the past ten days, and included in the above, you have captured forty-six pieces of field artillery and thirty-seven battle flags. You have never lost a gun, never lost a color, and have never been defeated; and notwithstanding the numerous engagements in which you have borne a prominent part, including these memorable battles of the Shenandoah, you have captured every piece of artillery which the enemy has dared to open upon you. The near approach of peace renders it improbable that you will again be called upon to undergo the fatigues of the toilsome march or the exposure of the battlefield; but should the assistance of keen blades, wielded by your sturdy arms, be required to hasten the coming of that glorious peace for which we have been so long contending, the General commanding is proudly confident that, in the future as in the past, every demand will meet with a hearty and willing response.

Let us hope that our work is done, and that, blessed with the comforts of peace, we may be permitted to enjoy the pleasures of home and friends. For our comrades who have fallen, let us ever cherish a grateful remembrance. To the wounded, and to those who languish in Southern prisons, let our heartfelt sympathy be tendered.

And now, speaking for myself alone: When the war is ended and the task of the historian begins—when those deeds of daring which have rendered the name and fame of the Third Cavalry Division imperishable are inscribed upon the bright pages of our country's history, I only ask that my name may be written as that of the commander of the Third Cavalry Division.

> G. A. Custer
> Brevet Major General Commanding
> L. W. Barnhart, Captain and A. A. A. G.

The third brigade of this division has done the heaviest fighting. This was formerly commanded by Custer.

In the Battle of Moorfield, on the 7th of August, 1864, the brigade distinguished itself in a most extraordinary manner. To its valor we are mainly indebted for that brilliant victory which gave us forty-two Rebel officers as prisoners, several hundred privates, four pieces of artillery and five battle flags. The cup of rejoicing at Moorfield was not without mingled emotions of sorrow; indeed, when it was known that Major S. B. Conger and Lieutenant L. Clark of the Third West Virginia Cavalry were among the killed, a great grief spread through the entire brigade. Two braver officers never drew swords in defense of a country. Peace to their memory. In the five days' fighting that took place in the vicinity of Bunker Hill, in the Shenandoah, the brigade again added fresh laurels to the many already acquired. These laurels, however, were not won without heavy loss. Among their captures were three battle flags and Early's headquarters wagons, as well as many prisoners. It again bore conspicuous part in the sanguinary Battle of the Opequan, fought on the 19th of September, 1864, and again at the Battle of Fisher's Hill, on the 22d. It had the right of the line, which they held against overwhelming odds, turning the enemy's left and probably deciding the battle in our favor. At Mount Jackson, on the 23d, it again behaved admirably. On September 24th, 1864, Colonel H. Capehart, of Ohio, was appointed to the command of the brigade. The appointment has fully vindicated the wisdom of the appointing power, as the Colonel has justly established a reputation of which any officer might well be proud. The first day the Colonel commanded the brigade, they killed seventeen of Rosser's Cavalry. On September 26th, the enemy was driven from Wier's Cave through Brown's Gap, and on the 27th was fought the Battle of Wier's Cave, in which we suffered severely. About the 6th of October the brigade bore an honorable part in the successful reconnaissance to Sperryville, as also later at Guard Hill, and still later it acquitted itself with honor in the two successive attacks at Milford. In the fearful Battle of Cedar Creek, on the 19th, our cavalry of which the Third was the most prominent brigade, held in check the enemy's cavalry, and prevented our forces from being flanked, and is thought by many to have changed the fortunes of that fearful day. On the 12th of November the Battle of Nineveh was fought by this brigade *alone*. It was one of the cleanest victories ever achieved in the valley. Among the captures were two pieces of artillery, two battle-flags, two hundred prisoners, and McCausland's entire wagon train.

At Waynesborough on March 2, 1865, the First and Second Brigades of the Third Division, under the immediate supervision of General Custer—who was on the field, carefully arranging the programme of the battle and inspiring all with his own spirit and determination—was massed and a part dismounted on the right, leaving the center open for the Third, which opportunity they at once improved, behaving, as the regiments composing this brigade have always done, in the very best possible manner. The work was short, decisive, and the victory complete, the chivalry running in the wildest confusion without system or order, and our men thundering at their heels. We charged them ten miles through Rockfish Gap, over fences, hedges, ditches and dikes, and through the deep mud, regardless of suffering and personal peril, until the dense darkness compelled a halt, when the results of victory were summed up as follows: Fourteen hundred and fifty prisoners, eleven guns, nine battle-flags, one hundred and fifty wagons heavily laden with every variety of stores, including General Early's headquarter wagons with his personal wares, &c, &c. Never was victory more complete or the route of an army more thorough. Again at the Battle of Dinwiddie Court House, the brigade distinguished itself. It had been in the rear of the wagon train, but at that critical moment General Custer sent for and hurried it up, a distance of eight miles on the gallop. The field was reached just at the opportune moment, and it was probably owing to its arrival that the enemy fell back during the night. At the fearful and decisive Battle of Five Forks, on the 31st of March, the position of the brigade was on the left of the line, where it distinguished itself by completely flanking the enemy and cutting off his retreat, and thus contributing greatly to break the lock that had so long kept us out of Richmond.

On April 3d the brigade signalized itself by its great bravery at the Battle of Sailor's Creek, capturing seven pieces of artillery, fifteen hundred prisoners, fourteen battle-flags, five Major Generals, viz.: Major General Ewell, Major General Kershaw, Major General Custus Lee, Major General Burton Corse, and Major General Semmes, also one hundred wagons. With a degree of impetuosity seldom equaled, and bravery equal to that of the Spartan band, this brigade alone charged and carried the enemy's works, which were defended by two lines of infantry. In the great charges of this war there has been few, if any, more brilliant.

SECOND CAVALRY DIVISION
General Henry E. Davis, Commanding

1st Brigade

10th N. Y. Cavalry
24th N. Y. Cavalry
1st N. J. Cavalry
1st Penna. Cavalry

FIRST CAVALRY DIVISION

General Thomas C. Deven, Commanding
Reserve Brigade, General Gibbs, Commanding

6th N. Y. Battalion
2d Mass. Cavalry
6th Penna. Cavalry

2d Brigade
Colonel C. L. Fitzhugh, Commanding

6th N. Y. Battalion
1st N. Y. Cavalry
20th Penna. Cavalry
17th Penna. Cavalry
9th N. Y. Cavalry.

1st Brigade
Colonel Peter Stagg, Commanding

6th Michigan Cavalry
7th Michigan Cavalry
1st Michigan Cavalry
5th Michigan Cavalry

Horse Artillery Brigade
Colonel James M. Robertson, Commanding

Battery C, 2d U. S.
Battery B, 2d U. S.
Battery L, 2d U. S.
Battery L, 5th U. S.
Battery D, 2d U. S.
Battery M, 2d U. S.
Battery C, 4th U. S.
Battery E, 4th U. S.
6th New York Independent Battery

Provost Marshal Generals' Brigade
General G. N. Macy, Commanding

2d Penna. Cavalry
1st Mass. Cavalry
3d U. S. Infantry

10th U. S. Infantry

Engineers Brigade
General W. H. Benham, Commanding

Battalion of Regular Engineers
15th N. Y. Engineers
50th N. Y. Engineers

SECOND BRIGADE, FIRST CAVALRY DIVISION

The following circular will give an idea of the work accomplished in one campaign by the 2d Brigade of this division:

Hdqrs. Second Brigade, First Cavalry Division
Middle Military Division, Nov. 6, 1864

Soldiers: The Brevet Brigadier General Commanding feels that he should not allow the present opportunity to pass without referring to and recalling the operations of his brigade during the late engagements.

Rapidly transferred from the Army of the Potomac to the Shenandoah Valley, you, on the second day's march, engaged a brigade of mounted infantry and in one hour drove them from two strong positions in utter rout. Again, at Front Royal, Smithfield, Kearneysville, and Shepherdstown, your sturdy arms and keen sabers on each occasion hurled back the serried masses of the foe. At the Battle of the Opequan, after charging and routing a superior force of the enemy's cavalry in your front, you whirled like a thunderbolt on the left of his infantry lines, and rode them down in the face of a withering fire, in two successive charges, capturing over five hundred prisoners and five battle flags.

When detached from the Division, and in advance during the long pursuits of Early's army from Fisher's Hill to Port Republic, your gallantry and daring while pressing the enemy called forth the highest praise. In the action of the 9th of October, taking the advance near Edinburg, you drove Lomax's Division "whirling" through Mount Jackson and across the Shenandoah, capturing his last gun and his train.

On the memorable 19th of October the crowning glory was reserved for you, of pursuing the enemy and reaping the fruits of that brilliant victory. After sturdily fighting from early morn with the gallant old Division to which you are attached, in its successful efforts to check and finally drive the enemy's right, you dashed across the bridge over Cedar Creek, under a heavy fire, charging and completely smashing the enemy's rear guard. Darkness did not relax your efforts, but on you pushed, capturing guns, trains and prisoners, until at near midnight, you had reached Fisher's Hill, eight miles from the battlefield.

At early dawn you charged and drove the enemy's cavalry from the hill, and pushed on to Woodstock after the fast flying foe who could not again be overtaken.

Twenty-two of the forty-three guns captured by the cavalry, fifty-nine wagons and ambulances, over four hundred prisoners (including a number of officers), and two battle flags, were the trophies of your success.

You have captured during this short campaign, twenty-four guns, nine battle flags in action, and over one thousand prisoners.

Tins brilliant success has not been effected without severe loss. One-third of your number, including forty officers, have been killed or wounded. They have fallen nobly at their post of duty.

Praise from me is superfluous. The record of your deeds is sufficient. You have done your duty, and the Brigade has maintained its old reputation.

Thomas C. Deven,
Brevet Brigadier General

FIRST BRIGADE, FIRST CAVALRY DIVISION

This brigade, now generally known as the Michigan or Custer's old brigade, is at present commanded by Colonel Peter Stagg, whose masterly management of the same during the spring campaign of 1865 has won both for it and himself imperishable laurels. It is composed of four Michigan regiments, the First, Fifth, Sixth and Seventh. The First, commanded by Lieutenant Colonel Maxwell, made a most brilliant charge at Five Forks, immediately under the eye of General Sheridan. Colonel Maxwell here lost a leg. The Fifth, commanded by Colonel Hastings, the Sixth by Lieutenant Colonel Vinton, and the Seventh by Lieutenant Colonel Briggs, all distinguished themselves at this the great fight of the season. At Sailor's Creek, April 6th, Colonel Stagg took his orders directly from General Sheridan, and with his brigade made two distinct and brilliant charges, for which he was complimented on the field. At Appomattox also it was hotly engaged, and was pressing the enemy heavily when the dirty white rag was displayed which virtually said treason was satisfied with war and desired peace. Thus, perhaps, may end the military career of one of the most noted brigades in the cavalry service.

RESERVE BRIGADE, FIRST CAVALRY DIVISION

This brigade was organized in March, 1863, as the Reserve (or Regular) Brigade, First Cavalry Division, as it was composed of the First, Second, Fifth and Sixth United States Cavalry only; which regiments have always been identified with the brigade, and have done the best of service. Various volunteer regiments have been attached to it from time to time, and done good duty in every respect. The brigade has been commanded, by the late Major General John Buford, while Brigadier General; Major General Wesley Merritt, while Brigadier General; the late Brigadier General Charles R. Lowell, while Colonel, and Brigadier General Alfred Gibbs, its present commander.

All will remember the reception on the day of its arrival; the streets were filled with joyful people—bands, glee clubs, church choirs and Sabbath school classes were playing and singing patriotic airs of welcome, and the wildest enthusiasm prevailed. The Division played a most conspicuous part upon that great battle-plain. Striking Lee in flank it brought him to bay in the right place, and then held him for one entire day, until General Meade could get his gallant army up and in position.

Buford's reputation was made from that day forward, and the Division carried with it the highest meed of praise. It participated in all the subsequent actions of the campaign—prominent at Falling Waters, Shepardstown, Brandy Station, Culpepper, and Raccoon Ford on the Rapidan River.

It participated in the most important reconnaissance that developed the design of General Lee to flank the Army of the Potomac in the fall of the same year, covering his left and rear from the south banks of the Rapidan river to the defenses of Washington without the loss of a *solitary wagon,* holding in check day after day the impulsive charges of Lee's best troops.

Especially did it distinguish itself at Stephensburg, Brandy Station, and Oak Hill. In the subsequent advance of the same season, it played a prominent part on the extreme right, south of Sulphur Springs. In this campaign the lamented Buford contracted the disease that cost him his life, to the sorrow of every officer and man in the division. Brigadier General Merritt succeeded him in command. In the spring of 1864 the corps was re-organized under

Major General Sheridan and Brigadier General Torbert was assigned to command of the division. General Merritt to the command of the Cavalry Reserve Brigade, General Curtis the First Brigade, and Colonel Deven the Second Brigade. The division became the right bower of Sheridan, and participated in all the engagements of the campaign against Richmond in 1864—including the raid around Richmond and Trevillian Station. Returning and crossing the James, it was employed on the left of the army, until, July, 1864, it embarked for the Shenandoah Valley. General Torbert was then made Chief of Cavalry, and General Merritt again took command of the division. To it and its gallant commander, in a peculiar measure belongs the glory of the Battle of Winchester, on the 19th of September; its captures during the bloody campaign were immense; it took part in every engagement, and captured more guns and materials on the 19th of October, at Cedar Creek, than it could remove during the entire night. Under command of Brigadier General Thomas C. Deven, on the 27th of February, 1865, it commenced its march with the corps to rejoin the Army of the Potomac, raiding through to the White House; thence via Deep Bottom to the left of the army. Again it led the advance to the Five Forks, and there, after three days of the severest fighting on record, carried the position, as shown by the dispatch of President Lincoln of April 2. Joining in the pursuit of the now routed Rebel army, it fought by day and marched by night until, the 9th of April, it locked hands with its gallant comrades around the terror-stricken minions of Secession at Appomattox Court House; returning to Petersburg with the corps, it hastily refitted, and marched upon Johnston in North Carolina, reaching the Don river; and the surrender of the enemy becoming known to the satisfaction of the authorities, it returned via Richmond to Washington.

The division *never lost a gun*—perhaps more than can be said of any other in this department; with its history is associated the greatest battles and the grandest victories and the most distinguished cavalry officers of the war. The names of Pleasanton, of Buford, of Merritt, of Torbert and Deven, of Gibbs and Stagg and Fitzhugh, are inseparably associated with the coming history of this war, and will be remembered in gratitude through generations to come.

The organization in the last campaign is as follows:

Division Commander, Brigadier General Thomas C. Deven. Brigade Commanders: Brigadier General Gibbs, Commander

Reserve Brigade; Colonel Peter Stagg, First Brigade; Colonel Charles L. Fitzhugh, Second Brigade.

The organization of the First Cavalry Division dates back to December 1, 1862, immediately after the ill-fated Battle of Fredericksburg, and was commanded by Brigadier General Alfred Pleasanton. It consisted of the First and Second Brigades, commanded respectively by Colonels Grimes Davis and Thomas C. Deven. It participated in the Battle of Chancellorsville, and won for itself an undying renown, see General Pleasanton's complimentary order of that date. Its gallantry in that engagement made its commander a full Major General, who shortly after took command of the Cavalry Corps. The division was for a short time afterward commanded by Colonel Thomas C. Deven, who fought it under the direction of Brigadier General John Buford, in the Battle of Beverly Ford, in June, 1863. The engagement was a severe one, and the division received the complimentary order of its commander. General Buford was shortly afterward assigned to the command, bringing with him to the division the "Cavalry Reserve Brigade," embracing all the regular cavalry in this Department, then commanded by Brigadier General Wesley Merritt. As thus reorganized, the division participated in the grand Pennsylvania campaign of 1863. At the Battle of Upperville it carried everything before it—gorging Stuart's thousands in the gapping rear of the town—turning its back upon the retreating foe, its march to Gettysburg was at once unprecedented—almost forty-eight hours in rear of the Army of the Potomac in developing to a *certainty* the ingenious design of the Rebel Lee, it marched past its faithful comrades with the speed of veteran patriots and reached the famous hills of Gettysburg twenty-four hours in advance of Meade's infantry.

LIST OF ENGAGEMENTS

Kelly's Ford, March 18, 1863
Fleming's Cross Roads, May 4, 1863
Beverly Ford, June 9, 1863—loss heavy
Upperville June 21, 1863
Gettysburg, July 1, 2 and 3, 1863—loss very heavy
Williamsport, July 6, 1863
Boonesborough and Funkstown, July 8, 9 and 10, 1863
Falling Waters, July 14, 1863
Manassas Gap, July 21, 1863

Brandy Station, August 1, 1863
Sudley's Church, October, 1863
Manassas Plains, October, 1863
Culpepper, November, 1863
Sulphur Springs, November, 1863
Mine Run, December, 1863
Todd's Tavern, May 7 and 8, 1864—loss heavy
Yellow Tavern (near Richmond), May, 1864
Meadow Bridge, May, 1864
Mechanicsville, May, 1864
Hanovertown, May, 1864
Haugh's Shop, May, 1864
Old Church, May, 1864
Cold Harbor, May, 1864—two days, loss very heavy
Deep Bottom, July, 1864
Stone Church (Shenandoah Valley), August, 1864
Newtown, August, 1864—loss heavy
Kernstown, September, 1864
Skirmishes on Opequan Creek, September, 1864
Winchester, September 19, 1864—severe
Milford, September 23, 1864
Luray Court House, September 24, 1864
Waynesborough, September 28, 1864
Mount Crawford, October 4, 1864
Fisher's Hill, October 8, 1864
Tom's Brook (Woodstock Races), October 9, 1864
Cedar Creek, October 19, 1864—loss heavy
Five Forks (skirmish), March 30, 1865
Dinwiddie Court House, March 31, 1865
Five Forks, April 1, 1865—severe
Sailor's Creek, April 6, 1865
Appomattox Court House (Clover Hill), April 9, 1865.
Lee surrenders

In addition to the above, the Second Massachusetts Cavalry, while attached to the Third Brigade, First Division (disorganized September 8, 1864), was engaged at Summit Point, Charleston, Halltown, Berryville Pike, and Berryville, in the Shenandoah Valley.

ARMY OF THE POTOMAC

NINTH ARMY CORPS

General John G. Parke, Commander and Staff

FIRST DIVISION

General O. B. Wilcox, Commanding. 1st Brigade, Colonel Samuel Harriman, Commanding

38th Wis. Infantry
27th Mich. Infantry
17th Mich. Infantry
27th Wis. Infantry
109th N. Y. Infantry
79th N. Y. Infantry

2d Brigade
Colonel Ralph Ely, Commanding

2d Mich. Infantry
46th N. Y. Infantry
50th Penna. Infantry
20th Mich. Infantry
100th Penna. Infantry

3d Brigade
General N. B. McLaughlin, Commanding

3d Md. Battalion
5th Mass. Infantry
14th N. Y. Heavy Artillery
59th Mass. Infantry

SECOND DIVISION
General S. S. Griffin, Commanding

1st Brigade
Colonel Sumner Carruth, Commanding

39th N. J. Infantry
48th Penna. Infantry
7th R. I. Infantry
45th Penna. Infantry
58th Mass. Infantry
36th Mass. Infantry
35th Mass. Infantry

~ 315 ~

51st N. Y. Infantry

2d Brigade
Colonel Herbert, Commanding

11th N. H. Infantry
56th Mass. Infantry
179th N. Y. Infantry
17th Vt. Infantry
31st Me. Infantry
186th N. Y. Infantry
2d Md. Infantry
6th N. H. Infantry
9th N. H. Infantry

THIRD DIVISION
General John G. Curtin, Commanding

1st Brigade
General G. S. Beale, Commanding

15th Me. Infantry
114th N. Y. Infantry
29th Me. Infantry
30th Mass. Infantry
1st Me. Battalion

2d Brigade
General E. P. Davis, Commanding

153d N. Y. Infantry
8th Vt. Infantry
12th Conn. Infantry
26th Mass. Infantry
47th Penna. Infantry

3d Brigade
General J. D. Fessenden, Commanding

173d N. Y. Infantry
160th N. Y. Infantry
162d N. Y. Infantry
133d N. Y. Infantry
30th Me. Infantry

Ninth Corps Artillery Brigade
General J. C. Tidball, Commanding

34th N. Y. Battery
7th Me. Battery
19th N. Y. Battery
11th Mass. Battery
27th N. Y. Battery
Battery D, Penna. Heavy Artillery

ARMY OF THE POTOMAC

SECOND ARMY CORPS
General A. A. Humphreys, Commander and Staff
Escort, Co. F, 1st New Jersey Cavalry

FIRST DIVISION
General John Ramsey, Commanding

1st Brigade
Colonel John Fraser, Commanding

61st N. Y. Infantry
31st Penna. Infantry
140th Penna. Infantry
26th Mich. Infantry
5th N. H. Infantry
2d N. Y. Heavy Artillery

2d Brigade
Colonel Robert Nugent, Commanding

69th N. Y. Infantry
28th Mass. Infantry
88th N. Y. Infantry
4th N. Y. Heavy Artillery
63d N. Y. Infantry

3d Brigade
General C. D. McDougall, Commanding

39th N. Y. Infantry
52d N. Y. Infantry

125th N. Y. Infantry
111th N. Y. Infantry
126th N. Y. Infantry
7th N. Y. Infantry

4th Brigade
Colonel S. A. Mulholland, Commanding

116th Penna. Infantry
53d Penna. Infantry
183d Penna. Infantry
145th Penna. Infantry
64th N. Y. Infantry
148th Penna. Infantry

Second Army Corps Artillery Brigade
Colonel J. G. Hazard, Commanding

Battery K, 4th U. S.
Battery B, 1st R. I.
Battery B, 1st N. J.
Battery M, 1st N. H.
10th Mass. Battery
11th N. Y. Battery

SECOND DIVISION
General Francis C. Barlow, Commanding

1st Brigade
Colonel William A. Ohnstead, Commanding

59th N. Y. Infantry
19th Me. Infantry
184th Penna. Infantry
36th Wis. Infantry
20th Mass. Infantry
19th Mass. Infantry
7th Mich. Infantry
1st Minn. Infantry
152d N. Y. Infantry

2d Brigade
Colonel J. P. McIvor, Commanding

8th N. Y. Heavy Artillery
170th N. Y. Infantry
155th N. Y. Infantry
164th N. Y. Infantry
69th N. Y. National Guard

3d Brigade
Colonel D. Woodall, Commanding

108th N. Y. Infantry
10th N. Y. Infantry
69th Penna. Infantry
1st Del. Infantry
4th Ohio Infantry
7th W. Va. Infantry
12th N. J. Infantry
14th Conn. Infantry
106th Penna. Infantry

THIRD DIVISION
General G. G. Mott, Commanding

1st Brigade
General R. DeTrobriand, Commanding

1st Me. Heavy Artillery
20th Ind. Infantry
110th Penna. Infantry
99th Penna. Infantry
40th N. Y. Infantry
86th N. Y. Infantry
73d N. Y. Infantry
124th N. Y. Infantry

2d Brigade
General R. B. Pierce, Commanding

17th Me. Infantry
105th Penna. Infantry
5th Mich. Infantry
93d N. Y. Infantry
141st Penna. Infantry
57th Penna. Infantry
1st Mass. Heavy Artillery

3d Brigade
General R. McAllister, Commanding

7th N. Y. Infantry
120th Mich. Infantry
11th Mass. Infantry
8th N. Y. Infantry
11th N. Y. Infantry

ARMY OF THE POTOMAC

FIFTH ARMY CORPS
General Charles Griffin, Commanding and Staff.

FIRST DIVISION
General J. H. Chamberlain, Commanding

1st Brigade
General A. L. Pearson, Commanding

198th Penna. Infantry
185th N. Y. Infantry

2d Brigade
General E. M. Gregory, Commanding

189th N. Y. Infantry
187th N. Y. Infantry
188th N. Y. Infantry

3d Brigade
Colonel J. Cushing Edmonds, Commanding

32d Mass. Infantry
20th Me. Infantry
91st Penna. Infantry
1st Me. Infantry
16th Mich. Infantry
155th Penna. Infantry
1st Mich. Infantry
118th Penna. Infantry
83d Penna. Infantry

SECOND DIVISION
General R. B. Ayres, Commanding

1st Brigade
General J. Hayes, Commanding

114th Penna. Infantry
5th N. Y. Infantry
146th N. Y. Infantry
140th N. Y. Infantry
15th N. Y. Heavy Artillery
61st Mass. Infantry

2d Brigade
General A. W. Dennison, Commanding

1st Md. Infantry
4th Md. Infantry
7th Md. Infantry
8th Md. Infantry

3d Brigade
General James Gwyn, Commanding

190th Penna. Infantry
210th Penna. Infantry
4th Del. Infantry
3d Del. Infantry
8th Del. Infantry
191st Penna. Infantry

THIRD DIVISION
General S. S. Crawford, Commanding

1st Brigade
General H. A. Morrow, Commanding

6th Wis. Infantry
7th Wis. Infantry
91st N. Y. Infantry
Independent Battalion Sharp Shooters

2d Brigade
General Henry Baxter, Commanding

11th Penna. Infantry
97th N. Y. Infantry
104th N. Y. Infantry
16th Me. Infantry
39th Mass. Infantry
107th Penna. Infantry

3d Brigade

64th N. Y. Infantry
142d Penna. Infantry
95th N. Y. Infantry
88th Penna. Infantry
121st Penna. Infantry
56th Penna. Infantry
147th N. Y. Infantry

Fifth Army Corps Artillery Brigade
General C. S. Wainwright, Commanding

Battery B, 4th U. S.
Battery H, 1st N. Y.
Battery B, 1st N. Y.
Battery D, 1st N. Y.
Battery D, 5th U. S.
Battery G, 5th U. S.

Every available space where human feet could stand or hands could cling, was appropriated long before the prancing steeds of Sheridan's cavalry led the advance up Pennsylvania Avenue. Stands, staging, boxes, tables, chairs, vehicles, lamp-posts, indeed everything that promised a lookout, was crowded to suffocation with eager people. Windows, balconies and housetops were even more densely packed. Indeed, the mass of civilians pressing their eager homage upon these soldiers coming home from the war, was a sight long to be remembered and attaining to the grandly sublime, as an independent pageant; but when the fiery cavalry steeds, prancing to their well-known bugle notes; the long lines of infantry with burnished arms flashing in the sunlight; the thundering rattle of artillery wheels in an unceasing surging mass, swept along through the day, how shall words be found to express the fervent, sacred emotions stirred within every heart?

The troops as they moved along Pennsylvania avenue presented a grand appearance, all arms of the service being represented in full force. The occasional insertion of a body of Zouaves served to relieve the sameness. The dark and light blue uniforms gave a fine effect to the spectacle. Looking up the broad Pennsylvania Avenue, there was a continuous moving line as far as the eye could reach of National, State, division, brigade, regiment and other flags. Some of them were new, the stars of gold leaf glittering in the sun, and these contrasted strongly with flags borne in the procession tattered in battle or mere shreds. Other flags were thickly covered with names and dates of battle-fields where victories were won by these proud veterans. The flagstaffs were decorated with flowers, and very many bouquets hung from the muzzles of muskets. These troops did not, as to dress, present a war-worn appearance; they were all well and cleanly clad, and their fine marching elicited praise from every tongue. On the south side of the avenue, fronting the Executive Mansion, a stand was built, handsomely and heavily festooned with National flags. At various points were the inscriptions, "Atlanta," "Wilderness," "Stone River," "South Mountain," "Shiloh," "Vicksburg," "Savannah," "Richmond," "Petersburg," and "Coal Harbor." This stand was in part occupied by President Johnson, members of the Cabinet, Generals Grant and Sherman, and other distinguished army officers. On the left were members of the diplomatic corps and their families, two hundred tickets having been issued to this class of spectators. On the stands provided for the purpose were George Bancroft and the following-named Governors of States: Crapo, Buckingham, Andrew, Fenton, Fairchilds, Bradford, Curtin, Smith; Senators Wade, Sherman, Wilson, Johnson, Chandler, Harris, Hendrickson, Dixon, Foster, Morgan, Conness, Lane of Kansas, and Representatives Schenck, Hooper, Marston, Lynch, Hayes, Porter, Kelley, Jenckes, Loan, and ex-Speaker Grow. There were at least thirty naval officers bearing the highest rank, and as many army officers, including Generals Hancock, Wilcox, Cadwallader, Hitchcock, Newton and Rawlins. As the corps and divisions passed in review of the President and Lieutenant General Grant, their commanders severally left the column and took seats on the platform, The Judges of the Courts, the Chiefs of the Government Bureaus, and other public officers were similarly accommodated. The crowd in that part of the city was extremely dense, it being the main point of attraction, and the reviewing place where was assembled the highest dignitaries.

General Custer rode a powerful horse; at times he became restive and ungovernable; when near the Treasury Department the animal madly dashed forward to the head of the line. The General vainly attempted to check his courser, at the same time endeavoring to retain the weight of flowers which had previously been placed upon him. In the flight the General lost his hat. He finally conquered his horse and rejoined his column. Passing the President's stand he made a low bow and was applauded by the multitude.

Five thousand children participated, handsomely decorated by red, white and blue rosettes, flags, banners, &c., &c, of all sizes and descriptions, supplied with a vast number of bouquets and wreaths. The officers and men received these bouquets by thousands, the children meanwhile singing, "When Johnny comes marching home again," and other patriotic songs. The absence of all the Negroes from the old Ninth Corps was noticed and freely commented on by those who may have forgotten that they were organized into a separate corps. From the portico of the Treasury Department the flag of the Treasury Guard Regiment was displayed, the lower portion tattered and torn, not by battle, but by the spur of Booth, the assassin, as he jumped from the box at Ford's Theater to the stage on the night of the assassination. A placard appended stated this fact, and it attracted much attention. Between the rear of the Ninth Corps and the advance of the Fifth Corps there was an interval of ten or fifteen minutes. An immense number of persons rushed into the opening which was in front of the stand occupied by President Johnson, General Grant and the members of the Cabinet, and gave each one repeated cheers. These gentlemen severally rose and bowed their acknowledgement of the honors.

The troops occupied six hours in the review, from nine o'clock in the morning until three o'clock in the afternoon. In military phrase, the "cadence step" was taken from the Capitol to Seventeenth street, from which point the various organizations proceeded on the march to their separate quarters. The review is spoken of as the greatest which has taken place on this continent. It was a grand affair and suggestive of the trials and victories of the Army of the Potomac.

Wednesday, May 24, 1865
Washington, D.C.
Second Day of the Grand Review

Today Washington had another bright, and in all other respects, charming day for the review of the Armies of the Tennessee and Georgia. The sidewalks of Pennsylvania Avenue, at all elevated points, were occupied by deeply interested spectators. Fresh arrivals augmented the already large numbers of strangers who had especially visited Washington to witness the grand military parade. The tastefully decorated stands near the Executive Mansion were again occupied by President Johnson, members of the Cabinet, and Lieutenant General Grant, together with distinguished army and navy officers, Chiefs of Executive Bureaus, the Diplomatic Corps and families, and other personages. The vicinity of the reviewing point was densely crowded over a larger area than on yesterday, this locality being the most attractive.

The Army of the Tennessee moved from the Capitol at nine o'clock, proceeding toward the Executive Mansion. At the head of the column rode Major General Sherman, who was vociferously cheered all along the line, while many clapped their hands and others waved their handkerchiefs and miniature flags. The greeting of this hero was in the highest degree enthusiastic. He had been presented with two large wreaths of flowers, one of which had been placed around his horse's neck, the other hung upon his own shoulder. Major General Sherman was accompanied by Major General Howard, formerly in command of the Army of the Tennessee. Next followed Major General Logan, Staff and Escort. On Tuesday he assumed command of this army. Major General Logan appeared at the head of the command. The Fifteenth Corps led the van, commanded by Major General W. B. Hazen, the hero of Fort McAllister. This Corps is composed of troops from Michigan, Missouri, Ohio, Indiana, Minnesota, Illinois, Iowa, and Wisconsin. The Seventeenth Army Corps was preceded by its commander, Major General Blair, with his Staff, followed by the Headquarters' Escort. The troops from this Corps are from Illinois, Ohio, New York, New Jersey, Wisconsin, Indiana, Minnesota and Michigan. The next in review was the Army of Georgia, Major General Slocum commanding, who rode at the head of the column.

The Twentieth Corps was commanded by Major General Mower, and composed of Volunteers from Connecticut, Pennsylvania, New York, New Jersey, Wisconsin, Massachusetts, Ohio, Delaware, Indiana and. Michigan. This was succeeded by the Fourteenth Army

Corps, Brevet Major General J. C. Davis commanding. It was composed of Volunteers from Wisconsin, Ohio, Indiana, Illinois, Michigan, New York, Minnesota and Kentucky. The respective commanders of the armies, divisions and brigades bore upon their persons profusions of flowers, which had been bestowed in acknowledgment of their heroic deeds; and as they passed along the line, cheers were given and handkerchiefs and flags waved by those who chose this mode of testifying their gratitude for the gallant services of both officers and men. None seemed to be weary of continuous gazing at the troops as there was always presented something of increased interest.

The armies represented all branches and divisions of the service—cavalry, artillery, and infantry, with sufficient variety in trimmings and appointments to relieve the general sameness of uniform; and several regiments of Zouaves contributed to produce this effect. There was an extensive flashing of drawn swords, bayonets, and polished brass cannon in the clear sunlight. Sections of pontoon bridges and ambulances and stretchers, and even heavy wagons, were features in the procession. There was also a fair representation of the spade and ax department, the implements being carried upon the shoulders of both white and black soldiers. Much amusement was occasioned by a display of pack-horses and mules. They were all heavily loaded with commissary supplies, including chickens. A coon, a dog, and a goat were comfortably fastened to three of the saddles; those were the pets of soldiers. Two black soldiers of largest size, riding on very small mules, their feet nearly touching the ground, was regarded as a comic scene in connection with this part of the display, and occasioned general laughter.

An interesting feature in the grand military parade was the exhibition of flags and banners of various patterns, some of them entirely new; others were carried, torn by bullets and reduced to shreds; while others, entire as to material, were faded by exposure to the weather or blackened by the smoke of battle. Several staffs were carried, from which the flags had been shot away. All the spear-heads were ornamented with flowers either in bouquets or wreaths. It was remarked, as in contrast to the Army of the Potomac, that the troops composing the Armies of Georgia and Tennessee wore the wide-brim felt hats, regulation pattern. Their appearance in all respects was equal to that of the Army of the Potomac, notwithstanding they had performed more marching service. Their general movements were much admired and accordingly applauded. The commander of each army, and corps and division, attended by one staff officer, dismounted after passing the General-in-Chief, and joined him until his army, corps or division had passed the reviewing stand, when he remounted and joined his command. Officers commanding regiments presented swords on passing the reviewing officer, but company officers were not required to make such salutes. Brigade bands or consolidated field music turned out and played as their brigades passed. One band to each division performed during the march from the Capitol to the Treasury building. After the troops passed the reviewing officer, they were marched to their respective quarters. Secretary Seward, notwithstanding his severe physical affliction, took a deep interest in the review. General Augur made him comfortable, and furnished him with a good position at the headquarters of the defenses of Washington, that he might witness the grand military display. The Armies of the Tennessee and Georgia occupied six hours in passing—the same length of time required for the review of the Army of the Potomac.

The following are a few of the incidents of the day: Previous to the march, a number of young ladies made their way through the crowds of spectators and soldiers on Capitol Hill, and festooned upon some of the officers bouquets, wreaths and garlands. It has already been stated that General Sherman led the advance today, accompanied by General Howard with bouquets in their hands, and their horses decorated with flowers. Upon reaching the western part of the city, a Veteran Reserve soldier approached General Sherman with another bouquet, but the horse of the latter became restive, and he motioned the soldier back. "Give it to Howard," shouted the multitude; but he, too, having but one hand, could attend only to his prancing horse; so the veteran returned to his seat with his offering amid cheers on all sides. Riding to the western entrance of the Executive Mansion, General Sherman dismounted, and with General Howard and staff joined the group on the stand. The reception given to General Sherman exceeded in enthusiasm that extended to any other officer. Generals Logan, John W. Geary and Frank Blair especially received the acclamations of the multitude. As the head of Major General Frank P. Blair's Corps reached Fourteenth street in the marching column, some one hundred and fifty gentlemen, mostly from Missouri, presented to the General a splendid banner, and to each of the officers of his staff a beautiful bouquet.

Any representation of Sherman's Army would have been far from being complete which omitted the celebrated Bummers' Brigade. These foragers, black and white, composed the most incongruous, as it was certainly the most comical, appendage ever seen with any army. After Blair's Corps had passed, came two diminutive donkeys, astride of which were two equally diminutive but gleeful darkeys; closely following this was a collection of mules, young horses, broken-down nags, upon which were loaded tents, baggage, utensils, kettles, swords, pigs, chickens, goats, dogs, raccoons, pickaninnies, black women; trudging along in the dusty rabble were the blackest of Negroes and all the thousand-and-one appurtenances of camp life. In fact it may be truly said that Sherman's Army presented the same general aspects on its way through the city as it did through the Carolinas, only with much more order. It is understood they choose a fresh camp tonight. This gave a varied picture of the way in which Sherman made war by living on the enemy; only by this means could he have cut loose from his base and made his admirable swoop down to the coast. The darkeys who have been picked up in the march were some of them armed with huge old pistols or captured knives. They seemed to understand well the part they were playing in the terrible drama of revolution, and received the uproarious shouts, laughter and jeers with soldierly unconcern. Any representation of Sherman's Army would have been incomplete which omitted the notorious Bummers accordingly. At the end of General Blair's Corps appeared the most ludicrous, and at the same time, the most interesting scene ever witnessed in connection with any army. The brigade of black servants, attended by the guards of the small baggage train, was preceded by two diminutive darkeys, whose self-complacency was only equaled by the imperturbable animals under them. Then came the strangest huddle of animation, equine, canine, bovine and human that ever civilian beheld, but which has been common enough in Georgia. Mules, asses, horses, colts, cows, sheep, pigs, goats, raccoons mounted on mules, chickens, dogs led by Negroes blacker than Erebus. Every beast of burden was loaded to its capacity with tents, baggage, knapsacks, hampers, panniers, boxes, valises, kettles, pots, pans, dishes, demijohns, bird cages, cradles, mirrors, fiddles, clothing, pickaninnies, and an occasional black woman. In effect Sherman gave us a sample of his army as it appeared on the march through the Carolinas. He is, in fact, moving to another camp, and today's display was a perfect picture of his progress, only more orderly and no foraging. Some of the Negroes appeared to have three days' rations in their ample pouches, and ten days' more on the animals they led. The fraternity was complete; the goats, dogs, mules and horses were already veterans in the field, and trudged along as if the brute world were nothing but a vast march with a daily camp. Thus are we shown how Sherman lived upon the enemy, and how he was enabled to live upon the enemy.

The Army of the West lost Hooker in the review, that of the East lost Sheridan. Meade's army has only a part of its infantry—Sherman's none of its cavalry. The superior conversance of Meade with Washington city enabled him to so defile his forces that not a gap occurred along the entire route, but Sherman's men once or twice broke in sections for long distances, marring the unity of his procession. Meade's army was composed of the most conventional levies—Sherman's of the most individual. The Army of the East was composed of citizens—that of the West of pioneers. A gentleman, socially so-called, would have preferred the display of Meade. His men had more readable faces, better characterization, and were less wild and *outre* in their expression. A pioneer would have most applauded the review of Sherman, because his men were hardier, knottier, and weightier. Meade represented the Army of the East, being a graceful and accomplished commander. Logan, and not Sherman, was the West's representative soldier. The Army of the West marched, as a rule, better than the East, if rigid mathematical time-keeping is the best of good training. Its constituents were, in physiognomy, just the men for dashing adventures, prolonged advances, and reckless fighting; but Meade's men bore the impress of intelligent patience like that which sat before Richmond four defeated years, and in the end had the pluck to pass over the bastions of Petersburg. The officers of Sherman were less punctilious in externals than those of Meade. His staff officers were not so neatly garbed, his line officers were more indifferent to their wardrobe. The West was the best army for a republic, the East for a standing army, and New York troops generally speaking were the best Meade had to show. Illinois troops, casually remarked, were the flower of Sherman's veterans. The absence of cavalry which quite embarrassed Sherman, so far as the spirit of his entertainment went, was made up by series of contrabands and many odd concomitants in the shape of mules, fowls and dogs, which the soldiers took along. Sherman had less artillery than Meade. The battle flags of both were equally riddled. Harmony prevailed among the partisans of both armies. The country was proud of them all. Their deeds are alike, the fames are equal; their reviews were the most wonderful panorama in American history.

SHERMAN'S RIGHT WING IN THE REVIEW
THE 15TH AND 17TH CORPS

The right wing, or Army of the Tennessee, commanded by Major General John A. Logan, is composed of the Fifteenth Corps, Major General W. B. Hazen, and the Seventeenth Corps, Major General Frank P. Blair.

Major General John A. Logan, the present commander of the Army of the Tennessee, was born in Jackson county, Ill., on the 9th of February, 1832, and is consequently about thirty-three years of age. Like Sheridan and other generals who have distinguished themselves during the present war, he was born of Irish parentage. Previous to the war he had acquired some popularity as a politician in his native State, having served in the State Legislature of Illinois and the National Congress. He entered the army in September, 1861, as Colonel of the Thirty-first Illinois Infantry, and participated in the battles of Belmont, Fort Henry and Fort Donaldson. At the latter fight he was wounded three times, and for conspicuous gallantry was promoted to a Brigadier Generalship. As Brigadier General he commanded a division at the siege of Corinth, and subsequently took command of the post at Jackson, Miss. In March, 1863, he received his commission as Major General, and took part in the Battle of Thompson's Hill. The Battle of Raymond was fought alone by General Logan, and during the engagement he had two horses killed. Subsequently General Logan, with his division, took part in the battles of Jackson, Champion Hills, Baker Creek and the siege of Vicksburg, for conspicuous gallantry at which he was by special order from General Grant assigned to the command of the Fifteenth Army Corps, vice General Sherman promoted to the command of the Army of the Tennessee. During the winter of 1864, Logan was in command of the District of Northern Alabama, headquarters at Huntsville. In all the subsequent engagements, far too numerous to mention, in which his corps participated and won undying fame, Logan has been distinguished for his good generalship and gallantry in the field.

By General Order No. 210, dated War Department, Adjutant General's Office, Washington, December 18, 1862, the Fifteenth Corps was organized under command of Major General W. T. Sherman, the present commander of the Military Division of the Mississippi. General Sherman was succeeded by Major General John A. Logan, who was succeeded by Major General W. B. Hazen, who led the successful assault on Fort McAllister last fall.

THE FIFTEENTH CORPS IN THE LINE
General W. B. Hazen, Commander and Staff

FIRST DIVISION
Major General C. B. Woods and Staff with the
Twenty-ninth Missouri Cavalry as an Escort

1st Brigade
Brigadier General W. B. Woods, Commanding

76th Ohio
27th Missouri
93d Indiana
31st and 32d Consolidated Battalion of Missouri
4th Minnesota
13th Indiana

2d Brigade
Colonel Gotterson, Commanding

93d Illinois
10th Ohio
46th Ohio
26th Illinois
100th Indiana
103d Illinois

3d Brigade
Colonel George A. Stone, Commanding

4th Iowa
9th Iowa
25th Iowa
26th Iowa
30th Iowa
31st Iowa

SECOND DIVISION
Major General Oliver, Commander

1st Brigade
Brigadier General Theodore Jones, Commanding

30th Ohio

6th Missouri
17th Iowa
55th Illinois
37th Ohio
6th Michigan
8th Missouri
116th Illinois
127th Illinois
10th Iowa

2d Brigade

Brigadier General Wells S. Jones, Commanding

53d Ohio
54th Ohio
47th Ohio
57th Ohio
26th Missouri
144th Illinois
83d Indiana

3d Brigade

Colonel Hutchinson, Commanding

15th Michigan
48th Illinois
56th Illinois
90th Illinois
70th Ohio

FOURTH DIVISION
Major General J. M. Corse, Commander and Staff

1st Brigade
Brigadier General A. V. Rice, Commanding

2d Iowa
7th Iowa
52d Illinois
66th Indiana
12th Illinois

2d Brigade
Brigadier General Clarke, Commanding

31st Ohio
64th Illinois
59th Indiana
18th Wisconsin
48th Indiana

3d Brigade
Colonel Rowell, Commanding

39th Iowa
57th Illinois
7th Illinois
69th Illinois
50th Illinois

Artillery Brigade
Lieutenant Colonel Ross, Chief of Artillery and Staff

Battery B, 1st Michigan
Battery H, 1st Illinois
Battery H, 1st Missouri
12th Wisconsin

The Fifteenth Corps since its organization has participated in nearly all of the important battles which have taken place during the memorable campaigns in the West, and has won immortal fame on the following battle fields, which are inscribed on its colors: Chickasaw Bayou, Arkansas Post, Siege of Vicksburg, Jackson, Chattanooga, Mission Ridge, Tunnel Hill, Sneak Creek Gap, Resaca, Dallas, Big Shanty, Kennesaw Mountain, Chattahoochee River, Atlanta, Jonesborough, &c.

THE SEVENTEENTH ARMY CORPS
General Frank Blair, Commander
Staff with Escort of Ninth Illinois Mounted Infantry

FIRST DIVISION
Brigadier General M. F. Force, Commander and Staff

1st Brigade
General J. W. Fuller, Commanding

27th Ohio
39th Ohio
18th Missouri
64th Illinois

2d Brigade
Brigadier General J. W. Sprague, Commanding

43d Ohio
63d Ohio
35th New York
25th Wisconsin

3d Brigade

Brigadier General John Tillson, Commanding

10th Illinois
22d Ohio
24th Indiana

THIRD DIVISION
Major General M. D. Leggett, Commander and Staff

1st Brigade
Brigadier General Ewing, Commanding

12th Ohio
16th Ohio
31st Illinois
45th Illinois
30th Illinois

2d Brigade
General R. K. Scott, Commanding

69th Ohio
7th Ohio
20th Ohio
20th Illinois

FOURTH DIVISION
Major General G. A. Smith, Commander and Staff

1st Brigade

Brigadier General B. F. Potts, Commanding

23d Ohio
32d Ohio
53d Illinois
53d Indiana

2d Brigade
Brigadier General Stolbrend, Commanding

32d Illinois
14th Illinois
15th Illinois

3d Brigade
Brigadier General W. W. Belknap, Commanding

11th Iowa
13th Iowa
15th Iowa
16th Iowa

Artillery Brigade
Major F. Welker, Chief of Artillery and Staff

15th Ohio
1st Minnesota
Battery C, 1st Michigan

On the flag, in front of General Blair's headquarters is inscribed the following laconic record of that Corps:

"Shiloh, Corinth, Iuka, Hatchie, Port Gibson, Raymond, Jackson, Champion Hills, Vicksburg, Meridian, Kennesaw Mountain, Nickajack Creek, Jonesborough, Atlanta, Savannah, Pocatalico, Salkehatchie, Edisto River, Orangeburg, Columbia, Cheraw, Fayetteville, Bentonville."

THE LEFT WING OF SHERMAN'S ARMY IN THE REVIEW
ARMY OF GEORGIA
Major General Slocum in Command

TWENTIETH CORPS
Major General Joseph A. Mower and Staff

~ 335 ~

This sterling corps was first organized on the 3d of April, 1864, in Lookout Valley, Tennessee. As originally constituted it was composed of four divisions, commanded by Generals Williams, Geary, Butterfield, and Rousseau; but the Fourth Division under the last named General has never served with the corps, having always been detached upon other duties. The First, Second, and Third Divisions were composed almost entirely of troops of the Eleventh and Twelfth Corps, when these organizations were disbanded. General Hooker commanded this corps up to the siege of Atlanta, and these are the boys that did the fighting above the clouds at Lookout Mountain,

FIRST DIVISION
Major General A. B. Williams, Commander

1st Brigade
Brigadier General James L. Selfridge, Commanding

5th Connecticut
46th Pennsylvania
123d New York
141st New York

2d Brigade
Brigadier General Hawley, Commanding

3d Wisconsin
2d Massachusetts
13th New York
107th New York
150th New York

3d Brigade
Brigadier General James S. Robinson, Commanding

31st Wisconsin
82d Ohio
82d Illinois
101st Illinois
143d New York

The First and Second Brigades of this division formerly belonged to the Twelfth Corps, while the First Brigade came principally from the Eleventh Corps. The First and Second Brigades were the real nucleus of the division. They originally composed General Williams' Division of the Second Corps, then commanded by General Banks, under whose leadership they fought the battles of Winchester and Cedar Mountain. After this battle the corps were reorganized and called the Twelfth. The division as the First of this new corps was engaged in the battles of Winchester, Antietam, Second Bull Run, Chantilly, Sulphur Springs, Chancellorsville and Gettysburg. Since then as a part of the Twentieth Corps, the division has participated in all its battles.

SECOND DIVISION
Major General John W. Geary, Commanding

1st Brigade
Brigadier General A. Pardee Jr., Commanding

5th Ohio
29th Ohio
66th Ohio
28th Pennsylvania
147th Pennsylvania

2d Brigade
General P. H. Jones, Commanding

33d New York
73d Pennsylvania
119th New York
134th New York
154th New York

3d Brigade
General H. A. Barnum, Commanding

29th Pennsylvania
111th Pennsylvania
60th New York
102d New York
137th New York
149th New York

This was formerly the Second Division of the Twelfth Corps. When the present organization was established it received the addition of one brigade from the Eleventh Corps. The troops of the

First and Second Brigades, prior to the formation of the Twelfth Army Corps in September, 1862, were under the command of Major General Banks, and during 1861 and 1862 were actively engaged in the Shenandoah Valley, and along the Upper Potomac. Some of the corps of the First Brigade fought in the battles in West Virginia, under General McClelland. The Second Brigade, formerly of the Eleventh Corps, prior to its formation, was under the commands of Generals Sigel and Fremont. Before the formation of the Twentieth Corps the troops of this Division in whole or in part, had been engaged in the following battles:

Rich Mountain, Laurel Hill, Carrick's Ford, Harper's Ferry, Winchester, two battles, Cross Keyes, Port Republic, Cedar Mountain, White Sulphur Springs, Second Bull Run, Chantilly, Antietam, Chancellorsville, Gettysburg, Wauhatchie, Lookout Mountain, Missionary Ridge and Ringgold.

The division was particularly distinguished at Lookout Mountain, which gallant action it fought and won without assistance. It has since participated in all the battles of the Twentieth Corps, Averysborough and Bentonville. Besides this it has fought singly the Battle of Mill Creek Gap. Since its organization it has been under the command of General Geary, formerly Brigadier, now Brevet Major General. It is generally considered the best disciplined division in the Twentieth Corps, and as such the crack division of Sherman's Army. It is a remarkable fact that this division has never lost a gun and but one stand of colors.

THIRD DIVISION
General W. G. Ward, Commander

1st Brigade,
General Benjamin Harrison, Commanding

70th Indiana
79th Ohio
102d Indiana
105th Illinois
129th Illinois

2d Brigade
General Daniel Dustin, Commanding
19th Michigan
22d Wisconsin
33d Indiana

85th Indiana
3d Brigade

General Cogswell, Commanding

20th Connecticut
26th Wisconsin
33d Massachusetts
55th Ohio
73d Ohio
136th New York

This division is mainly composed of Western troops. The First and Second Brigades are exclusively so, and a portion of the Third Brigade is also from the West. These troops, prior to the organization of the corps, had been guarding railroads and Government property in Kentucky and Tennessee, and had never been engaged in battle. The remainder of the men had participated in all the battles of the Eleventh Corps. Since the formation of the Twenty-first Corps, the division has been engaged in nearly all the battles of the Ninth Corps, and has fought gallantly in them all.

ARTILLERY BRIGADE
Captain C. E. Winegar, Commanding

Battery I, 1st N. Y.
Battery M, 1st N. Y.
Battery C, 1st Ohio
Battery E, Ind. Penna.

THE FOURTEENTH ARMY CORPS IN THE REVIEW
Major General Jeff. C. Davis, Commander.

The present organization of this corps was effected in October, 1863, at Chattanooga, under the command of Major General Palmer. It participated always with credit in all the battles of the Atlanta campaign, and fought the Battle of Jonesborough (below Atlanta) unsupported, driving a large force of the enemy from the works and capturing two four-gun batteries. It participated in the pursuit of Hood, and has since formed with the Twentieth Corps the left wing (now the Army of Georgia) of Sherman's Army. At the Battle of Bentonville it sustained the first shock of Johnston's attack, and resisted so stubbornly that time was given for the arrival of the

Twentieth Corps, when the Army of Georgia repulsed all Johnston's attacks, which, finding fruitless, he withdrew to Smithfield. The history of the Fourteenth Corps has been an eventful one, but is so nearly like that of the Twentieth Corps with which it has been so closely connected, that to give a lengthened sketch of its services would be to indulge in needless repetition. This corps is commanded by Major General Jefferson C. Davis, who has been heard to thank God that he had a C. in his name.

FIRST DIVISION
General Charles C. Walcutt, Commander and Staff

1st Brigade

21st Wisconsin
42d Indiana
33d Ohio
88th Indiana
94th Ohio
104th Illinois

2d Brigade
Brigadier General Buell, Commanding

21st Michigan
60th Ohio
13th Michigan
3d Brigade
21st Ohio
38th Indiana
14th Ohio
79th Pennsylvania

This division left Louisville (the First Division of the old Fourteenth Army Corps) on the 1st of October, 1862; fought at Perryville, October 1, 1862; reached Nashville in November; participated in the hard fought Battle of Stone River, December 31, January 1, 2 and 3. At Murfreesborough the division was reorganized, and started in January, 1863, on the Tullahoma campaign; was in the battles of Horner's Gap, June 21, and Chickamauga, September 19 and 20, Brigadier General Baird being then in command. At Chattanooga it was reorganized, since which time it has been actively engaged in all the battles of the present Fourteenth Corps. Since its organization it has had the following commanders: Brigadier General Rousseau, Brigadier General Baird, Brigadier General Rousseau again, Brigadier General Johnson, Brigadier General King, Brigadier General Carlin, and Brigadier General Walcutt, its present leader.

SECOND DIVISION

General James D. Morgan, Commander

1st Brigade
General Vandevers, Commanding

10th Michigan
14th Michigan
10th Illinois
60th Illinois
17th New York

2d Brigade

121st Ohio
113th Ohio
108th Ohio
98th Ohio
34th Illinois
78th Illinois

3d Brigade

35th Illinois
80th Illinois
110th Illinois
125th Illinois
52nd Ohio
22d Indiana
37th Indiana

This division was organized October 10, 1863, under command of Jeff. C. Davis, then Brigadier General. It has participated in all the battles of the Fourteenth Corps, and at Jonesborough particularly distinguished itself. In this action there were, to quote the words of General Morgan's official report, "two four-gun batteries taken, one by the First and one by the Second Brigade; three hundred and ninety-four prisoners, one Brigadier General, twenty-four commissioned officers, over one thousand stand of small arms, and six battle flags." It was detached to capture Rome, Georgia, and succeeded. In its attack on Kennesaw Mountain it lost one thousand three hundred men in twenty minutes, and five field officers.

THIRD DIVISION
General A. Baird, Commander

1st Brigade
Colonel M. C. Hunter, Commanding

17th Ohio
1st Ohio
89th Ohio
92d Ohio
82d Indiana
23d Missouri detachment
11th Ohio detachment

2d Brigade
Colonel Gleeson, Commanding

105th Ohio
2d Minnesota
75th Indiana
87th Indiana
101st Indiana

3d Brigade
General S. S. Green, Commanding

14th Ohio
38th Ohio
10th Kentucky
18th Kentucky
74th Indiana

Fourteenth Army Corps Artillery Brigade

Battery C, 1st Illinois
Battery L, 2d Illinois
5th Wisconsin Battery

This division, like the preceding, was organized at Chattanooga in October, 1863, and has sustained an excellent reputation in all of the numerous battles in which it has been engaged. At Jonesborough its loss was very heavy, but the works in its front were gallantly carried. At Bentonsville it was ordered forward, unsupported by the other divisions, and made a successful reconnaissance of the enemy's position. Its men still proudly remember that they belonged to Major General George H. Thomas's Division at the first successful Battle of the war—Mill Spring, where Zollicoffer met his death.

COMMENT ON THE GRAND REVIEW
AFTER IT PASSED

The grand review is over. The two days of deserved apotheosis of the two great armies of the Republic have come and gone, and one hundred and fifty thousand veterans have been reviewed, not merely by Grant and Sherman and Meade, but by the people, the grateful millions. Your faithful correspondents have already given you by telegraph the story of the marching in serried columns, the huzzas of the multitude, and the names of commanding officers from those of corps to those of regiments. I shall only add a few observations, reflections and recollections.

To civilians looking on, perhaps the most amazing thing was the number that marched by. Unused to armies, they sat seven hours on yesterday and seven hours today, while the men with sabers and the men with bayonets, in close order and at brisk pace, marched past and still the wonder grew where all the soldiers came from. And yet only one-quarter of the loyal forces now under arms in the country were seen by them. So the dense, swift, long columns were the greatest wonder, because they were dense and swift and long.

The next wonder was that the soldiers seemed so little excited. They tramped along with a certain easy satisfied, every-day nonchalance that was the perfection of the *nil admirari*. They scarcely looked right or left, and any pride and exultation they did show was grim and bronzed like their faces and their uniforms. There were, however, some exceptions. When a shout of "Hurrah for Massachusetts " would be raised by a group of Bay State spectators, or an enthusiastic Sucker would call for and get rousing cheers for Illinois, as regiments from their respective States passed by, then the rank and file would look eagerly to where the shout came from, and scan each man's face as though hoping to see a familiar one. Again, when a Colonel on passing the main pavilion would ask for cheers for the President and General Grant, the imperturbable faces would become transfigured into wild animation and pride, and old rusty caps, grasped by tawny hands and swung high by brawny arms, would circle in the air, while lungs made strong by years in the field and throats familiar with the whoop of the charge and the cheer of victory, would send up a noise like that of the many waters of many Niagaras. And yet not one in fifty would turn his eyes to see the faces of those they were cheering. Whether the seeming want of curiosity was the result of discipline which commanded "eyes to the front, all," or whether they really did not deign to appear to be curious, I can't say.

There never was so perfectly happy a set of men as those in the main pavilion—the President and Cabinet, General Grant, and the score or two of other distinguished officers. Not that they grinned and bowed in self-approbativeness, for there was not a bit of that. It wasn't self-complacency, but a sort of calm quiet; a settled peace and gratitude, seemed to pervade them all. When the crowd would surge up to the stand, at any brief interval in the procession and demand a sight of their favorites, the President would rise and bow repeatedly, but say never a word. Grant, when called for, would but rise for an instant, with lifted hat, and if his face told any story at all it was one of shyness and surprise.

To the stranger in Washington who had never seen the men on that stand, it was well worth while the rushing up as the rear of a division or corps passed, the hurried glance, and the scamper back when the head of the next column approached. There were the President and Cabinet, Sherman, Meade, Hancock, Howard, Slocum, Logan, Hunter, Humphreys, Custer, and fifty others only less famous—a collection of names that will pass into history among the giants.

Yesterday the favorites among the officers who rode by were clearly Merritt, Custer, Humphreys, Griffin and Miles. Custer is the Murat of the war, Humphreys has worthily succeeded to the command of Hancock's old corps (the Second), and Griffin to Warren's (the Fifth). It should not and does not detract from the latter, that the men raised cheer after cheer for Warren, than whom an officer was never more idolized by his soldiers. It may not be inappropriate to say here that it is understood that Warren stands today entirely exonerated from any fault on the day that he was relieved from his corps by Sheridan, and that he and Sheridan are now the best of friends. The statement is confirmed by Warren's late assignment to an important command at the West.

Today the heroes have been Sherman, Logan, Slocum and Geary. Howard having taken charge of the Freedmen's Bureau, and yielded the Army of the Tennessee, did not ride with the troops; but everybody asked for him, and an ovation was waiting for this one-armed hero.

You know before the war Logan was an *awful* Democrat, and in his speeches actually committed himself against "coercion." But when Sumter was fired upon, and his political chief, Douglas, wheeled about and pronounced for coercion, then he, too, began to reconsider. It is said that he wrote to Douglas to know what to do, and that the latter replied, "Raise a regiment, John." Logan did so, and was commissioned Colonel by an old political antagonist, Governor Yates. During the first year of the war he remained very much of a Democrat—fought for the Union with Slavery. He dates his Abolitionism from the day he entered some Southern city—I think it was Nashville—and found no welcome except from the Negroes. Last fall his wife bet a span of mules with General Singleton that her husband would vote for Lincoln—and won them. A few weeks before the election he was given leave of absence, and announced that he would speak; but, desirous of getting at his old political associates, refused to say upon which side he would speak. He got a tremendous audience, and pronounced for Lincoln; and then spoke twice each day till election. As the direct result, the political revolution in Southern Illinois was the most remarkable thing in the last campaign.

Yesterday the best horse in the line was Custer's, today Geary's. Major General Geary was Scott's Military Governor of the City of Mexico, has been mayor of San Francisco, Governor of the Territory of Kansas, and has fought through this war, beginning as colonel. How he sat on his horse today!—a tall, shining black horse, whose neck was clothed with thunder, whose tail was carried like a banner, whose step bespoke the pride of Lucifer—a kingdom for *that* horse were not so bad a bargain!

One thing, both yesterday and today, never failed to call forth cheers, and that was the old flags, the tattered, torn, stained flags, frayed to shreds, staffs with a few sprays of a lint-like silk—these were loudly cheered every three times. Sometimes a regiment would show two of these old flags, and alongside it a broad new silken "glory" bearing the names of the battles in which it had participated. One Massachusetts Regiment had affixed to an old staff to which still clung a few shreds of the old flag, a score of bright new streamers, each having the name of one of the battles of the regiment—and wasn't *that* cheered!

The Army of the Potomac reviewed yesterday is mainly composed of Eastern troops, while the Army of Georgia (Slocum's), and the Army of Tennessee (Logan's, late Howard's), are mainly Western troops. The exception in the one case consists in a dozen Western regiments scattered through the different divisions. In the latter the exception is the Twentieth Corps (the Eleventh and Twelfth consolidated), which went West under Hooker. Naturally a comparison was provoked in the minds of the spectators between the Eastern and Western troops. It was noted that the Western men had the advantage in physique, were taller men, with fewer boys, and scarcely any foreigners among them, that their marching step was several inches longer, and that yellow and red beards, and light hair, worn long, predominated. Officers of the Army of the Potomac conceded that they marched better, that they moved with an elastic, springy, swinging step that does not belong to the Eastern boys, and that their faces were more intelligent, self-reliant and determined. One could not distinguish officers from men except by their uniforms—the privates and the officers seemed equal in intelligence and manly bearing, and in station when at home. On the other hand, the Eastern troops showed more pure discipline, more drill. There was a marked distinction between the officers and the men in point of culture. The officers were more gaily dressed, and evidently belonged to more elegant, or at least more presuming walks of life than those of the general rank in the Western armies. The Eastern men all wore the close-fitting regulation skull-cap; the Western men the soft slouch hat. The former were exact, prim, stiff— the latter, easy, don't-care, independent, and pioneerish.

It was remarkable to see how the Twentieth Corps transplanted, as it had been, from the East, had taken on many of the characteristics of their new comrades. They had learned the same swinging stride, exchanged caps for hats, and become military cosmopolites.

Bringing up the rear of each brigade today were the jack mules, heavily laden with the camp fixtures of the commands, and with the plunder of the long march from Atlanta to Washington. Indeed the mules themselves were found on the way. They were led by Negroes—also found on the way. Tied to the backs of the mules were a number of big red roosters and fighting cocks. Crosswise the back of one, with feet either pannier, was a grave billy-goat. Following one brigade, led by Negroes, was a pair of small white original jackasses and several cows. These things elicited much merriment and shouting among the thousands looking on, to whom the "bummers" of a large army were a revelation. A half dozen pickaninnies not ten years old, of both sexes, astride mules, evidently the protégés of regiments, were funny enough.

Commanding a brigade in this corps was General H. A. Barnum, of Syracuse. Your correspondent once wrote that man's obituary—after the seven days' battles. The surgeon reported him dying, and he was left on the field, after having sent his last words to his wife and little boy. However, he came down from Richmond on the first flag-of-truce boat, and lived to fight at Fredericksburg, at Chancellorsville, at Gettysburg, at Lookout Mountain—where he was again wounded—and now to lead a brigade in "Sherman's march to the Sea." You wouldn't have thought as you saw him backing a wild horse today, receiving the bouquets that were brought him, and bowing acknowledgement to the cheers that greeted him, that he still has an unhealed wound from Malvern Hill yet such is the case. You could put your whole hand into the raw cavity in his side that still remains, and will never heal, but since he received that wound he stormed Lookout Mountain, and was chosen to go to Washington bearing the thirty-five flags captured there.

Commanding the Third Division of the Fourteenth Corps was Brevet Major General J. M. Corse, of Ohio, a young man of twenty-eight. Six or eight years ago he was dropped from the roll of cadets at West Point for incompetency—inability to maintain the required rank in his class. But the knowledge of tactics gained in the year or two he was there, gave him at the commencement the adjutancy of an Iowa regiment. He couldn't do the mathematics of West Point, nevertheless he was a natural soldier, and, young as he is, has won his present rank by sheer fighting, by sheer *ability*

in fighting. When Hood struck Sherman's communications, Corse, with twelve hundred men was garrisoning the important point of Altoona. By the inspiration which he infused into his men he beat off half of Hood's army, and was brevetted Major General for it— but he couldn't get through West Point. His career is a beautiful comment on the assumption and presumption of some of those who do not get through that questionable institution known as "West Point." I never saw General Corse till he rode by today, but I think I am correct as to his failure at West Point, as I know I am in regard to his brilliant record in the army.

The Army of the Potomac lacked in this review one of its best corps—the Sixth, General Wright commanding since Sedgwick fell. The Sixth was necessarily detained at Danville and vicinity until last week, and only left Richmond for this city yesterday morning. Its absence yesterday is much to be regretted, for no corps has a better record.

And so the last review is over. The war is over. The boys are going home.

"When shall their glory fade?"

The Army of the Potomac marched back to their camps on the other side of the river, but Slocum's armies have gone into camp on this side, north and east of the city.

Thursday, May 25, 1865

Washington, D.C.

The Rebel General Johnston has published a letter stating the causes which induced him to surrender to General Sherman. He says: "The consequence of prolonging the struggle would only have been the destruction or dispersion of our bravest men, and great suffering of women and children, by the desolation and ruin inevitable from the marching of two hundred thousand men through the country. Having failed in an attempt to obtain terms giving security to citizens as well as soldiers, I had to choose between wantonly bringing the evils of war upon those I had been chosen to defend, and averting those calamities with the confession that hopes were dead, which every thinking Southern man had already lost. I made this convention to spare the blood of this gallant little army, to prevent further suffering of our people by the devastation and ruin inevitable from the marching of invading armies, and to avoid the crime of waging a hopeless war."

New Orleans, Louisiana

Rebel deserters and escaped prisoners of the Thirty-third Iowa Regiment just arrived from Texas, report that the Union prisoners confined at Tyler, Texas, were allowed to escape in large numbers, the guards saying that, when they are all gone, they will have nothing to do, and then can go home. The interior of Texas is in a. terribly disorganized condition. A telegraph line is to be constructed from San Antonio and Austin to Matamoras.

Boston, Massachusetts

The United States gunboat Tuscarora, from Fortress Monroe, with Alexander H. Stephens and Postmaster Reegan on board, arrived below this port this morning, and anchored in the Narrows. The Rebel party will be lodged in Fort Warren today.

Saturday, May 27, 1865

Kirby Smith's Surrender, War Department, Washington, D.C.

Major General Dix: A dispatch from General Canby, dated at New Orleans, yesterday, the 26th inst, states that arrangements for the surrender of the Confederate forces in the Trans-Mississippi Department have been concluded. They include the men and material of the army and navy.

Edwin M. Stanton,
Secretary of War

Tuesday, May 30, 1865

Special Field Orders No. 76
Washington D. C.

The General commanding announces to the armies of the Tennessee and Georgia that the time has come for us to part; our work is done and armed enemies no longer defy us.

Some of you will be retained in service until further orders; and now that we are about to separate, to mingle with the civil world, it becomes a pleasing duty to recall to mind the situation of national affairs.

When but little more than a year ago we were gathered about the twining cliffs of Lookout Mountain, and all the future was wrapped in doubt and uncertainty, three armies had come together from distant fields, with separate histories, yet bound by one common cause, the union of our country, and the perpetuation of the Government of our inheritance.

There is no need to recall to your memories Tunnell Hill, with its rocky face mountain and Buzzard Roost Gap, with the ugly forts of Dalton behind. We were in earnest, and paused not for danger and difficulty, but dashed through Snake Creek Gap, and fell on Resacca, then on to the Etowah to Dallas, Kennesaw, and the heats of summer found us on the banks of the Chattahoochee, far from home, and dependent on a single road for supplies.

Again we were not to be held back by any obstacles, and crossed over and fought four heavy battles for the possession of the citadel of Atlanta. That was the crisis of our history. A doubt still clouded our future, but we solved the problem and destroyed Atlanta, struck boldly across the State of Georgia, secured all the main arteries of life to our enemy, and Christmas found us at Savannah.

Waiting there only long enough to fill our wagons, we again began our march, which for peril, labor and results will compare with any ever made by an organized army; the floods of the Savannah, the swamps of the Combahee and Edisto, the high hills and rocks of the Santee, the flat quagmires of the Peedee and Cape Fear Rivers were all passed in mid-winter, with its floods and ruins, in the fare of an accumulating enemy, and after the Battle of Averysborough and Bentonville we once more came out of the wilderness to meet our friends at Goldsboro.

Even then we paused only long enough to get new clothing to re-load our wagons and again pushed on to Raleigh, and beyond, until we get our enemy suing for peace instead of war, and offering to submit to the injured laws of his and our country. As long as that enemy was defiant, nor mountains, nor rivers, nor swamps, nor hunger, nor cold had checked us, but when he who had fought us hard and persistently offered submission, your General thought it wrong to pursue him further, and negotiations followed which resulted as you all know in his surrender.

How far the operations of the army have contributed to the overthrow of the Confederacy, to the peace which now dawns on us, must be judged by others, not by us; but that you have done all that men could do has been admitted by those in authority, and we have a right to join in the universal joy that fills the land because the war is over, and our Government stands vindicated before the world by the joint action of the volunteer armies of the United States.

To such as remain in the military service your General would only remind you that successes in the past are due to hard work and discipline, and that the same work and discipline are equally important in the future. To such as go home I would only say that our favored country is so grand, so extensive, so diversified in climate, soil, and productions, that every man can surely find a home and occupation suited to his tastes, and none should yield to the natural impotence sure to result from our past life of excitement and adventure.

You will be invited to seek new adventure abroad; but do not yield to the temptation, for it will lead only to death and disappointment.

Your General now bids you all farewell with the full belief that as in war you have been good soldiers, so in peace you will make good citizens, and if unfortunately a new war should arise in our country, Sherman's army will be the first to buckle on the old armor and come forth to defend and maintain the Government of our inheritance and choice. By order of

> W. T. Sherman,
> Major General
> L. M. Dayton,
> Assistant Adjutant General

Friday, June 2, 1865

General Orders No. 108
Washington, D.C.

Soldiers of the Armies of the United States:

By your patriotic devotion to your country in the hour of danger and alarm, your magnificent fighting, bravery and endurance, you have maintained the supremacy of the Union and the Constitution, overthrown all armed opposition to the enforcement of the laws, and of the proclamations forever abolishing Slavery—the cause and pretext of the Rebellion—and opened the way to the rightful authorities, to restore order and inaugurate peace on a permanent and enduring basis on every foot of American soil. Your marches, sieges and battles, in distance, duration, resolution and brilliancy of results, dim the luster of the world's past military achievements, and will be the patriot's precedent in defense of liberty and right in all time to come. In obedience to your country's call, you left your homes and families and volunteered in its defense. Victory has crowned your valor and secured the purpose of your patriotic hearts; and with the gratitude of your countrymen and the highest honors a great and free nation can accord, you will soon be permitted to return to your homes and families, conscious of having discharged the highest duty of American citizens. To achieve these glorious triumphs and to secure to yourselves, your fellow countrymen and posterity the blessings of free institutions, tens of thousands of your gallant comrades have fallen and sealed the priceless legacy with their lives. The grave of these a grateful nation bedews with tears, honor their memories, and will ever cherish and support their stricken families.

U. S. Grant
Lieutenant General

Thursday, June 8, 1865

Washington, D.C.

The review of the Sixth Corps, Major General Wright, has been the incident of today. The corps consisted of three divisions, nine brigades and forty-four regiments, and consumed two hours in passing. Reviews here seem to have lost their interest, for the turnout of the people was very small, though it was to witness the marching of gallant men who have borne the brunt of battle for four years. The arrangements also were conspicuously bad, the tickets of admission to the central platform having been sagaciously sent to General Meade's headquarters at Fort Albany, five miles from the city, the result of which was that the platform was not half full, while Senators and members of Congress, Generals, heads of Bureaus and reporters were obliged to keep to the street. The pavilion, occupied by the President, Secretary McCulloch, Secretary Stanton, Generals Meade, Wright and Heintzelman, Admiral Davis and others, was beautifully decorated with flags and flowers as before. The Vermont Brigade, Major General L. A. Grant, was greatly admired for their fine appearance. Major General Casey, whose praise is worth having, says their marching was of a superior order, indicating excellent discipline, and that this was the only brigade that saluted the President correctly. These troops received a hearty welcome from the Vermonters, with Governor Smith at their head, who occupied a stand opposite the pavilion. A noticeable feature of the procession, also, was the One Hundred and Sixty-eighth New York, Colonel A. N. McDonald. This regiment was the first to march into Petersburg. Other New York regiments and the New Jersey Brigade came in for their meed of praise. The Thirty-seventh Massachusetts also attracted great attention and applause, as on the recent grander review. There were no colored soldiers in line to receive any portion of the popular homage for their bravery and fidelity. They have all been sent off to Texas, where they are for the present safe from the applause of their grateful countrymen and from the sneers of those officers who are jealous lest black men share the honors of the day of victory.

Friday, June 9, 1865

Twenty-third Army Corps,
Greensboro, North Carolina

The mustering out of a portion of the Twenty-third Corps begins today. A portion of the old Fort Fisher Brigade, the first of the Second Division, Tenth Corps, is about to start for home. It consists of the One Hundred and Twelfth, One Hundred and Seventeenth, and One Hundred and Forty Second New York, commanded respectively by Colonel Ludwig, Colonel Myers, and Colonel Burney, with Brevet Brigadier General Daggett as Brigade Commander. Their horses have already been sent to Gaston, Whence the troop follow by rail, and march thence to City Point, where they take transports. This brigade was the first to storm and take Fort Fisher, during which every officer and man covered himself with glory, and saw the colors first planted on the parapet of the fort. I saw it done. Why is this brave body of troops to be mustered out here, and to lose all the time between the date of muster out and their actual payment at home? They must retain their organization until they reach home. This is complained of as unjust and unusual.

Wednesday, June 29, 1865

Washington, D.C.
Headquarters of the Army of the Potomac

Soldiers: This day two years ago, I was assigned command of you under the orders of the President of the United States. Today, by virtue of the same authority, the army ceasing to exist, I have to announce my transfer to other duties and my separation from you.

It is unnecessary to enumerate all that has occurred in these two eventful years, from the grand and decisive Battle of Gettysburg, the turning point of the war, to the surrender of the Army of Northern Virginia at Appomattox Court House. A grateful county will honor the living, cherish and support the disabled and sincerely mourn the dead.

In parting from you, your Commanding General will ever bear in memory your noble devotion to your country, your patience and cheerfulness under all the privations and sacrifices you have been called on to endure.

Soldiers, having accomplished the work set before us, having vindicated the honor and integrity of our Government, and flag, let us return thanks to Almighty God for his blessing in granting us victory and peace, and let us earnestly pray for strength and light to discharge our duties as citizens, as we have endeavored to discharge them as soldiers.

> George G. Mead
> Major General, U.S.A.

The hanging of the Lincoln Assassination conspirators
From Left to Right
Mary Surratt, Lewis Paine, David Herrold, George Atzerodt
July 7, 1865

Addendum
POW Prison Camps Comparison

Camp Chase, Columbus, Ohio

Established in 1861 and originally constructed for 4500 to 5000 prisoners. At times, as many as 7000 prisoners were incarcerated there. In 1865, after the barracks had been enlarged, the total exceeded 10,000. During the war as many as 25,000 Confederates passed through the gates at Camp Chase. Over 2000 died there.

Elmira Prison
Elmira New York

Established in May of 1864 and closed in July 1865. 12,122 Confederate prisoners were incarcerated there. Of this number, 2,963 died of sickness, exposure and associated causes.

Elmira Prison, POW Camp
Elmira, New York

Belle Island POW Camp
Richmond, Virginia

~ 365 ~

Established on an island in the James River, this 6 acre camp was designed to hold around 3000 prisoners in 1862. Nearly 30,000 Union prisoners were held on this island and a thousand or more died there. Starvation, disease and exposure to the elements were the main cause of death for the prisoners. There are no records indicating the total deaths on Belle Isle but one diary account states that 15 to 25 deaths occurred daily.

Libby Prison
Richmond, Virginia

Libby Prison – Union Prisoners were kept on the top two floors, the windows were barred but open to the elements. Conditions were terrible and lack of sanitation and over-crowding resulted in many deaths from disease. At one time, over one thousand Union prisoners were packed into the top two floors.

From an article published by the "Daily Richmond Enquirer":
"Libby takes in the captured Federals by scores, but lets none out; they are huddled up and jammed into every nook and corner; at the bathing troughs, around the cooking stoves, everywhere there is a wrangling, jostling crowd; at night the floor of every room they occupy in the building is covered, every square inch of it, by uneasy slumberers, lying side by side, and heel to head, as tightly packed as if the prison were a huge, improbable box of nocturnal sardines."

Libby Prison
Richmond, Virginia

Andersonville
Andersonville, Georgia
Andersonville...the worst of the worst. Established in 1864 as a place to move the many prisoners that had been kept in and around Richmond.

From Kevin Frye, Andersonville Historian:
The pen initially covered about 16 1/2 acres of land enclosed by a 15 foot high stockade of hewn pine logs. It was enlarged to 26 1/2

acres in June of 1864. The stockade was in the shape of a parallelogram 1,620 feet long and 779 feet wide. Sentry boxes, or "pigeon roost" as the prisoners called them, stood at 30 yard intervals along the top of the stockade. Inside, about 19 feet from the wall, was the "DEADLINE ," which the prisoners were forbidden to cross upon threat of death. Flowing through the prison yard was a stream called Stockade Branch, which supplied water to most of the prison. Two entrances, the North Gate and the South Gate, were on the West side of the stockade. Eight small earthen forts located around the exterior of the prison were equipped with artillery to quell disturbances within the compound and to defend against feared Union cavalry attacks. The first prisoners were brought to Andersonville in February, 1864. During the next few months approximately 400 more arrived each day until, by the end of June, some 26,000 men were confined in a prison area originally intended to hold 13,000. The largest number held at any one time was more than 32,000- about the population of present-day Sumter County- in August, 1864. Handicapped by deteriorating economic conditions, an inadequate transportation system, and the need to concentrate all available resources on the army, the Confederate government was unable to provide adequate housing, food, clothing, and medical care to their Federal captives. These conditions, along with a breakdown of the prisoner exchange system, resulted in much suffering and a high mortality rate.

Over 45,000 Union prisoners were incarcerated here and 12,912 of them died there. Death by starvation, dehydration, disease and suicide were common daily occurrences.

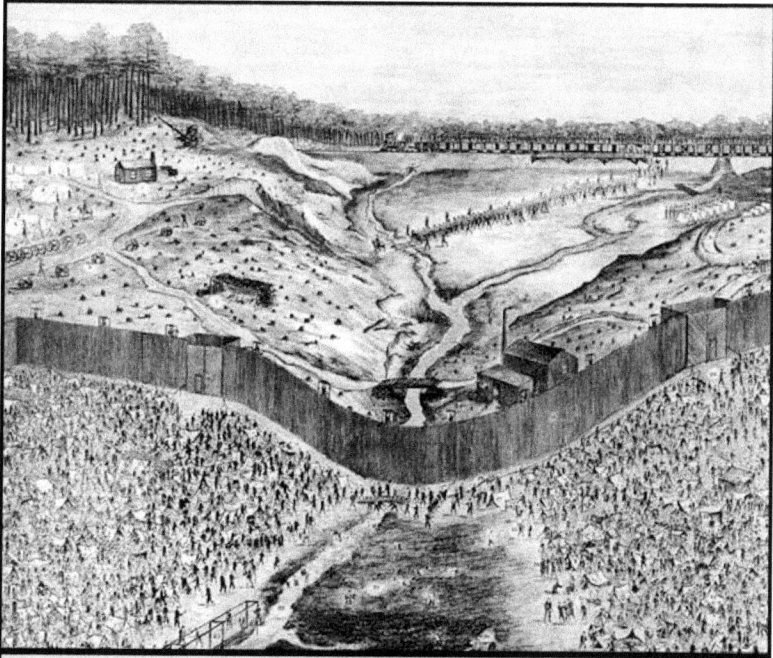

Andersonville
Drawn from memory by Thomas O'Dea, ex-prisoner

Some who lived through it...for a while at least.

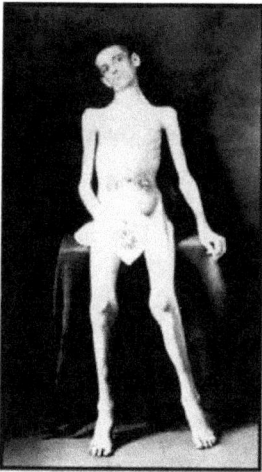

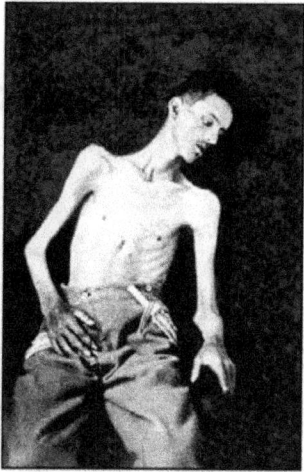

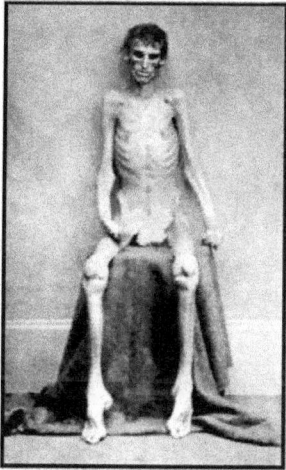

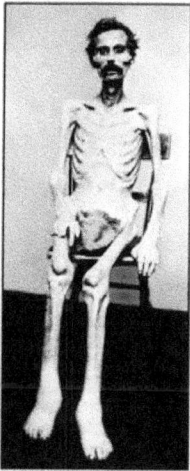

Captain Henry Wirtz
Commandant Andersonville Prison
Executed at Washington D.C. on November 10, 1865

For more great stories from our nation's past, please visit the Historical Collection at our website.

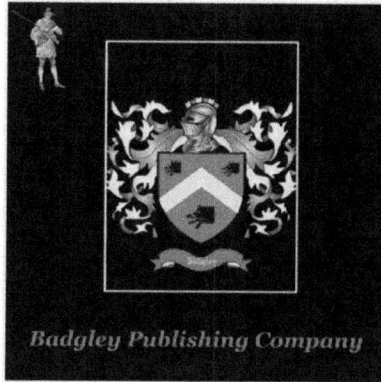
Badgley Publishing Company

www.BadgleyPublishingCompany.com

www.ingramcontent.com/pod-product-compliance
Lightning Source LLC
LaVergne TN
LVHW051448080426
835509LV00017B/1703